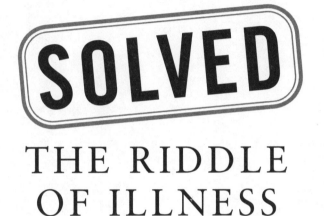

THE RIDDLE
OF ILLNESS

FOREWORD BY DR. WAYNE DYER

SOLVED

THE RIDDLE
OF ILLNESS

Stephen E. Langer, M.D.,
and James F. Scheer

McGraw·Hill

New York   Chicago   San Francisco   Lisbon   London   Madrid   Mexico City
Milan   New Delhi   San Juan   Seoul   Singapore   Sydney   Toronto

The **McGraw·Hill** *Companies*

Library of Congress Cataloging-in-Publication Data

Langer, Stephen E.
        Solved: the riddle of illness/Stephen E. Langer and James F. Scheer.—4th ed.
            p.   cm.
        Previously published: Los Angeles: Keats, 2000.
        Includes bibliographical references and index.
        ISBN 0-07-147057-3 (alk. paper)
            1. Hypothyroidism—Popular works.   2. Hypothyroidism—Complications.
        3. Health.   I. Scheer, James F.   II. Title.
        RC657.L3 2006
        616.4'44—dc22   2006001323

1 2 3 4 5 6 7 8 9 10 11 12 13 14 15 16 17 18   FGR/FGR   0 9 8 7 6

ISBN-13: 978-0-07-147057-5
ISBN-10:   0-07-147057-3

McGraw-Hill books are available at special quantity discounts to use as premiums and sales promotions, or for use in corporate training programs. For more information, please write to the Director of Special Sales, Professional Publishing, McGraw-Hill, Two Penn Plaza, New York, NY 10121-2298. Or contact your local bookstore.

This book is printed on acid-free paper.

Dedicated with love and light to my family:
Debra, Stuart, Caroline, George, Lilly, and Gavin.
STEPHEN E. LANGER, MD

Spring blossoms in the heart of winter
No one wants this dream to end.
—KUAIPU

For Joan—
On the pathway of dreams to you
My feet never touch the ground.
JAMES F. SCHEER

Contents

Foreword   ix

Acknowledgments   xi

Please Note!   xiii

Special Note   xv

A Salute   xvii

1 "Nothing Organically Wrong"   1

2 Why So Much Hidden Hypothyroidism?   18

3 What's Sabotaging Your Thyroid?   27

4 Care and Feeding of the Thyroid   33

5 The Great Controversy: Synthetic Versus Natural   43

6 Body Heat   47

7 Thyroid and Sex—for Women   56

8 Thyroid and Sex—for Men   64

9 How to Enhance Fertility and Pregnancy   72

10 Thyroiditis: A Growing Menace   88

11 How to Beat Hyperthyroidism   93

12 Selenium Deficiency and Hypothyroidism   100

13 A New Look at Iodine   103

14 Better Skin, Better Living   109

15 Mind and Emotions: The Thyroid Connection   116

16 Reversing Depression   122
17 Medical Look-Alikes:
    Hypoglycemia and Hypothyroidism   127
18 Diabetes: A Preventable Illness   132
19 How to Prevent a Heart Attack—Your Own!   142
20 Be Kind to Your Arteries!   154
21 Dramatic Treatment for Circulatory Problems   165
22 Guard Yourself Against Cancer   173
23 Alzheimer's Disease or Something Else?   179
24 Better Coping with Menopause   188
25 Is Fibromyalgia Really Incurable?   191
26 Stress and Free Radicals   196
27 Overweight? How to Be a Good Loser   203
28 Tobacco and Alcohol: Thyroid Gland Enemies   209
29 How to Thrive in a Polluted World   214
30 Live Longer, Healthier, and Younger   229
31 Some Things You Ought to Know . . .   239
32 For Doctors Only   244
33 Conclusion   262

    Afterword   265
    Notes   267
    Bibliography   281
    Index   283

Foreword

In *Solved: The Riddle of Illness*, thyroid gland authority Stephen Langer, MD, and health editor–writer James F. Scheer show you simple ways to understand and manage your thyroid gland so you can make the most of your life physically, mentally, and emotionally.

Supercharged energy and a wholesome emotional outlook are basic to living and functioning positively for goal achievement, social adjustment, and happiness—difficult or impossible to achieve if your thyroid gland isn't working properly.

One of the most important books of our time—its first edition was a perennial bestseller—the enlarged and updated edition of *Solved: The Riddle of Illness* reveals in simple and colorful terms the secrets of abundant health—physical, emotional, and mental.

In this age of astronomical health care costs that threaten to bankrupt the individual as well as the nation, *Solved: The Riddle of Illness* offers new hope, because it deals with underlying causes for a multitude of ailments, rather than just symptoms.

One of the most prevalent basic ailments and one of the least diagnosed—contributing to horrendous medical costs—is hypothyroidism (low thyroid function).

There are more than sixty symptoms of low thyroid function, the most prevalent of which are two of today's most common disorders: fatigue and depression.

Among many novel features of *Solved: The Riddle of Illness* is a no-cost, self-administered temperature test that you can take to indicate whether you are hypothyroid. This is called the *Barnes Basal*

Temperature Test. If your temperature runs low, according to given parameters, it is time to see your family doctor to get more extensive and verifying tests.

Dr. Langer and James F. Scheer show you how to reverse a widespread illness that saps your physical vigor, reduces your sexual vitality, steals your ability to think and remember, and undermines your emotional life.

Why is it that normal thyroid function is so key to functioning at 100 percent in this highly competitive world? Every one of your trillions of cells requires thyroid hormone, just as the cylinders of your car require a rapid succession of sparks to ignite the fuel and power them.

Without bright sparks, your car engine falters, runs weakly, or quits entirely. Without adequate thyroid hormone, your cells—and you—respond in a similar way.

This fourth edition of *Solved: The Riddle of Illness* deserves a permanent place on your health and wellness bookshelf, just as it now has on mine!

DR. WAYNE DYER

Acknowledgments

A PRIME MOVER in clinical research on the thyroid gland for half a century, the late Broda O. Barnes, MD, PhD, was also a prime mover behind the writing of this book, by liberally giving his time, abundant information, encouragement, and inspiration to my coauthor, James F. Scheer, and me. I know of no one else in the world who has done so much as a medical doctor, writer, lecturer, and talk show guest to alert millions to the often hidden causes of illness, as well as to simple ways to stay well for life.

This revised, updated, and enlarged version of *Solved: The Riddle of Illness*—as with the original edition—is intended to carry the Barnes tradition forward—to reveal the unsuspected reasons for illness and sound ways of achieving and maintaining wellness.

Credit for encouraging the writing of *Solved: The Riddle of Illness* also goes to George Shutt of Glendora, California, founder of Shutt Medical Technologies and an inventor-pioneer in arthroscopic surgical instrumentation.

For many years, George Shutt served as Dr. Barnes's volunteer publicist. He has made a second career—concurrent and nonprofit—of disseminating information on subnormal thyroid function. By forming a private enterprise, he has realized funding to launch a hypothyroidism foundation to educate the public and the medical profession and to facilitate research efforts in this critically important area.

In addition, thanks go to biochemist Jeffrey Bland, PhD. I drew some of the book's material from a talk he gave when we were speakers, with Dr. Barnes, at the Webster-Barnes Foundation in Dallas, Texas.

I am also grateful to William H. Philpott, MD, from whose superb book, *Victory Over Diabetes*, I used some material with permission from Nathan Keats, founding publisher of Keats Publishing, Inc., and publisher of his book and previous editions of this one.

Edward R. Pinckney, MD, and his wife Cathey of Beverly Hills, California, both prominent medical writers, generously supplied key material from several of their books and other publications for use in *Solved: The Riddle of Illness*.

It's impossible to give enough thanks to two individuals who contributed mightily to this edition: Mary Shomon and John C. Lowe, DC. Mary is the author of *Living Well with Hypothyroidism: What Your Doctors Don't Tell You . . . That You Need to Know* and writer-editor of the Web site on thyroid disease (www.thyroid-info.com). Mary introduced us to Dr. Lowe, who supplied much of the cutting-edge information for the chapter on fibromyalgia. Our gratitude goes to Richard Passwater, PhD, best-selling writer, consultant to the health food industry, and a human treasury of biochemical information, always available to fill us in on his innumerable areas of expertise.

Our deep thanks also to Lee Swanson, president of Swanson Health Products. We thank Lee for his friendship, advice, and encouragement through many years.

Please Note!

Solved: The Riddle of Illness suggests a way of life for reaching and maintaining peak health. It is based on the best of the latest research and the best of time-tested methods—some of the latter long forgotten.

Although the medical profession encourages us to take more responsibility for our health, seeking wellness should be done in cooperation with a doctor. More and more physicians are becoming aware of the benefits to be derived from preventive methods—among them optimal nutrition.

This book is not to be considered a prescription. You are unique. You have your own set of individual variations—physical, mental, and emotional. Only the doctor who knows, examines, and treats you can prescribe for you. For this reason, the authors and publishers cannot take medical or legal responsibility of having the contents of this book considered a prescription for anyone.

With regard to case studies used in this book, we have made every effort to conceal the identity of all individuals in order to preserve their privacy. To this end, all names, physical descriptions, and even professions have been changed.

Special Note

THE FIRST EDITION of *Solved: The Riddle of Illness* was written more than a decade ago. Since then it has been found that certain conditions other than hypothyroidism (such as chronic viral infections) can reduce a person's basal body temperature, too.

Therefore, it is incumbent for any practicing physician to perform a complete battery of thyroid tests—total and free T3, T4, TSH, and antithyroid antibodies, anti-TPO, and antithyroglobulin—in addition to the basal temperature test before prescribing thyroid supplementation.

Happily, with the new, ultrasensitive thyroid tests, a high percentage of patients with low basal body temperature also show abnormalities in their lab workups, and these are the patients for whom I now routinely prescribe thyroid supplementation.

Make no mistake, the Barnes Basal Temperature Test (underarm temperature reading) is often the first indication a person is hypothyroid; and I urge all of my readers to see their family doctors as soon as possible for a complete thyroid evaluation if the morning thermometer consistently registers less than 97.8°F.

A Salute

A MAN WHO worked medical miracles.

That sums up the life and career of the late Broda O. Barnes, MD, PhD, who worked miracles in the lives of millions of patients—his own as well as those of more than one hundred other doctors—and readers of his many books.

This book picks up where Dr. Barnes's writings leave off—actually a little before that. As authors, we were privileged and blessed to have known Dr. Barnes intimately and benefited from his rich store of knowledge and experience.

After the release of the first edition of *Solved: The Riddle of Illness*, many individuals wrote or asked us for additional personal information about Dr. Barnes. Therefore, we are now delighted to summarize his life—a lot of which is covered in the text of this book—because his accomplishments convince us that he is worthy of the Nobel Prize in medicine and research.

Perhaps you will agree.

Way back in the mists of history, a man named George slew a firebreathing dragon that had eaten the innocent citizens of a distant city. He was showered with thanks and great acclaim and eventually was sainted. That's how plain George became St. George.

In more recent years, a Fort Collins, Colorado, medical doctor slew a different kind of dragon, which—directly or indirectly—had killed many innocent inhabitants in every land.

Unlike St. George, Dr. Barnes received only limited attention and never stood a chance of being sainted. However, that was all right with him. He wanted attention drawn not to himself but to the slain dragon, the myth that wholesome and nutritious cholesterol-containing foods should be minimized or eliminated to avoid cardiovascular ailments. He wanted attention drawn to the real reasons for clogged arteries, strokes, and heart attacks and to the simple ways to prevent them.

We salute Dr. Barnes for his lifelong studies and discoveries about the thyroid gland and how, when functioning properly, it contributes to preventing heart attacks (as well as cancer, chronic fatigue syndrome, premature aging, and a medical book full of minor to devastating ailments).

His contributions to the health and well-being of people around the world place him among the giants in the modern history of medicine and biochemistry: Tom Spies, MD, Roger J. Williams, PhD, Hans Selye, MD, Wilfrid Shute, MD, Evan Shute, MD, Albert Szent-Györgyi, PhD, and Linus Pauling, PhD. You will understand why when you meet Dr. Barnes in the pages of this book.

Just who is Dr. Broda Barnes? What events and information shocked him into the realization that medical researchers were looking at the wrong evidence to solve the riddle of epidemic heart disease and that, of course, they were coming up with the wrong answers?

As we knew him, Dr. Barnes, a stocky, bespectacled, white-haired, small city medical doctor, had a folksy way of talking and an irreverent wit. He was born on April 14, 1904, in a log cabin desperately clinging to a steep and rocky slope of the Ozark Mountains in southern Missouri.

"A couple wheels of my parents' covered wagon broke off there, giving me plenty of time to be born. Ten years later, they had the wheels fixed, and we moved westward," he admitted.

Driven by powerful inquisitiveness as a youngster, he became enchanted with research as a chemistry student at the University of Denver. For two years he taught physiological chemistry at Western Reserve University, where he had received his master of science degree in 1930. At the University of Chicago, he earned a doctorate in physiology in 1931.

It was there, while studying under Anton J. Carlson, PhD, world-renowned physiology professor, that he reluctantly began investigating the thyroid gland.

"My interest in the thyroid gland grew out of necessity, rather than choice," he told us. "Professor Carlson arbitrarily assigned this subject for my doctoral thesis when I entered his department many years ago.

"I would have preferred another subject, but during the Great Depression—actually it wasn't that great!—one was happy to find any job permitting the continuation of education. . . .

"As time passed, the wisdom of this great educator's decision was more than justified. He was aware that many secrets of this tiny gland remained undiscovered, but I'm sure he had no idea that this humble beginning would solve such an incredible range of medical problems. Neither of us foresaw the solution of the major health problems of the century through proper care of the thyroid gland: everything from overwhelming fatigue to the devastating diseases—heart and artery ailments and cancer—and, least suspected, common emotional disorders such as depression."

Dr. Barnes taught physiology at the University of Chicago for five years, then studied for his medical degree, completing this work in 1937 at Rush Medical College (Chicago), interning at Illinois Research Hospital. He began practicing medicine while serving for two years as assistant professor of medicine at the University of Illinois.

The brilliance of his research papers on thyroid function led to his being named chairman of the Health Education Department at the University of Denver. He served in the military between 1943 and 1946 and intermittently until 1951. Then he was appointed professor affiliate in the department of physiology at Colorado State University (1963–1968).

During more than forty years in private medical practice, Dr. Barnes was decades ahead of his time in stressing prevention of illness, rather than just treatment. Although a general practitioner, he always specialized in the thyroid gland, because its insufficiency and improper function were the unsuspected causes of a host of illnesses.

More than one hundred of his publications on the thyroid gland and related topics appeared in leading medical and scientific journals throughout the world and in three books.

Without the contributions of Dr. Barnes, millions of individuals would be energyless, living vegetables, old far before their time, emotionally disturbed without understanding why, unable to think or remember (believing that they had Alzheimer's disease) and being treated for symptoms, rather than for the easily correctable, underlying condition responsible for more than sixty common medical ailments suffered by an estimated 40 percent of the population.

You may be among that 40 percent.

After reading this book, you will understand fully why Dr. Barnes is worthy of a Nobel Prize!

1

"Nothing
Organically Wrong"

"Dr. Langer, I hate sex!"

Tears glistened in the eyes of the attractive thirty-year-old woman seated across the desk from me.

"Maybe it's my fatigue," she continued. "Half awake, in a mental fog, I drag around the office. At home in the evening, I collapse, exhausted, when my husband wants me most. Yet how can I even think of having sex when my body cries out just for survival?"

Particularly upsetting to this patient, whom I'll call Connie, was the assessment of her condition by previous doctors: "There's nothing organically wrong."

Allison's problem was somewhat different. She enjoyed sex but usually turned off her mate with icy cold hands and feet. Tired, drowsy, anxious, often depressed, she caught every cold that came her way and had frequent sinus and upper respiratory infections and severe headaches.

"My doctor can't find a thing wrong," she told me. "He calls me the world's foremost hypochondriac."

Eloise had no complaints about her sex life, only her sex. Difficult menstruation, which had started prematurely at age ten, caused her to miss school and, now, time from her prosperous advertising agency. To cope with exhaustion and with being cold, she drank mug after mug of hot coffee. She often experienced acute anxiety and occasional feelings of doom.

"My former doctor—and I do mean former—made me furious during my last office visit," she explained. "He told me, 'I advise you to take a more wholesome view of your health, because there's nothing organically wrong.'"

Like these women, Phil, a brilliant twenty-nine-year-old computer designer, had a mixed bag of problems—sudden inability to perform sexually, increasing difficulty producing innovative ideas, and minimal energy and endurance.

"My sexual failure is humiliating," he admitted, "but mental sluggishness and lack of energy are threatening my income and career. Coffee and pep pills don't do a thing for me. It's as if somebody pulled the plug on my power source."

His previous physician had tried a series of testosterone injections, which had given him only a minor charge and no improvement in his sex life or performance in business. Too young to be old, Phil was naturally dejected.

The four patients had two things in common: frustration and the same basic ailment. During their individual consultations with me, I informed them:

"Your thyroid function needs checking."

Their reactions could be summed up in the words: "Not another test!" All of them had gone through exhaustive tests, including one for thyroid function, at a cost of hundreds of dollars.

"This won't cost you a cent," I assured them. "You can do the Barnes Basal Temperature Test yourself at home."

They were puzzled. Who had ever heard of a no-cost test? Then I explained how to do it.

"Before going to bed tonight, shake down a thermometer. Leave it on the bedside table. As soon as you wake up in the morning after a good night's sleep—no later—tuck the thermometer snugly under your arm for ten minutes as you lie there.

"If your thyroid function is normal, your temperature should be in the range from 97.8 to 98.2 degrees Fahrenheit. If it's lower, you are probably hypothyroid—your thyroid gland is underfunctioning—and your physical problems and related ones have probably been caused or at least influenced by that. The test should be done on two consecutive days."

To the women, I said, "You get the most accurate readings if you're not menstruating (temperature fluctuates at that time) or on the second or third days of menstruation."

Reported results confirmed my suspicions: all were indeed hypothyroid. The treatment—Armour natural desiccated thyroid supplement—brought gratifying results: freedom from their ailments in less than two months. Eloise was ecstatic about painless menstruation and normal body temperature.

Appreciative husbands of Connie and Allison told me that thyroid supplement had saved their sex lives and marriages. Phil went even further. He said, "It saved my whole life."

Over thirty years as a medical doctor, I have been privileged to help many Connies, Allisons, Eloises, and Phils. In fact, I seem to specialize in patients whose symptoms are not readily diagnosed—persons who have been through the traditional system and possibly have been rejected as psychosomatic cases or as hypochondriacs. A graduate of the State University of New York College of Medicine at Buffalo, I spent some time studying psychiatry before realizing that I couldn't accept one of the basic assumptions of traditional Western allopathic medicine—the sharp cleavage between mind and body. I was troubled that patients should be branded as "psychiatric problems" or as having "psychogenic problems," as opposed to having "ailments of the body." It seemed that the twain would never meet.

In my frame of reference, mind and body are two expressions of the same thing. As I moved out of psychiatry, I realized another key fact about my professional stance. I couldn't build a shrine before the double-blind approach so highly revered in medical schools. It is certainly valid, but it is just one belief system among many. Belief systems should be used pragmatically, not be regarded as sacred. They should be continually transcended if something better comes along—even if that something doesn't fit into the tidy training mold of medical doctors.

Because of this position, I can draw upon the best of today's medicine and still think and act independently. Therefore, if patients have no clinical findings to back up a laundry list of complaints, I don't automatically conclude that they are hypochondriacs, neurotics, or psychotics. After an examination and the taking of a thorough history (which may not reveal reasons for their problems), I still do not paste a negative label on them.

After all, no medical system or doctor is infallible. Often there is a physical basis for many symptoms, a cause not always apparent within the framework of traditional clinical medicine.

One major basis frequently overlooked is hypothyroidism—underfunctioning of the thyroid gland. Even a seemingly slight deficiency in thyroid hormone can cause an incredible number and variety of sabotaging physical, emotional, and mental ailments.

For the benefit of my patients and the expansion of my professional horizons, I am thankful that I stumbled across the monumental research in this area of Broda O. Barnes, MD, PhD, one of the world's foremost authorities on the thyroid gland. This wealth of information revolutionized my practice of preventive health maintenance more than any other single factor.

Speaking from almost fifty years of clinical experimentation, Dr. Barnes stated that no less than 40 percent of the adult population of the United States suffers from an often hidden condition known as hypothyroidism. In medical school, we saw a few cases, but no one paid much attention to them. The 40 percent figure struck me as a gross exaggeration until I followed the Barnes method in my practice and found the percentage running slightly higher.

Lecturing to physicians and laypeople worldwide, Dr. Barnes warned that serious hypothyroidism was going virtually undetected, because of doctors' almost total reliance upon laboratory blood tests. Why should millions suffer needlessly from the insidious effects of hypothyroidism when a simple, accurate thyroid function test was available to everyone? After all, his underarm test had been painstakingly checked for accuracy against basal metabolism results in thousands of persons in the late 1930s and early 1940s, and a paper on the subject had been published in one of the most prestigious medical journals.

His hypothesis was interesting enough for me to investigate it. Why not give it a fair trial? Obviously, Dr. Barnes was not out to sell something, because thyroid hormone is one of the cheapest substances on the market.

He did not claim that an underactive thyroid was the sole cause of a host of ailments, only that it played a significant role in them, and that many traditional treatments for chronic degenerative diseases would not work smoothly—or at all—until the thyroid gland was properly tested, and, if necessary, supplemented. Certainly he never claimed that thyroid hormone was a panacea.

About this time, I began appearing as a guest on television and radio talk shows, as well as conducting my own question-and-answer radio show in the San Francisco area, and I set up a phone interview with Dr. Barnes, then practicing medicine in Fort Collins, Colorado. For two hours, Dr. Barnes answered my questions and those from the audience so directly, factually, and convincingly that I was prompted to take my own basal temperature; I found it somewhat low. Shortly after I started using a small daily dosage of natural desiccated thyroid supplement, remarkable changes occurred: my energy shot up, my ability to concentrate improved dramatically, and many minor nagging symptoms disappeared.

Then I judiciously began using the Barnes Basal Temperature Test on a number of problem patients and, when it was indicated, prescribed the thyroid supplement. Their quick, positive response made me a believer. Soon I found that this test is the key to treating a number of chronic degenerative illnesses that I couldn't touch by conventional methods. I learned what most doctors know: that there is always a population of people who defy many of our best clinical approaches. My surprise was in seeing how large that population is.

Unusual success and satisfaction with Dr. Barnes's methods stirred up questions in my mind. How did he discover that temperature is a more reliable indicator of thyroid function than the pride of modern medical technology—lab tests? How did he learn that even slight hypothyroidism—often not detectable by conventional measuring devices or systems—can cause or contribute to serious ailments in women, men, and children?

Once I became well acquainted with Dr. Barnes, I learned firsthand the fascinating facts that have helped me treat the neglected gland of hundreds of patients in a proper manner so that they could become revitalized. Here is how he tells it:

> In the early 1930s, even before planning to become a physician, I was assigned to study the thyroid gland for my doctorate in physiology at the University of Chicago, under Dr. Anton J. Carlson, a giant in the field.
>
> Soon I had a PhD after my name, and Dr. Carlson assigned me to teach endocrinology to future physicians. One of my duties was to show a motion picture to demonstrate the powerful influence of the thyroid gland on every living cell of every body system.
>
> Students were shocked at the rapid deterioration of a small rabbit after removal of its thyroid. Previously warm at room

temperature, active, and alert, the animal now shivered with cold, moved in slow motion, drugged with fatigue—as if old and feeble.

Its fur was dry, its skin was scaly, its mucous membranes were infected—particularly in the respiratory system—and its heartbeat and muscles were weak. My respect for the tiny thyroid gland increased with every class.

Striving to increase my effectiveness as an instructor, I completed the medical curriculum, not realizing that I would soon do more doctoring than teaching. Upon completion of my internship in 1937, I took the Hippocratic oath, and the philosophy of Hippocrates, the Father of Greek medicine, is still branded on my brain, particularly the following statement: "It is not to be expected that he should know the remedies of illnesses who knows not their origin."

Treating the symptoms, the usual approach in modern medicine, was not enough. I wanted to probe to the roots of illnesses, to causes. Now, licensed to practice, I had an immediate opportunity.

Charlotte, my wife, who developed tuberculosis, became my first patient. Galen, the celebrated physician of the second century, had said, "If you develop tuberculosis, go to the mountains and buy a cow."

We did both, settling in the then clean-air countryside near Denver, where we not only drank fresh milk but picked and ate ripe vegetables and fruit from our garden and trees. Charlotte and I took a small amount of thyroid daily to compensate for hypothyroidism.

Her rapid recovery and my boundless energy and endurance demonstrated the value of natural, nutrient-packed food—a major part of the foundation for good health—and thyroid supplementation.

Lessons learned from the rabbit helped with my first paying patient, a woman who had complained of female problems, coldness, lack of energy, anxiety, low blood pressure, and one infection after another. She had been thoroughly examined and treated in a world-renowned midwestern clinic, where no physical reason for her symptoms could be found.

"Doctor, I spent a small fortune there and came away with no satisfaction. What makes me indignant is that they think I'm a hypochondriac."

I put her on a daily grain of natural thyroid extract and she soon improved, recovering completely in seven weeks.

That rabbit continued to make me look good. This grateful woman sent me friends who had one or more similar complaints with no apparent measurable causes: sexual dysfunction, little or no vaginal sensation, feeling cold, excruciating menstrual pain (then commonly treated with aspirin and bedrest), too frequent periods, too copious blood flow, acute headaches, fatigue, irritability, hair-trigger temper, and infections (mainly in the vagina and urinary tract).

Small doses of natural desiccated thyroid improved or eliminated these conditions. Husbands began coming to me. Spectacular recoveries of women and men enlightened and puzzled me. Surely so many of my patients would not have been helped by thyroid if it had not been necessary. Yet other doctors had given them comprehensive physical exams, including a basal metabolism test (the then accepted measurement of thyroid function), without detecting hypothyroidism. Could it be that thyroid deficiency too slight to be recorded contributed to or caused many illnesses?

Could the basal metabolism test be so far wrong that it actually concealed hypothyroidism? Could known symptoms of low thyroid function be a more reliable indicator than the basal metabolism test?

Searching for answers—even clues—I paged through countless journals in the Denver Medical Library and found a revealing, detailed description of the first acute hypothyroid patient who had symptoms similar to those of my patients, though far more exaggerated.

In 1877 Dr. William N. Ord, a brilliant London clinician, had made a milestone discovery while performing an autopsy on a mature woman.

Medical records disclosed that she had been constantly cold and exhausted, prone to fall asleep if not moving around, incapable of thinking or speaking without extreme effort, unable to sew because of numb and clumsy hands, and inclined to suffer frequent headaches and menopausal problems, as well as infections and a kidney ailment causing bloody urine.

He was fascinated by her unsightly physical degeneration: a moon face too swollen to change expression (a feature of cretinism) and body skin and connective tissue bloated with fluid. When Dr. Ord cut into her skin, expecting water to run off (as in kidney failure), a thick, gluelike substance called *mucin* remained fixed there. To give a name to this condition, he took the Greek word for mucin, *myx,* and wedded it to *edema,* the description for water-logged tissue, calling it *myxedema.*

The woman's arteries showed advanced atherosclerosis. Coronary, kidney, and brain arteries were almost clogged. He was amazed at the sight of the woman's thyroid gland, so overgrown and choked with fibrous tissue that it had stopped functioning. He concluded that this was what had caused myxedema and atherosclerosis.

Mulling over the woman's list of symptoms, I found six common denominators in my far milder cases of hypothyroidism: subnormal temperature, fatigue, drowsiness, depression, female problems, and infections.

Despite exhaustive study of the thyroid gland, I still thought it incredible that this tiny, lightweight (less than an ounce), coral-colored bow tie semicircling the windpipe under the Adam's apple could be so critical to living and to the quality of life. Yet numerous well-designed experiments had already shown that production of thyroid hormone can make or break a person's health.

All of your blood—approximately five quarts—circulates through the thyroid gland once every hour, bringing iodide, the material your thyroid needs to make hormones, as well as a hormone from the anterior pituitary gland to stimulate production from the thyroid. Your thyroid also stores and discharges thyroid hormone in the bloodstream for delivery to your cells where and when needed.

Too little thyroid hormone (in hypothyroidism) causes your motor to run poorly. Heartbeat slows, blood pressure drops, circulation becomes sluggish (contributing to discomfort from cold, particularly in the hands and feet), energy and endurance are low, digestion slows down, constipation is common, headaches occur frequently, hair becomes lifeless and falls out more readily, nails are brittle, wounds heal slowly, thinking is slow, memory undependable, and sex urge weak or dormant. The effects of hypothyroidism are felt in each of your trillions of cells in every organ and tissue of your body.

Too much thyroid hormone, in hyperthyroidism, makes your motor race. Heartbeat increases, blood pressure rises, blood volume swells; you flush from overheating, often to the level of a mild fever; you perspire profusely, are nervous and sleepless, and you may have diarrhea. (Similar symptoms may occur if a hypothyroid is given too much thyroid supplement.)

Teamwork of the thyroid and pituitary glands in infants, children, and youths encourages growth of the skeleton and sexual organs and contributes to eruption of teeth and development of the brain.

One of the most succinct and colorful summations of the dramatic function of the thyroid (which I happened upon considerably later) is in the writings of endocrinologist Herman H. Rubin, MD: ". . . a few grains of thyroid may be the main difference between a captain of industry and the office boy who is always dragging his feet." [1] Then he added that a close and sympathetic relationship exists between the thyroid and sex glands of men and women, that sexual function really is an expression of energy. Due to the fact the thyroid is the governor of our uses of energy, we shouldn't be too surprised by the association. Alertness, animation, fire, and sparkle result from a properly functioning thyroid. These qualities show themselves particularly in glamour and sexual attractiveness.

In my reading, I came across another succinct summary on the critical importance of the thyroid gland by the late Louis Berman, MD, world-renowned endocrinologist:

"Without thyroid, there can be no complexity of thought, no learning, no education, no habit formation, no responsive energy for situations, as well as no physical unfolding of faculty and function. No reproduction of kind with no sign of adolescence at expected age and no exhibition of sex tendencies thereafter." [2]

With no thyroid gland, you and I would not be human at all; we'd be vegetables!

In a continuing search of the literature, I noticed that subnormal temperature appeared to be a common denominator in hypothyroidism. Many decades of pioneering research in England had demonstrated that if metabolism is low, temperature is also low. Each hypothyroid patient who came to my office was a verification of this fact.

Could temperature give a more accurate indication of hypothyroidism than the basal metabolism test? I decided to find out. In my private practice and, later, as professor of Health Education at the University of Denver, I took the oral temperature of hundreds of male and female patients and students and also gave them the basal metabolism test, making sure that no subjects had an infection, which would have caused a false reading.

I then compared results of both measurements with known symptoms of hypothyroidism and learned that temperature was the more accurate indicator by far.

In a subsequent study of one thousand college students, reported in the August 1942 issue of the *Journal of the American Medical Association*, I again found that the relationship of subnormal temperature to accepted major symptoms of hypothyroidism was significantly greater than to basal metabolism readings.

Dr. Joseph Ehrlich and I, while U.S. Army medical officers in Kingman, Arizona, during World War II, refined the test, taking oral, rectal, and armpit temperatures of one thousand soldiers. We found that, barring sore throats, sinusitis, or colds, which raise oral temperature, mouth and armpit temperatures are nearly identical.

Out of these experiments came the Barnes Basal Temperature Test, which, for many years, had been listed in the *Physicians' Desk Reference* (the *PDR*). Many physicians now rely on this test because by using it they have discovered tens of thousands of hypothyroid individuals who were rated normal by conventional tests. But even though the temperature test's accuracy has been abundantly demonstrated, we do not lean exclusively on its results. We verify them with classical symptoms of hypothyroidism and the patient's thorough medical history, carefully correlating and interpreting data.

Any less painstaking procedure can lead to possible error. A Mayo Clinic study by Drs. Joseph C. Scott, Jr., and Elizabeth Mussey, made this point clearly when they found that a patient can be regarded as mildly hypothyroid by one physician and normal by another, based on results of just one office interview or test. "No single test or procedure will define the status of the thyroid gland," they write. "Further, any combination of methods may lead to erroneous interpretation or to inconsistent results. The clinician must have the faculty of correlating the clinical appearance of the patient with laboratory findings."[3]

Despite the validity of this position, present-day doctors, enchanted by the laboratory test, often make it the sole and final authority. Is this wise or otherwise?

You be the judge.

The Centers for Disease Control routinely sends out specimens to 980 licensed laboratories—some 7 percent of all laboratories in the United States. Between 8 and 25 percent of the tests yield erroneous results, according to an article in *American Medical News*.[4] These labs process all kinds of tests, including critical ones for thyroid function.

Edward R. Pinckney, MD, former associate editor of the *Journal of the American Medical Association*, wrote an earth-shaking article for the *Archives of Internal Medicine* on the accuracy of medical testing. It says, in part: "Hardly a week goes by when the FDA [Food and Drug Administration] does not recall several in-use laboratory reagents that are contaminated, defective, or inaccurately labeled. Other surveys have reported that one out of every two sphgymomanometers [the common blood-pressure checking device] gave erroneous readings, that thousands of ECG [electrocardiogram] machines were found to be improperly calibrated, and that hundreds of X-ray machines, often operated by inadequately trained technicians, were producing thousands of useless roentgenograms [X-rays]." [5]

Dr. Pinckney reveals that in an American Medical Association survey, three out of four doctors admitted ordering X-rays, ECGs, and a multitude of laboratory and other procedures for the sole purpose of having a better defense in the event of a malpractice suit.

"The American College of Physicians is in the throes of evaluating the usefulness of medical tests," writes Dr. Pinckney. "To date, it has declared some fifty tests to be of no proven value, unreliable, or obsolete."

Admitting that medical journals are constantly reporting controversy, confusion, and contradictions about the significance of tests, Dr. Pinckney advocates the old-fashioned approach to doctoring: comparing results of medical tests against the physician's clinical judgment. If the doctor doesn't do this, what good are his or her training and experience?

"In three separate but similar studies, one conducted at the Mayo Clinic, the physician's history and physical examination detected twice as many alcoholics as did detailed laboratory data," writes Dr. Pinckney.

As early as 1959, a nationally recognized authority on the thyroid gland, Dr. A. S. Jackson, had published a paper in the *Journal of the American Medical Association*, declaring that low thyroid function is the most common disease entering the doctor's office and the diagnosis most missed.[6] The situation is much the same today, except that there are more tests, more misdiagnoses, and more people.

Like Drs. Jackson and Barnes, I continue to see numerous previously undetected cases of hypothyroidism. For this reason, it was no surprise to learn that biochemist Roger J. Williams, PhD, discoverer of pantothenic acid (vitamin B_5), says: "There are doubtless a great many people who are mildly deficient in thyroid hormone and would be benefited by taking it orally but are not ill enough to see a physician."[7]

The findings of James C. Wren, MD, reported in the *Journal of the American Geriatric Society*, bear out those of Dr. Williams, as well as those of Drs. Barnes and Jackson.[8] In a five-year research project with 347 atherosclerotic patients—174 women and 173 men—only 31 were shown by laboratory tests to be hypothyroid.

Yet when thyroid supplements were given to all subjects, measurable improvement was shown in a significant number of patients. Further, their mortality rate was less than half that of the run of this category of untreated patients. Why were results of thyroid treatment apparent across the board if only thirty-one subjects—9 percent—were hypothyroid according to conventional laboratory tests? (Later chapters will offer additional revealing data on how hypothyroidism relates to heart and artery diseases.)

In a medical journal article, "Hypothyroidism: A Treacherous Masquerader," Gerald S. Levey, MD, an endocrinologist and the vice chancellor of medical sciences and dean of the David Geffen School of Medicine at UCLA, warns that hypothyroidism is often such an extremely subtle disease that physicians can misinterpret its symptoms.[9]

The correct diagnosis is often missed, because a broad range of symptoms is not generally associated with hypothyroidism, he says: severe muscle cramps, particularly at night; persistent low back pain; blood abnormalities (easy bruising, minor bleeding, heavy blood loss in menstruation, and anemia); excessive blood uric acid; stiffness of joints (mild arthritis); and a decrease in heart contractility.

These conditions can be improved or relieved by thyroid hormone therapy, he says. Dr. Levey feels that traditional routine screening for thyroid function may leave something to be desired, inasmuch as many factors—among them drugs and certain systemic states—can distort results of such tests.

Various researchers have estimated that one-fourth of the United States population is hypothyroid—considerably under the forty-plus percentage of my new patients.

You may be among them.

Now, however, you don't have to wonder whether you are or aren't. You can gather the evidence through the Barnes Basal Temperature Test, a careful review of your medical history, and a check of your symptoms against the following telltale physical and emotional signs: (1) weakness; (2) dry, coarse skin; (3) lethargy; (4) slow speech; (5) swelling of face and eyelids; (6) coldness and cold skin; (7) diminished sweating; (8) thick tongue; (9) coarse hair; (10) pale skin; (11) constipation; (12) gain in weight; (13) loss of hair; (14) labored, difficult breathing; (15) swollen feet; (16) hoarseness; (17) loss of appetite; (18) excessive and/or painful menstruation; (19) nervousness; (20) heart palpitation; (21) brittle nails; (22) slow movement; (23) poor memory; (24) emotional instability; (25) depression; and (26) headaches.

If your temperature, medical history, and symptoms indicate that you are hypothyroid, report to your doctor with the facts and request treatment. Most physicians are now familiar with Dr. Barnes's method of treatment and his extensive list of publications in medical journals.

It is not my intention to indicate that additional thyroid hormone is a cure-all for anything or everything that might ail you. This would be simplistic, ignoring many other considerations, including biological and biochemical differences, which make you and me individuals with varying needs.

What I am saying is that a broad and serious blind spot exists today in physical diagnosis, one that needs immediate recognition. The purpose of this book is to serve as a newly ground, polished set of lenses to bring all parts of this area sharply into our visual fields.

Awareness of widespread hypothyroidism and the three-way approach to its accurate diagnosis will enable you to do one of two things: rule it out entirely or get proper treatment for it. This condition is too important to go ignored and untreated. It only worsens. Remember that the thyroid—the neglected gland—can have a mild to profound effect on every aspect of living: energy, endurance, body heat, sexuality, mind and emotions, resistance to colds and other respiratory ailments, and condition of hair, skin, and nails, as well as protection against diabetes and diabetic complications, heart and artery diseases, and cancer. It affects how long and how well you live!

2

Why So Much Hidden Hypothyroidism?

OFTEN WHEN I'M a guest on radio or TV programs, people who call in usually ask the following question: "How can hypothyroidism possibly be so widespread, with iodized salt available to everyone?"

A good question deserves a good answer.

Iodized salt was never intended to prevent hypothyroidism, just one manifestation of it: goiter, enlargement of the thyroid gland on the front and sides of the neck. It would not be practical or healthful for us to increase salt use in an effort to get all the iodine necessary to assure normal thyroid function. Overuse of salt is implicated in a host of ailments—insomnia, obesity, stomach ulcers, edema, high blood pressure, and heart disease, among others.

The Recommended Daily Allowance (RDA) of iodine is 100 micrograms (mcg) for women and 120 mcg for men, although up to ten times that amount has not produced toxic effects in persons with a normal thyroid. Residents of Japan thrive on nearly four thousand times as much iodine as Americans, all from large amounts of seafood, kelp, dulse, and sea lettuce. (*Warning*: it could be hazardous to one's health to ingest so much iodine in supplement form.)

Goiter, premature gray hair, and symptoms of hypothyroidism are rare in Japan. Is it any wonder? Much of the nation's population lives near the coast, and both soil and water are iodine-rich at or near seashores. So are vegetables, fruit, and grains grown there, as well as readily accessible seafood and ocean plants.

Although we require only a minute quantity of iodine for our thyroid glands, the world's goiter belts supply just one-seventh of that amount. Goiter belts are found in mountainous or inland regions, such as the Alps, Carpathian, and Pyrenees mountains of Europe, the Himalayas of Asia, the Andes mountains of South America, and various parts of North America, including the valley of the St. Lawrence River, the Appalachian mountains, the Great Lakes basin, and westward through Minnesota, South and North Dakota, Montana, Wyoming (and adjoining areas of Canada), the Rocky Mountains, and into the northwest (parts of Oregon, Washington, and British Columbia).

Over the course of many centuries, soils of mountain and inland areas become iodine bankrupt because rain washes this trace mineral away into streams and, eventually, into the oceans. Low iodine content in the soil, however, is not the sole reason for subnormal thyroid function. Another weighty factor is inheritance. Several studies show that goiters and hypothyroidism without goiters run in families, many of whose members are hypersensitive even to minute iodine lack. Individuals prone to hypothyroidism are often revealed to have subnormal thyroid function, despite what appears to be an adequate intake of iodine.

Why did 7 percent of 8,000 schoolchildren with adequate iodine intake, surveyed in Georgia, Kentucky, Michigan, and Texas, have goiters? Why did a Centers for Disease Control study of individuals in ten states from California to Massachusetts end up with almost the same results? Again, more than 99 percent of those surveyed reported an acceptable intake of iodine.

A research project by Eduardo Gaitan, MD, of the Veterans Administration Medical Center and University of Mississippi Medical School, Jackson, led him to believe region-specific environmental factors were often to blame. Returning to his native Colombia, South America, he studied this problem in the Cauca-Patia Valley area of the Andes mountains.[1] In 1948, more than half of all schoolchildren there had goiters. The correct amount of iodine was added to the daily diet, but a 1978 survey revealed that 15 percent of the population still had goiters. Dr. Gaitan wanted to know why within this 800-kilometer-long valley the goiter incidence ranged from 1 percent to 42 percent.

His investigation permitted him to rule out insufficient iodine intake, other dietary shortcomings, and socioeconomic factors. "It is certain chemicals in the water supply," he told an American Chemical Society meeting in Seattle, and elaborated his reasons for this belief. He had found a high-goiter area and a low-goiter area in Candelaria, a nonindustrial city in the Andes with a population of eight thousand. This confused him until he learned that two different wells supplied these areas. Dr. Gaitan had water samples analyzed by an impartial testing laboratory, and the chemical culprits emerged in water from the high-goiter district—10 to 100 parts per million of resorcinol and phthalate esters. Resorcinol has a documented reputation as a cause of goiters. The phthalate esters (normally added to various plastics to give them flexibility) also contain substances that encourage goiters. No resorcinol and negligible amounts of phthalates could be found in the water samples from the low-goiter area.

What puzzled Dr. Gaitan is how resorcinol and phthalates could enter the water, inasmuch as they are common products of the industrial world, and Candelaria has no industry. Pipes from the well with the high level of contaminants were not made of plastics and plastic containers were not used in gathering or storing water samples. Dr. Gaitan finally concluded that these chemicals came from organic soil constituents 200 feet down.

For self-protection, it would be wise for us to avoid or minimize our consumption of beverages stored in plastic containers and to check with officials of the municipal water supply to make sure it does not have a harmful content of resorcinol or phthalate esters from industrial wastes.

While Dr. Gaitan's findings may well apply to previously unexplained goiter prevalence in areas amply supplied with iodine, individual variation in size and capability of thyroid glands may also play a big part.

Roger J. Williams, PhD, whose studies on the size and functional variation of human organs have revolutionized physiology and biochemistry, writes in his book *Free and Unequal* that, among what are called normal individuals, thyroid glands vary in weight from 8 grams to 50 grams. Undoubtedly size and activity of one's thyroid gland make a difference.[2] Heredity is also an important factor.

One would have thought it possible that, in the course of several generations, marriages between hypothyroids and persons with normal thyroids would decrease hypothyroids in the population. Actually, there appear to be few such intermarriages, as many physicians conversant with thyroid problems have observed. Hypothyroids usually attract other hypothyroids for a basic reason: they have low energy and high sleep requirements in common. Even when short, impulsive courtships bring hypothyroids and those with normal thyroids to the altar, these couples soon realize their glaring energy mismatch and, in time, may end up in the divorce court.

In my early days of prescribing thyroid, I discovered it was a serious mistake to treat just one person of a hypothyroid couple. One of my patients was a pudgy, sluggish, no-energy man who hardly made it through a workday, mechanically munched a TV dinner with an equally dragged-out wife, then collapsed heavily into a sexless bed. A daily grain of thyroid and a diet without junk foods brought about a remarkable change in him in less than three months. He lost weight, gained energy, slept less, and began going out at night, insisting that his weary wife join him in partying and attending concerts and the theater. Their contrasting energy levels triggered repeated quarrels.

Rather than let them live unhappily ever after, I insisted that the wife take her basal temperature. Learning that it was way below par, I prescribed natural desiccated thyroid. Now this couple has made new breakthroughs in marital harmony.

The growing population of persons with subnormal thyroid glands is not entirely due, however, to the procreation of hypothyroid couples. Medical ingenuity has something to do with it. Antibiotics have made hypothyroids less susceptible to infectious diseases that in years past would have annihilated them. Less than a century ago, almost 50 percent of all children died before becoming adults. Only those who could resist infectious diseases survived. At that time, medical science contributed little to the ability to survive. Today, over and above those who are normally infection-resistant, there is a new population segment—hypothyroids with low resistance to infectious diseases, who are kept alive by the physician's arsenal of antibiotics.

Dr. Broda Barnes draws a sharp focus on the historic battle to survive in pointing out that humanity is constantly threatened by a grim competition of diseases: "Smallpox led the pack for many years, wiping out babies and children. Then an obscure physician, Edward Jenner, MD, discovered that smallpox could be prevented by vaccination. Soon the champion killer was dethroned, and a larger segment of the population could live longer. Then a new menace moved in, tuberculosis, which, for more than two generations, decimated young adults, until bedrest, improved diet and, particularly, antibiotics knocked it out. Again, life expectancy rose, making the biggest advance in medical history. One disease or another keeps proving our mortality. Due to our longer life through the conquest of many infectious diseases, another killer has now claimed the championship—heart and circulatory ailments," he says.

Like Dr. Barnes, other medical doctors, clinical researchers, and scientists over more than eight decades have found that thyroid supplements have won skirmishes, battles, even wars, against myriad ailments in addition to the so-called hypochondriacal conditions: fatigue, physical and sexual coldness, infectious diseases, every kind of female problem, emotional illnesses, migraine headaches, skin abnormalities, heart disease, arthritis, diabetic complications, and cancer.

It is time for medical researchers and doctors to take a fresh look at the thyroid—the neglected gland—at present laboratory tests for thyroid function, and at treatment of its subnormal function.

Often I am asked why, if patients are revealed to be hypothyroid, they cannot correct their condition simply by supplying more iodine to their thyroid glands through seafood or kelp. Sometimes they can. In first-generation hypothyroidism, such compensation often proves helpful. However, in most cases, hypothyroidism has persisted for generations, so iodine supplementation may be too little, too late. This is not my finding alone. Dr. Barnes and more than one hundred of his physician followers have discovered the same phenomenon. Through experience, we have discovered that natural desiccated thyroid supplement helps make sure that enough thyroid hormone is available. It takes less than 1/100,000 ounce of this substance to keep us healthy.

A commonsense approach now assists doctors in administering thyroid supplement safely and effectively. The fear of prescribing it is slowly disappearing. The secret is to balance the amount of the supplement with the amount of hormone secreted by the thyroid gland, so that an oversupply does not lull the gland into complacency and stop it from working.

When the blood level of thyroid hormone drops below normal, the hypothalamus gland in the brain senses this and discharges thyroid-releasing hormone (TRH). TRH influences the pituitary, the boss of the glandular company, to release thyroid-stimulating hormone (TSH), which tells the thyroid to get to work. Once sufficient thyroid hormone has been produced, the pituitary puts the thyroid gland on hold.

A thyroid whose function is limited by lack of iodine, by a hereditary flaw, or by a tumor or some other defect can't carry out the orders of the pituitary gland. Then it needs help from the outside.

When the subnormal working of the thyroid results from the gland itself, this is called *primary hypothyroidism*. When underproduction is caused by imperfect function of the hypothalamus or the pituitary gland, this is called *secondary hypothyroidism*. Both kinds usually respond to thyroid hormone supplementation.

I start hypothyroid patients with a moderate daily dose of natural thyroid—one-quarter to one-half grain of Armour desiccated thyroid preparation—and increase their dosage in one-quarter grain increments every fourteen days until I obtain a dosage that achieves desired clinical results.

Usually, a child under age three requires no more than a quarter grain until he or she reaches age six, at which time a half grain is most frequently the optimum amount needed. Teenagers generally work up to a full grain, and adults go as high as two to three grains. I monitor patients carefully, and if symptoms disappear, I keep them at this level.

I also advise that patients take a multivitamin and mineral supplement rich in B vitamins, inasmuch as, according to Murray Israel, MD, a pioneer in thyroidology, B vitamins are essential to efficient transport of oxygen inside the cells. Originally, Dr. Barnes used thyroid hormones alone—with success—but, impressed by Dr. Israel's results, he added vitamin B supplements to his treatment.

Dr. Israel's career in recognizing and managing widespread, unsuspected hypothyroidism also helped focus my attention on this much-neglected area of medicine. Startling results with his first case, described at an annual meeting of the American College of Endocrinology and Nutrition, left an indelible impression on me.[3]

Called in to treat an elderly woman so far gone that her family had brought in a priest to administer the last rites, Dr. Israel found her breathing shallow, heart sounds faint, blood pressure high, coronary artery severely atherosclerotic, and hypothyroidism pronounced. She had stark white hair and her pale face was flecked with dead skin. Fresh out of internship, Dr. Israel had a critical decision to make. From the standpoint of conventional medicine, the woman had two incompatible conditions, atherosclerosis and hypothyroidism. The usual treatment was to remove the thyroid gland surgically. The easy way out would have been to do nothing, but Dr. Israel decided to do something. Surgery would only make her hypothyroidism worse, so he administered 10 milligrams (mg) of thyroid along with brewer's yeast three times daily. (Brewer's yeast was then the best available vitamin B-complex source.)

He continued this regimen, and in a few days, the patient turned the corner. Within two weeks, she was mentally alert and perky and walked to church. Soon her dead, pale skin peeled off, leaving her complexion pink and smooth. Black strands of hair eventually began to replace some of the white. She lived actively and enthusiastically for another twenty years.

This milestone case set a pattern of treatment for Dr. Israel, that, over the course of many years, he used successfully in over a thousand similar cases. In addition to alerting modern medicine to a more effective approach for managing coronary atherosclerosis and hypothyroidism, his triumphs spared patients with these ailments the harmful, unnecessary, and costly removal of the thyroid gland and showed doctors that judicious supplementation with natural desiccated thyroid can be helpful and safe.

What excited Dr. Israel particularly was that the thyroid treatment had an apparent rejuvenative effect on patients. These results also intrigued a young medical doctor, Nathan Masor, MD, who later joined Dr. Israel's research staff. After injecting Dr. Israel's formula into elderly atherosclerotic patients each week for a month, along with supplements of vitamins C and B complex, he noticed marked physical and emotional improvement: more energy, faster movements, more endurance, better sleep, and less irritability, anxiety, and depression.

Encouraged, Dr. Masor did additional research, eventually concluding that organic and functional diseases are intertwined, showing two basic manifestations—fatigue and anxiety—which, in turn, cause myriad satellite symptoms, among them headache, hot flashes, depression, drowsiness, insomnia, irritability, loss of memory, inability to concentrate, impotence, guilt, and inferiority feelings.

In his book *The New Psychiatry*, Dr. Masor states that symptoms of so-called hypochondria can mimic those of any organic disease, and that when fatigue and anxiety begin to disappear, so do satellite symptoms in varying degrees.[4] He explained his thyroid/vitamin therapy to the Second International Congress for Psychiatry in Zurich, Switzerland.

Dr. Masor is skeptical about the accuracy and helpfulness of the usual laboratory tests for thyroid function and asks if it isn't possible that such modern tests are incapable of detecting every case of malfunctioning thyroid gland. "This is strongly suspected in the condition of metabolic insufficiency (hypothyroidism)," he says, "wherein all tests prove normal, but the individual may suffer from a fully developed fatigue and anxiety state."[5]

On the same subject, Dr. Israel's findings are even more decisive than those of his protégé. In almost forty years of practice, studies, and experimentation at the Vascular Research Foundation in New York, which he founded, he observed that laboratory tests failed to uncover even a minute fraction of hypothyroids.[6] Standard tests indicated that 85 percent of his patients had normal thyroid function. Yet all of them showed marked and consistent benefits from thyroid supplementation, including comfortable body temperature and increased energy and vitality.

With so much undiagnosed hypothyroidism, it is no wonder that patients with legitimate emotional, mental, and physical symptoms are sometimes written off as hypochondriacs and, even worse, left untreated, living lives of quiet desperation.

3

What's Sabotaging
Your Thyroid?

THERE'S MORE TO keeping your thyroid healthy than an ample amount of iodine, vitamin B complex and other nutrients—as crucially important as they are. Chapter 2 touched lightly on some key factors.

Studies by Eduardo Gaitan, MD, chief of endocrinology at the University of Mississippi School of Medicine, reveal that an estimated four hundred million people worldwide have slightly enlarged thyroid glands to full-fledged goiters—some as large as the belly of a pregnant woman. Such conditions indicate reduced thyroid gland function.[1]

One-quarter of these individuals—one hundred million people—have goiters that can't be traced to a lack of sufficient dietary iodine. They may be victims of goiter-producing geological factors, states Dr. Gaitan.

Like what?

Environmental pollutants in drinking water tend to limit thyroid function and cause goiters. In certain Appalachian coal-mining areas of Kentucky, "as many as 37 percent of the children have large goiters," writes Gaitan—this, despite an adequate intake of iodine.

He notes that children are more susceptible to goiter than adults. And this condition is especially harmful to children, because they are in the formative stage. Therefore, they can suffer both physical and mental problems if this condition is not treated.

An extreme example of this is *cretinism*, defined in *Webster's Collegiate Dictionary* (11th Edition) as "a congenital, abnormal condition marked by physical stunting and mental retardation and caused by severe hypothyrodism." Adult cretinism is attributed to the cumulative damage from low thyroid function over many generations.

Studies by Dr. Gaitan and associates in these Kentucky regions revealed resorcinol, a well-known thyroid inhibitor, present in much of the well water there.

"We also found other compounds in the water—phthalates— which, under the action of bacteria, can be transformed into dihydroxybenzoic acids: thyroid inhibitors," Dr. Gaitan told *Science News*.[2] He also reported finding them in his research in high-goiter areas of Colombia, South America, as stated in Chapter 2.

Why are these substances that apply the biochemical brakes to thyroid function so prevalent in the Kentucky regions mentioned? Both resorcinol and dihydroxybenzoic acids are waste materials in the coal-mining process, says Dr. Gaitan. So, it is likely that they may be present in any coal-mining areas of the world.

Other harmful chemicals discovered by Dr. Gaitan in drinking water in high-goiter areas of Kentucky, but not Colombia, are methoxyanthracene and bromoform. In investigating children in these Kentucky regions, he and associates found that one-third of affected children "make antibodies against their own thyroid glands" —a serious disorder called *autoimmune thyroiditis*.

Citing studies by other researchers, Dr. Gaitan mentions that buffalo rats given methoxyanthracene and bromoform develop autoimmune thyroiditis, a condition more fully covered in a later chapter.

Another key piece in the goiter jigsaw puzzle was discovered some years ago by Sir Robert McCarrison, MD, a noted English medical doctor who traveled worldwide searching for environmental sources of goiter.[3] He found that, although people in Hunza, high in the Himalaya mountains in northern Pakistan, were eminently healthy and living long, with no goiters, inhabitants in nearby areas where climate, soil (and its iodine content), and water were similar, suffered goiters, other forms of hypothyroidism, and less than ideal health.

Why? Dr. McCarrison observed that the Hunzas were close to pure water sources, pristine white snow and ice, and kept their drinking water clean in roofed tanks and cisterns, protected from environmental contamination and animals.

However, near Hunza, nine villages on the mountainside, one below the other, share water that rolls down through an open channel. This water is used for drinking, bathing, washing clothing and household utensils, crop irrigation, and to drain off manured fields, wrote Dr. McCarrison. Each village receives pollution-laden water from villages above, and the last one suffers the most accumulated pollutants. Other researchers have found that such contaminated water usually contains the poison cyanide, a well-established thyroid depressant. Dr. McCarrison's census of goiters shows a steady increase from the highest village to the lowest.

However, contaminated water is not limited to people in Third World countries. It exists in many parts of the United States. Government surveys reveal that goiter is nearly always more prevalent in rural areas. Many, if not most, wells yield polluted water. So individuals who escape to rural areas for freedom, homegrown food, and well water may be little better off than residents of the nine villages below Hunza.

During floods, brooks and rivers fill up with organic matter and chemical fertilizers. When a drought follows, the contaminants become more concentrated, and the cyanide content of the water increases. This is when goiter epidemics usually occur.

Ever since 1854, it has been known that fluoride is one of the most potent inhibitors of thyroid function, particularly in areas where soils and water are iodine deficient. Individuals who drink fluoridated water regularly and show a low temperature on the Barnes Basal Temperature Test may experience thyroid suppression—an excellent reason for using pure, bottled, spring water. In most instances, eliminating fluoridated water restores thyroid function to normal.

Certain drugs and chemicals suppress thyroid function. Many barbiturates contain cyanide and produce hydrocyanic acid in the body. In a number of studies, sulfa drugs and antidiabetic agents interfered with the formation of thyroid hormones by blocking iodine uptake. As indicated previously, it has been shown that prednisone should be judiciously used in known or suspected hypothyroidism, because in pharmacologic doses, it indirectly worsens already subnormal thyroid function. So does estrogen in pharmacologic doses, an important consideration for women on birth control pills or hormone replacement therapy.

Various medications can contribute to hypothyroidism—among them some cough medicines, amiodarone HC1 (Cordarone) and lithium (used as an antidepressant or for treating bipolar disorder)—by blocking the secretion of both major thyroid hormones: T4 (thyroxine) and T3 (triiodothyronine). Dopamine and corticosteroids suppress the pituitary gland's secretion of thyroid-stimulating hormones (TSH), essential for proper functioning of the thyroid gland. Corticosteroids also decrease thyroxine-binding globulin (the carriers of this hormone to the body's trillions of cells) and block the conversion of thyroid hormones T4 and T3.

Many doctors who have their patients take an aspirin or two a day to prevent blood clotting and to protect the heart may not be aware that aspirin and other salicylates—painkilling drugs—can contribute to hypothyroidism. The main ingredient in oil of wintergreen used in rubbing liniments to soothe muscles, salicylates may interfere with the binding of T4 to its transport proteins and decrease the amount of T4 in the blood.

Heavy smokers and those who share their polluted environment with nonsmokers should be aware that cigarette smoke contains thyocyanide (among its arsenal of other health destroyers), a fairly strong thyroid gland inhibitor. However, it isn't just noxious chemicals in the air we breathe, the fluids we drink, and foods we eat that suppress thyroid function. There are thousands of food additives whose relations to thyroid function have never been studied—a good reason for eliminating processed foods from our diets, or at least for minimizing them.

Certain otherwise wholesome foods—some of them found to contain anticancer substances—lower thyroid gland efficiency by reducing the amount of iodine available for synthesizing the two thyroid hormones, T3 and T4: cabbage, cauliflower, kale, kohlrabi, mustard greens, rutabaga, and turnips. These vegetables are most noted for this action in that they contain progoitrin, which is transformed by the body into goitrin. However, unless the person eats large amounts of these vegetables frequently and lives where iodine is deficient in the food and water, there's little chance of thyroid suppression from them.

A clue to the damage caused by excessive eating of cabbage and turnips was observed by food researchers in Europe as early as World War I. During that time of limited food supply, isolated pockets of individuals subsisted only on cabbage and turnips. Soon most of the people there developed goiters. To test these findings, researchers fed animals a diet almost exclusively made up of cabbage and turnips, and most of them developed goiters. Inasmuch as there are trace amounts of cyanide in these vegetables, they concluded that cyanide was the cause of suppressed thyroid function.

Other of the best-known food contributors to low thyroid function are soy products and walnuts—that is, if eaten frequently and in large amounts. Certainly, they should be minimized by individuals who are hypothyroid, at least until their condition is corrected or supplemented with thyroid hormone.

Millet, a highly nutritious breakfast food and a staple in developing nations, now appears to diminish thyroid function. Data from researchers Robert Cooksey and associates at the Veterans Administration Medical Center in Jackson, Mississippi, the University of Alabama (Birmingham), and the National Research Council of Canada (Saskatoon) reveal that substances in the hulls of millet are changed into resorcinol (mentioned earlier) by intestinal bacteria. Additionally, it is broken down to what are called "substituted resorcinol dihydroxybenzoic acids, ferulic acid, and thiocynate—all powerful thyroid suppressants:[4]

Depressed serum T4 levels, however, are not necessarily accompanied by below normal serum T3. . . . When severe iodine inadequacy is present, serum T3 tends to remain stable or even rise as T4 levels drop. . . . This relationship occurs because T3 contains less iodine, weight for weight, then does T4. . . . It is more metabolically active, and, hence, is produced by the thyroid when iodine is scarce. . . . Only in extreme iodine deficiency, when there is inadequate iodine even to produce T3, does its level decline. However, the T4 to T3 conversion requires the catalytic selenoenzyme iodothyronine-deiodinase. As a consequence, T4 and T3 deficiencies together are commonest in individuals living in environments depleted in both iodine and selenium. In contrast, depressed T3, without unusually low serum TO is characteristic of populations in regions where diets contain adequate iodine but lack selenium. Furthermore, animal studies suggest that, just as excess iodine consumption results in lowered serum T4 levels, an elevated intake of selenium may depress serum T3.

Cooksey believes that heavy and frequent intake of millet in Third World countries may explain, at least in part, why there is so much hypothyroidism—indicated by the high incidence of goiter—in these parts of the world. In most instances, moderate and occasional eating of millet brings some health benefits and should not prove harmful to anyone but extreme hypothyroids. However, in Third World nations, it is often eaten daily, sometimes more than once a day.

A further alarming discovery by Cooksey and colleagues is that when millet is cooked and stored—not an uncommon practice in developing nations where refrigeration is almost nonexistent—its thyroid suppression increases sixfold.

It is important to know and avoid environmental enemies, because in undermining the thyroid gland's function, they lower body temperature enough to bring on myriad illnesses.

4

Care and Feeding of the Thyroid

Don't take your thyroid gland for granted! Even if it is now normal, it may not stay that way unless properly fed, as one of my patients learned.

Mark's subnormal temperature, symptoms, and medical history indicated hypothyroidism.

"How can that be?" He was genuinely surprised. "I take kelp tablets for iodine."

Mark had been a vegetarian for a few years, eating raw and lightly cooked vegetables, with an emphasis on carrots, sweet potatoes, spinach, tomatoes, rutabagas, cabbage, and turnips.

After carefully examining a list of his daily foods, I observed, "Your diet seems short on protein and on at least three vitamins necessary to keep your thyroid working normally, particularly vitamin A."

That puzzled him.

"Something's wrong here, Dr. Langer. I get plenty of vitamin A in carrots, sweet potatoes, spinach, and tomatoes."

"Correction. What you get in these vegetables is carotene, a precursor of vitamin A. An underactive thyroid gland cannot efficiently convert carotene to usable vitamin A. In addition, vegetables such as rutabagas, cabbage, and turnips, eaten daily, may suppress thyroid function even more."

That was just the surface aspect of Mark's thyroid deficiency. I pointed out that he lacked vitamins B_2, B_6, and B_{12}, the former two further reducing his thyroid gland function. He rejected the idea of eating liver, which would have satisfied requirements of the B vitamins, so I recommended almonds, milk, wheat germ, and brewer's yeast for vitamin B_2; bananas, barley, wheat bran, wheat germ, and brewer's yeast for vitamin B_6; the best sources of vitamin B_{12}—eggs, Swiss and muenster cheese, and two kinds of fish, haddock and sole. I also put Mark on a grain of thyroid until the new diet could return his thyroid function to normal. Several months later this happened, and he is healthy again.

Although Mark's case was quite straightforward, that of Kathleen, a girl in her early teens, had mystified several other doctors and now challenged me. Once rather plump, ridiculed by schoolmates, she had opted for vegetarianism, despite parental objection, and had shed thirty-four pounds. Now she suffered from daily diarrhea, extreme sluggishness, and a seeming wasting-away of muscles. She wore sunglasses even in my office.

"Is the light too bright?" I asked.

"Yes."

"Do you have any other eye problems?"

"It's a little hard for me to see at night," she replied.

"On a vegetarian diet, it is sometimes difficult to take in enough protein—and enough of certain vitamins and minerals—to sustain you."

"My parents make me take a protein supplement twice every day," she responded.

That stopped me for an instant. However, her case triggered recall of a fascinating study done some years ago in India. Mass suffering from the protein deficiency disease *kwashiorkor* by tens of thousands of children prompted an American medical relief team to fly in to alleviate the situation. In kwashiorkor, the most prominent symptoms are wasting tissues, physical and mental sluggishness, swollen bellies, eye ailments—sometimes blindness—and even mental retardation. Immediately, the medical team fed the children a good grade of protein—powdered skim milk—expecting a reversal within weeks. Nothing beneficial happened, however, and they were baffled. Weeks ran into months, and the children grew steadily worse.

A second medical team flew in to help—doctors expert in eye ailments. To the protein-enriched diet, they added vitamin A, a nutrient essential to good health of eyes. In a short time, eye ailments began clearing up, and the children recovered from symptoms of protein deficiency. These doctors then ran painstaking tests and evaluated results, concluding that vitamin A must accompany protein to make it available to the body.

Kwashiorkor is a common disease in countries like India and parts of Africa and South America, where poverty prevents millions from eating enough protein and vitamin A-rich foods such as meats, eggs, fish, and dairy products. Now how could a teenage girl in California show some of the symptoms of kwashiorkor? Apparently by following a diet not too different from those of kwashiorkor victims. I told my patient what had happened to the children in India, got her agreement to add milk products and eggs to her diet, and gave her a good vitamin A supplement, vitamin B complex, and half a grain of thyroid to compensate for a malnourished thyroid gland. She did an amazing about-face. Today, she is a beautiful, slender, healthy young woman.

Unless one is an experienced nutritionist and knows the pedigrees of vegetables and fruits—that is, how they are grown, where, and with what kinds of fertilizers—it is difficult to secure enough protein and B vitamins from them.

Many years ago, William A. Albrecht, PhD, of the University of Missouri, investigated protein and vitamin content of commercially available vegetables and found that their food values had declined steadily because growers did not replace all the trace minerals that the plants remove from the soil. Numerous more recent studies have shown the same alarming trend. (Of course, this does not apply to organically grown produce available in an increasing number of stores.)

Furthermore, vegetables and fruits contain only a negligible amount of vitamin B_{12}. Most of us require just an infinitesimal amount of vitamin B_{12} daily—one microgram (one-millionth of a gram). If we don't get that much, however, we run the risk of pernicious anemia, neurological damage and, possibly, death. I recommend that strict vegetarians (vegans) take a vegetarian vitamin B_{12} supplement as dietary insurance.

It is impossible to forget a chilling article that I read in the nationally syndicated newspaper column of Lawrence Power, MD, that demonstrates the hazards of uncompromising vegetarianism.

Dr. Power cited a hospital report on twenty-five infants born in a religious community that adheres to a strict vegetarian diet. Of the twenty-five deathly ill babies rushed to the hospital, three were dead on arrival. Five more died a few hours after admittance, all from malnutrition. The remaining seventeen—severely malnourished—were returned to good health by more complete nutrition. Upon entry into the hospital, the surviving infants had enteritis, pneumonia, and anemia. Nine had acute rickets. The remainder showed involuntary muscle twitching.

I admire the moral, ethical, religious, and ecological principles that motivate vegetarians. Countless studies show that vegetarians have less cardiovascular disease than nonvegetarians, fewer cancers, less diabetes and arthritis, and fewer menopausal complications.

A monumental study by Gladys Block, PhD, a biochemist at the University of California, Berkeley—170 research projects in seventeen nations—reveals that those who eat the most vegetables and fruit slash by 50 percent their chances of developing all types of cancer over those who ate the least.[1]

A study by the German Research Center in Heidelberg demonstrates that natural killer cells in the blood of male vegetarians attack cancer cells twice as viciously as those in the blood of meat eaters.[2]

Twenty-six thousand Seventh Day Adventists in a twenty-one-year research project showed vegetarians to be half as likely as nonvegetarians to become diabetics. Many diabetics living on complex carbohydrates were able to stop taking insulin. [3]

Many other studies highlight the benefits of vegetarianism. In speaking with biochemist Richard Passwater, PhD, best-selling nutrition writer and consultant to the food industry, he summed it up well: "The total vegetarian diet has merit, but it must be well-designed, containing all nutritive factors that the body needs."

These body needs include nutrients that support the life-giving thyroid gland. Vegetarian diets are often deficient in vitamin B_{12}, vitamin D, omega-3 fatty acids, zinc, and iron.

There's so much harmful omega-6 in popular foods that it overwhelms omega-3—a ratio of anywhere from ten to thirty to one, estimate authorities. Omega-6 comes in innocent-looking oils—corn, sunflower seed, soy, and safflower—and products including them: margarines, mayonnaise, shortenings, and sandwich spreads. It reduces immune system function and promotes inflammation.

Omega-3 boosts the immune system, fighting inflammatory action that clogs arteries and ages us before our time. Further, it helps to combat inflammation characteristic of thyroiditis. Omega-3 supports thyroid function in taking part in cell respiration and metabolism. Thyroid sets the speed of oxidation, but to do this it needs fuel from this fatty acid.

Individuals who eat wild, cold-water fish—not farm-raised—at least twice a week usually derive enough omega-3. Likewise, they can get its benefits from fish liver oils. Certain brands in health food stores are warranted to be uncontaminated.

Often my vegan patients are deficient in omega-3 fatty acids, simply because it's difficult to find vegetarian omega-3. However, now that has changed. There is a vegetarian omega-3 product derived from sage and chia seed in health food stores.

Many other well-known nutrients support thyroid gland function. *Vitamins in Endocrine Metabolism*, a biochemistry classic by Isobel Jennings, of the University of Cambridge (England), names them and tells us exactly how they work to prevent hypothyroidism.[4]

Among many illuminating points, Jennings makes one that is pertinent to the malnutrition that infants mentioned earlier endured. Beta carotene, a vitamin A precursor, is not easily translated into vitamin A, particularly by hypothyroids.

Infants (as well as adults with gastroenteritis) have a much reduced capacity for converting carotene to vitamin A. In hypothyroids and diabetics, this ability is nearly suppressed. Without enough vitamin A, the infants could not make their limited protein supply available to their bodies.[5]

Studies cited by Jennings show that when animals are short-changed on vitamin A, their ability to produce thyroid-stimulating hormone (TSH) is limited. Vitamin A deficient cattle and sheep show degeneration of pituitary gland basophils, the cells where TSH is synthesized.[6]

In the world of glands, the pituitary is king; it controls the structure and output of the thyroid gland by means of TSH and makes sure that there is enough thyroid hormone circulating in the blood to service the living cells. When this level has been reached, thyroid hormone shuts off production of TSH and inhibits the release of added thyroid hormone. Vitamin A deficiency also influences the thyroid gland directly in two ways: the rate at which this gland can take up its major nutrient, iodine, is reduced, along with the amount of thyroid hormone secreted.

A Danish researcher, Birthe Palludan, PhD, found that after two weeks of severe vitamin A deficiency, thyroid secretion of pigs was reduced by 40 to 50 percent. In other experiments, when thyroid glands were removed from rabbits, they developed bulging eyes, a condition called xerophthalmia. Administration of vitamin A corrected the eye disorder. Carotene didn't. Researchers conclude that without a functioning thyroid—or adequate supplementation—vitamin A can be metabolized, but carotene cannot.

Like vitamin A, vitamin B_2 (riboflavin) exerts a powerful influence on how well or how poorly the thyroid gland works. Jennings cites animal experiments that reveal that in a vitamin B_2 shortage, function of the ovaries or testes is often depressed, and that changes occur in all glands—particularly in the thyroid and adrenals—which fail to secrete their hormones efficiently.[7]

Another powerful member of the vitamin B family, B_3 (niacin), helps assure the good health of your thyroid and other glands. All living cells require niacin, since it assists in respiration and in the metabolism of carbohydrates, proteins, and fats. This vitamin is essential for keeping your cells—including those of your endocrine glands—in good working order.[8]

A thyroid gland starved for vitamin B_6 (pyridoxine) cannot utilize its iodine raw material efficiently in making the hormones that are a matter of life or death. Some physiologists believe that insufficient B_6 may reduce the pituitary gland's ability to synthesize and release thyroid hormone.[9]

Unless we feed the thyroid gland properly, we can't efficiently absorb another critical vitamin, B_{12} (cyanocobalamin). In laboratory tests, rats without thyroid glands could not absorb vitamin B_{12} at all.[10]

Earlier we mentioned that acute vitamin B_{12} deficiency could cause pernicious anemia and death. It can also contribute to other serious symptoms such as mental illness, neurological disorders, neuralgia, neuritis, and bursitis. This vitamin is one of the most temperamental of the B family. It can't be manufactured in our intestines and, therefore, must be ingested in foods or supplements. Some of us are not well enough supplied with what is called "the intrinsic factor," which makes it possible to absorb vitamin B_{12}. Subnormal thyroid function is undoubtedly a little-known reason why many of us cannot make the best use of ingested vitamin B_{12}.

Although I administer vitamin B_{12} shots to patients desperately low in this nutrient, I make certain, first, that their thyroids are normal to assure proper absorption. Then, I recommend the richest sources of B_{12}: beef liver, beef kidney, and beef round. For vegetarians, I suggest a vegetable-based B_{12} supplement. Fortunately, nutrition stores sell many good vitamin B_{12} supplements. Sublingual, tiny, red, pellets of B_{12} quickly dissolve under the tongue and enter the bloodstream. Hypothyroids usually show dramatic uptake of vitamin B_{12} once their blood levels of thyroid hormone are raised with natural desiccated thyroid supplement. Most vegetarians request and get synthetic thyroid supplements from me, pills containing both thyroxine (T4) and triiodothyronine (T3).

One of the most common nutrients, vitamin C (ascorbic acid) is uncommonly necessary to the thyroid gland. Guinea pigs, unlike most of the lower animals, cannot make their own ascorbic acid from foods. If they are made deficient in this vitamin, their thyroid gland capillaries begin bleeding, a condition that becames even worse in acute scurvy.[11] Additionally, in long-standing vitamin C deficiency, their normal thyroid gland cells multiply at an abnormal rate—a condition called hyperplasia—and secrete too much hormone, as if the governing influence of the pituitary gland had been nullified. Once the guinea pigs are well supplied with vitamin C, all three negative conditions disappear.

As is the case with depletion of ascorbic acid, experimental animals (rabbits) deficient in vitamin E showed unnaturally rapid multiplication of normal thyroid gland cells, as well as too little TSH synthesized by the pituitary gland.[12]

Rats demonstrated the same basic response to deficiency of vitamin E, and in, addition, transmitted hyperplasia to litters born to them. Most of the young failed to survive.[13]

A sense of horror comes over me when I think of the true significance of the last two experiments mentioned, namely, that a shortage of vitamins C and E brings about a condition that appears to be hyperthyroidism—overproduction of thyroid hormone and a racing of the metabolic motor. What appalls me is that, from the turn of the century until the late 1950s, it was standard surgical procedure to remove the thyroid gland that was over- or underproductive. A great number of such operations might have been avoided merely by compensating for certain vitamin deficiencies.

Various surveys indicate that nearly 70 percent of the population is deficient in vitamin D, the sunshine vitamin, integral to all glands secreting their hormones, to energy metabolism, and to regulating cell growth. This means it is vital to healthy thyroid function. Unless you're a lifeguard, farmer, fisherman—or a worker in other outdoor jobs—or live in the tropics, chances are you're deficient in vitamin D, which results from the sun's ultraviolet rays interacting with your skin.

In addition, many people tend to minimize or avoid eating vitamin D–rich foods, because they're high in fats: egg yolks, eggs, shrimp, sardines, liver, butter, and cheese. Most large fish such as shark, salmon, codfish and tuna—and their oils—are high in fat and may also be contaminated with mercury. Several studies have shown that the amount of vitamin D added to milk is often overstated.

A 1,300-page report by David Feldman, MD, of Stanford University's School of Medicine, covering vitamin D research from one hundred labs, reveals that people are depriving themselves of a nutrient that defends them against cancer, diabetes, multiple sclerosis, osteoporosis, and gum disease and makes it possible for immune system T cells to develop normally.[14]

Feldman's most spectacular nugget is research by JoEllen Welsh, PhD, at the University of Notre Dame. Her lab studies revealed that vitamin D caused breast, colon, and prostate cancer cells to differentiate, stop growing, and die. Welsh told *Science News* that "we've shown that if you give a chemical analog of 1,25-D to an animal that already has a mammary tumor, that tumor will regress."

Aside from widespread use of sunscreens, a cause of vitamin D deficiency disclosed by leading atmosphere scientists is increasing air pollution that is diminishing the amount of sunlight reaching the earth's surface—a decrease of more than 10 percent from the 1950s to the 1990s. The city of Hong Kong showed the steepest decline: 37 percent.[15]

Follow-up research disclosed that areas experiencing the greatest dimming are cities of 100,000 population or more and their surrounding areas where most of the world's industry is located: in the latitudes 10° north to 40° north.[16]

Despite this, it is possible for those living in the temperate zone of the United States to store enough vitamin D from as little as ten to fifteen minutes daily sun exposure in spring and summer to last through fall and winter. This means exposing face, hands, and arms to sunlight for a sane interval. It doesn't mean getting "well done" and therefore risking skin cancer. Otherwise, they can figuratively eat their sunlight in vitamin D-rich foods mentioned.

A consensus of authorities indicates that at least 400 IU of vitamin D_3 daily—some suggest as much as 1,000 to 2,000 IU per day are needed—to compensate for a deficiency that weakens bones. Likewise, they assert that there should be a two-to-one ratio of calcium to magnesium. People taking 1,200 mg of calcium supplementation daily for this purpose should also take in at least 600 mg of magnesium. A deficiency of magnesium can cause calcium to be drawn out of the bones.

To sum it all up, it is possible in some instances to correct unbalanced thyroid hormone production—too much or too little—merely by compensating for certain vitamin deficiencies.

Certain facts of life about nutrition and the thyroid have been known for the past thirty or forty years. Yet they have never seen print in anything but medical publications, and there only rarely. One of this book's missions is to fill in the broad knowledge gap—to make you and your doctor aware that how and what you eat may be slowing down, speeding up, or even injuring your thyroid gland.

Suboptimal nutrition is not the only cause of reduced thyroid function. As we mentioned in Chapter 3, certain drugs and chemicals can suppress it as well. In a number of studies, sulfa drugs and antidiabetic agents interfered with the formation of thyroid hormones by inhibiting iodine uptake. It has been shown that prednisone should be used judiciously in known or suspected hypothyroidism, because, in pharmacologic doses, it indirectly worsens this disorder. So does estrogen in pharmacologic doses, an important consideration for women on birth control pills or hormone replacement therapy.

Aside from thyroid-limiting medicines and foods, there is a mainstream protocol for prescribing thyroid hormone that is now seriously questioned. This is the subject for the next chapter.

5

The Great Controversy:
Synthetic Versus Natural

IT WAS A quiet war.

On one side stood the vast army of traditional medical doctors, schooled to prescribe synthetic thyroid formulas for hypothyroidism. On the other side stood a small number of holistically oriented doctors, influenced by the great success of Dr. Barnes in treating hypothyroidism with Armour natural desiccated thyroid. Traditional doctors had a crushing advantage: an army of hundreds of thousands versus tens of thousands. It was David versus Goliath all over again.

Clearly, the vast army felt secure that levothyroxine, the generic name for thyroid brands such as Euthyrox, Levothyroid, Levoxyl, and Synthroid with thyroxine (T4), was superior to natural forms of thyroid that contain both thyroxine (T4) and triiodothyronine (T3).

Then, just before the twentieth century gave way to the energy-charged twenty-first century, an article in the *New England Journal of Medicine* sent a shock through the medical community.[1] Research by Lithuanian endocrinologists at Kaunas Medical University and others at the School of Medicine at the University of North Carolina at Chapel Hill revealed that T4 hormone alone is not nearly as beneficial in treating hypothyroidism as is a combination of T4 with T3.

Thirty-three patients were studied for two five-week periods. These patients all suffered from hypothyroidism caused by an autoimmune disease in which the immune system attacks the thyroid gland or by surgical removal of the gland to treat cancer. In one five-week period, patients were issued their regular dose of T4 only. In the next five weeks, they were given both T4 and T3. Twenty of the thirty-three patients reported more energy, better ability to concentrate, and feeling better overall on the combination T4 and T3. Patients on the combination of hormones performed better on neuropsychological tests, and their emotional health improved.

In some physiological readings, such as pulse, blood pressure, and cholesterol, the differences between the T4 and T4/T3 combination were small. However, the researchers observed that the treatment with "thyroxine plus triiodothyronine improved the quality of life of most patients."

Patients who don't improve on the synthetic T4 might well improve on the combination. I have found this to be true in my own practice, as well; most hypothyroid and thyroiditis patients prescribed only T4 respond well to Armour desiccated thyroid that contains both naturally occurring T4 and T3 .

Despite this, most doctors object to natural thyroid because, they say, naturally occuring hormones in animals cannot be uniformly standardized, as synthetics can. Further, they claim that natural thyroid contains a higher amount of T3 in relation to T4 than synthetic T4/T3 combinations.

In the medical practices of Dr. Barnes and myself, natural thyroid hormone worked better in almost all cases. In fairness, however, I must admit that on rare occasions, when a patient was either sensitive to the natural hormone preparation or was a vegetarian who objected to taking animal-derived thyroid, I have successfully used synthetics containing both T4 and T3.

One fact overlooked by many doctors and researchers in favor of natural thyroid is that it also contains both diiodothyronine (T2) and monoiodothyronine (T1). These hormones wouldn't be secreted by human beings and animals if they didn't serve a purpose. Not knowing the purpose doesn't mean there is none. This has proved true for so-called vestigial organs once thought to be useless, such as the appendix, the tonsils, and even the spleen. For centuries the appendix was removed without cause until it was found to be part of the immune system, helpful in preventing some forms of cancer. As Dr. Barnes once told me, drug companies making synthetics arbitrarily decide on a single ingredient as the key corrective factor, ignoring other seemingly less important accompanying factors, as is the case of synthetic T4. If synthetics are intended to substitute for natural products, why not imitate nature faithfully in every respect? The theory of the synthetic T4 treatment that prevailed since the 1970s held that some of the secreted T4 is converted to sufficient T3, the more effective and body-usable hormone. Arem Ridha, MD, in *The Thyroid Solution* states that, "When taken on a daily basis, thyroxine as T4 allows for a steady and continuous production of T3 in bodily organs."[2]

Unfortunately, steady and efficient conversion of T4 to T3 is not automatic, a slam-dunk. In this age of stress, the adrenal glands of many— if not most—people are overworked and weakened. Even mild adrenal insufficiency can slow down this conversion. The adrenal glands must be strengthened for thyroid supplementation to be effective.

In a journal article, "The Diagnosis and Treatment of Hypothyroidism," Michael Schachter, MD, FACAM, stated essentially this same fact. If this T4 conversion doesn't happen, the patient experiences symptoms of an overactive thyroid gland: rapid heartbeat, palpitations, and increased sweating.[3] Symptoms of a weak adrenal system include allergies, asthma, breathing difficulties, acne, eczema, psoriasis, lupus, flaky dry skin, arthritic pains, and wide emotional swings. Previously, low production of T4 was thought to be the major cause of hypothyroidism. Now Dr. Schacter asserts that it is due, in large part, to an inability to convert the less active T4 to the more active T3. Beyond tired adrenal glands, he feels a valid cause could be weight loss or low protein diets lacking the amino acid tyrosine and iodine, essential to secreting thyroid hormone. Additionally, insufficient selenium could block T4 from converting to T3. (More about selenium in a later chapter.)

It is important to compensate for adrenal exhaustion, in order to improve hypothyroidism. Your own nutritionally oriented physician may be able to help strengthen your adrenals by placing you on a small amount of hydrocortisone (5 mg four times a day, after meals and before bedtime). This regimen has been clinically tested for many decades by William McKendree Jeffries, MD, and I urge you to have your doctor read his book, *The Safe Uses of Cortisone*, which documents why and how to use cortisone to help restore you to peak health."

On her thyroid Web site (www.thyroid-info.com), Mary Shomon writes:

> For years, patients have been told that all they need is levothyroxine treatment to get them into normal TSH (thyroid-stimulating hormone) range, and thyroid treatment is considered complete. Time and again, people who still suffered with symptoms—including fatigue, depression, cognitive problems, and more—were told that once their thyroid range was normal, these problems were no longer related to the thyroid. Instead, they were now depression, stress, PMS, or simply in your head. Patients who had done well on Armour, then switched to Synthroid, for example, and complained of not feeling well, were told they were getting old.[4]

Ever since research demonstrated that the T4/T3 combination is more effective than T4 alone, the thousands of medical doctors once branded as mavericks have been proved right by no less a mainstream authority than the *New England Journal of Medicine*.

6

Body Heat

DR. BRODA BARNES never thought of himself as a maverick. It was obvious to him that natural thyroid would treat hypothyroidism more effectively than the synthetics. It was also obvious to him that temperature should be a major consideration in diagnosing hypothyroidism. After all, he had seen the normal rabbit grow cold, shivering, and sick after its thyroid gland had been removed. And almost all hypothyroid patients were cold when others in the room were comfortable—especially their hands and feet.

Intuitively, he knew that subnormal temperatures handicapped patients more than just in their social, work, and sex lives. He suspected that many hypothyroid patients are ill because low body temperature inhibits their bone marrow's ability to produce red and white blood cells properly.

Red blood cells are responsible for transporting oxygen to the body's trillions of cells for metabolism, producing energy and heat, and building tissue. Such red blood cell disturbances lead to lower metabolic activity and still lower temperatures. Ability of white blood cells, soldiers of the immune system army, is reduced, too, making hypothyroids vulnerable to repeated colds, flu, sinusitis, sore throat, pneumonia, and other respiratory ailments.

While a physiology instructor at the University of Chicago many years ago, Dr. Barnes witnessed a dramatic demonstration that normal body temperature is essential to the production of sufficient blood cells. A PhD candidate was puzzled as to why red and white blood cells were being formed only in the bone marrow of certain bones—

the ribs, spine, and the pelvis. "He suspected that it was a matter of temperature, body organs being warmer than the extremities (the arms and legs)," explains Dr. Barnes.

"To test this hypothesis, he devised a special needle in whose hollow he inserted a small, thin thermometer to check bone marrow temperature in a white rat. He found only yellow, non-blood-making marrow in the rat's long tail, which had a temperature lower than that of the blood-producing backbone.

"Then he curved the rat's tail, and made a small incision in the animal's belly, temporarily inserting and suturing the tail there. Soon the marrow in the tip of the tail, now warmed by the body, was transformed into blood-producing red marrow, while the marrow of the bony structure of the tail's curve remained yellow and unable to make blood cells."

Years later in his medical practice, this graphic demonstration helped Dr. Barnes understand why anemic women often remain dragged out, pale, and depressed, even after having been administered extra iron. Several hundred sickly patients regained a new, fuller life when he gave them thyroid supplementation, which raised their temperature and increased their bodies' ability to produce blood cells, particularly red corpuscles.

Supplemental iron therapy is usually only temporarily useful in the treatment of hypothyroid anemia, because it treats the symptoms, rather than the cause, which is well taken care of by thyroid hormone therapy. Foods rich in iron—liver, fish, fowl, meats, fruits, green vegetables, raisins, and brown rice—are of limited value in a person whose anemia is caused by a hypothyroid condition.

At best, the body absorbs little more than 10 percent of available iron. Vitamin C (ascorbic acid) greatly aids the absorption of iron from the digestive tract. Research done by Paul R. McCurdy, MD, of Georgetown University School of Medicine, and Raymond J. Dern, of Loyola University Stritch School of Medicine, revealed that between 200 and 500 mg of ascorbic acid made it possible for the body to absorb twice as much iron (ferrous sulphate, 15 to 120 mg) as without this vitamin.[1] An accompanying dose of 500 mg of vitamin C resulted in a much higher absorption of iron from the gut than when smaller doses of this vitamin were given. A Swedish study, in fact, revealed that the U. S. government's recommended daily allowance (RDA) of 60 mg of vitamin C will do nothing to help absorb iron.[2]

Once absorbed, iron is constantly recycled by the body to manufacture new red blood cells from worn-out ones. Women, however, lose iron with their menstrual flow, and must therefore replace it in their diets. After absorption, iron must be assimilated by the cells in order to manufacture the hemoglobin necessary to carry oxygen throughout the body. To enable this to happen, another essential mineral, copper—found in liver, other organ meats, legumes, molasses, nuts, raisins, and seafood—must be present.[3] If, as is often the case, copper is in short supply, the blood's oxygen-carrying efficiency may be sharply diminished.

Hypothyroidism may reduce the uptake of copper from the gastrointestinal tract. In addition, a decreased body temperature, common to an underactive thyroid, can cause brain wave changes, which may be misinterpreted by a clinician as neurological damage, but which will in most instances be entirely reversible when thyroid therapy is instituted.

Slower reaction time is caused by lowered body temperature, as illustrated by polar explorers subjected to extreme cold who develop hypothermia. Anyone who is hypothyroid may have similar complaints.

Emanuel Donchin, PhD, a psychologist, and Noel K. Marshall, an electrophysicist, both of the Cognitive Psychophysiology Laboratory at the University of Illinois, discovered that seemingly small daily changes in body temperature—one or two degrees below normal—reduce certain brain responses in test subjects.[4] Even slightly depressed body temperatures slow down our movements and higher thought processes. Although we may not be aware of it, our brains respond more slowly to sound.

Brain wave peaks have a readily recognizable pattern. Nerve damage in the brain is a good possibility if wave peaks either don't appear or come later than they should. In hypothermia, the brain wave peaks are markedly delayed. Yet when temperatures are normalized, the brain waves speed up and become normal.

Donchin and Marshall caution doctors diagnosing such cases to consider body temperature of patients before concluding that they have irreversible brain damage. This recommendation was based on their experiments with fifteen test subjects. They discovered that even small temperature changes caused changes in their test subjects. The efficiency of sensory processing and coordination dropped with subnormal body temperatures and rose when temperatures reached normal.

These scientists relate their findings to those of G. A. Kerkhof, PhD, and his colleagues at the University of Leiden (Netherlands), who discovered that body temperatures actually do influence the brain in a manner that correlates with how subjects rate their performance of various tasks.[5]

Sometimes we put ourselves into categories—as "morning" or "evening" people—according to our work efficiency. Dr. Kerkhof discovered that temperatures were normal at peak performance times and lower than normal at other times. Not only was execution better at peak times, but subjects could also concentrate longer when working.

Experiments by Kerkhof and Donchin and Marshall offer laboratory proof of the handicaps of those individuals with a chronically low temperature, as in hypothyroidism. Frequently hypothyroids register temperatures from 1 to 2½ degrees below normal, as I have observed many times in my practice.

Now we can better understand why persons with extremely low thyroid function—and correspondingly low temperatures—show some of the following symptoms: slow-motion response, thick-tongued speech, poor coordination, impaired memory, and a slowing of mental activity.

If, indeed, 40 percent of the American population suffers from hypothyroidism, an incredible amount of mental and physical potential is being lost needlessly, because no condition can be more readily and inexpensively treated than hypothyroidism. Yet none is more frequently untreated and, even worse, unsuspected. Unless this condition is corrected, the thyroid gland, in partnership with the adrenal glands, cannot properly operate the body's heat-regulating system.[6] That is why, as indicated earlier, so many hypothyroids are cold when everybody else in the room is warm.

Not only do these glands regulate body heat for everyday living, they raise the body's temperature in disease states to produce a fever, which protects us from infection. Ever since the first thermometer was invented, there has been a difference of opinion about fever. Is it a friend or an enemy? The only point doctors have agreed on in the past hundred years is that fever is a sign of illness.

In the early twentieth century, the eminent physician Sir William Osler, MD, labeled fever as one of the three great scourges of mankind, the other two being famine and war: "By far the greatest, by far the most terrible is fever," he concluded.[7] However, even the eminent can be wrong. In 1960, two scientists, I. L. Bennett, Jr., and A. Nicastri, did a thorough review of medical literature and, although not as extreme in their judgment as Dr. Osler, they found no convincing evidence that fever benefits us in our continual warfare with microbes.[8]

Then researcher M. J. Kluger and his associates blasted this opinion with a stunning discovery on infected lizards. Lizards do not have a built-in fever-generating system such as ours and must find fever-inducing sources on the outside.[9] The Kluger team learned that sick lizards have an instinct that makes them seek hot environments in order to raise their body temperatures to fever level when they are sick. Infected fish, too, swim to warmer water to raise their temperatures and combat illness.

Various experimenters have discovered that fever encourages quick inflammation in the immediate area of an infection and keeps it from spreading. Apparently fever is triggered in the brain first by a hormonelike substance from macrophages, immune system cells that attack invading germs. Then the thyroid gland and adrenal glands work together to speed up metabolism to produce extreme heat.

Experiments by G. W. Duff and S. K. Durum showed that at 2°C of fever, certain immune system defenders—T cells and antibodies—increased by 2,000 percent over their number at normal body temperature.[10] Similar findings were reported by another research team. Antibody production in the spleen cells has been found to increase dramatically during a fever. Scientists have concluded that the hormonelike substances, called *interleukin-1* set off body defense cells to fight infection and also send the brain signals to increase body temperature to provide an ideal climate for the multiplication of defense cells. Many physiologists believe that human beings are equipped with a temperature regulation system that puts a ceiling on fever at approximately 41.11°C (106°F). In heatstroke and malignant hyperthermia, temperature breaks through to killing levels.

How is fever controlled? Scientists are not sure. Some believe that fever lingers as long as the infection lasts and recedes when there is no longer need for it.

If fever increases our ability to fight diseases, do subnormal temperatures make us more susceptible to them? Very likely. Hypothyroidism and its accompanying subnormal temperatures are stressors that lower the body's innate ability to fight off infection.

We are always under attack by infectious agents—bacteria and viruses. Countless invisible enemies mass on the skin, in the mouth and throat, and in the intestinal tract. Yet that is only half the bulletin from the war zones. Our built-in resistance, our own defense network, is the other half. If we keep our resistance high enough, the enemy cannot win the battle. He is neutralized until some stress weakens us and permits him to multiply and grow stronger.

Low thyroid function is far from the only stress that invites attack. Devastating emotional shock, long exposure to extreme heat or cold, physical exertion, poor nutrition, and insufficient sleep are other common causes of weakened resistance. But, hypothyroidism is definitely a major stress. Subnormal body temperature and too little thyroid hormone can reduce the strength and resistance of every cell, including the billions involved in the immune system. One of the most common results of hypothyroidism that I see daily in my office is recurrent colds, throat and nose infections, and other respiratory ailments.

Between sniffles and a hacking cough, a patient named Beverly let out all her frustration on the first visit to my office:

"Dr. Langer, I feel as if the common cold was invented exclusively for me. I'm sick at least four times a year—winter, spring, summer, and fall. I've had every respiratory ailment through the alphabet from A to Z."

Beverly's sardonic humor fascinated me, because it seemed too vigorous in contrast with her many symptoms typical of hypothyroidism: low energy, cold extremities, an assortment of respiratory ailments, tight, masklike facial skin, and a more-than-plump figure.

A Barnes Basal Temperature reading of 96.4°F confirmed my suspicion. I started Beverly on a grain of natural thyroid, a high potency B-complex formula, 10,000 units of vitamin A, and 3,000 mg of vitamin C daily. Several weeks later, she returned, looking great, weighing six pounds less, all smiles, and no sniffles.

"This treatment seems to have broken my monopoly on respiratory ailments," she proudly announced.

And she was right.

Diane, another new patient, a single woman in her late thirties, had a similar problem but one with sad social overtones. Naturally auburn-haired, she would have been striking, except for many symptoms of respiratory problems—a slightly swollen, reddish nose, watery green eyes, and a nervous habit of continually clearing her throat.

"Doctor, I simply can't shake this cold, no matter what cold remedies I take." She covered a sneeze with a tissue. "I go through a big box of tissues every other day. I'm desperate. I don't know what to do."

Diane's condition depressed her because, with her frequent sneezing, nose blowing, throat clearing, and headaches, men avoided her.

"Nobody wants me and my cold," she said. "I'm like Typhoid Mary." Tears of frustration began rolling down her cheeks.

Diane had so many obvious symptoms of hypothyroidism that I didn't delay giving her a grain of natural thyroid even before getting a report on her temperature, which, it turned out, was two degrees subnormal. Nothing dramatic happened for three weeks. Then Diane phoned to say the mucus was clearing from her head: "I'm beginning to feel like a human being." After three months, she was a total human being, and an extremely beautiful one. The headaches and respiratory ailments had all disappeared. She hadn't had any symptoms of a cold for weeks and felt great.

"You probably don't recognize me without a wad of tissues in my hand," she said during her last office visit, when she promised to stay on thyroid supplementation for the rest of her life. I haven't seen Diane for years. I know I would have if she weren't feeling well. What a pleasure to lose a patient to good health!

Diane's case is not uncommon. Often I have found unyielding colds and related respiratory ailments interfering with patients' love lives. The same goes for headaches, a frequent symptom of hypothyroidism. Many headaches in the bedroom are not just bedroom headaches. They are real ones. I have helped hundreds of patients get rid of them without aspirin.

Every part of the body suffers when insufficient thyroid hormones are available, including the skin and even the erogenous zones. A poor complexion is often a revealing sign of hypothyroidism, although far less dependable than subnormal basal temperature. Sophisticated electronic measuring devices have shown that in extreme cases of low thyroid function, the skin may be deprived of 75 to 80 percent of its normal blood supply, severely reducing the amount of nourishment delivered to the cells and delaying the removal of harmful waste products.[11] All sorts of strange, embarrassing skin conditions can result—

disorders damaging to social and sexual acceptance: blackheads, whiteheads, pimples, boils, carbuncles, acne, eczema, icthyosis (fish skin), and psoriasis, among others. Thyroid therapy brings about almost unbelievable improvement, and often complete disappearance of these conditions, because circulation has been stepped up. Further, the sensitivity of erogenous zones to touch and friction is heightened, making sex more enjoyable. Conditions that make sex less enjoyable—fatigue, headaches, respiratory ailments, and being physically cold—tend to diminish or vanish with thyroid supplementation.

To the hypothyroid with low body heat and a string of related physical problems, survival is higher on the priority list than lovemaking. But in time, thyroid supplements may be able to effect a remarkable change in priorities!

7

Thyroid and Sex— for Women

OUT OF THE memorable Broadway musical *Flower Drum Song* came an exuberant song, "I Enjoy Being a Girl," which unfortunately does not express the sentiments of many women just before and during the menstrual period. Ever since Eve, women have agonized each month, losing valuable time from work, education, social activities, recreation, and sports, while the male-dominated medical profession had done little or nothing to help.

Likewise, ever since the bedroom went public in the sexual revolution, women—and men—have developed feelings of inferiority about their contributions to lovemaking, comparing them to survey results and fictional standards. I know this from my own practice in preventive medicine and from discussions with numerous physicians, including gynecologists.

Few women or men know that a properly functioning or supplemented thyroid gland can bring new excitement to their sexuality. Even fewer know that the Pill, an effective birth control method, can cause severe bodily damage in hypothyroidism.

In this chapter, I will discuss menstrual disorders, sexual problems, sexual enjoyment, and birth control as they relate to proper thyroid function.

To help women cope with menstrual problems, I have administered, although unwillingly, painkillers, aspirin, relaxants, and tranquilizers. These are alien chemical substances that can be harmful, and therefore I prefer to use natural means. By administering desiccated thyroid, I have seen the correction or at least the lessening of such menstrual disorders as inordinate pain, irregularity, too copious flow, or premature or delayed menses.

Dr. Broda Barnes managed almost two thousand such cases successfully by this method and gave me access to his findings. He told me that he almost felt like shouting "Eureka!" when he first found thyroid supplementation to be helpful for these problems.

"I experienced the exultation of a pioneer until medical history revealed that, as early as 1899, Eugene Hertoghe, MD, of Antwerp, Belgium, had discovered that many female problems result from mild to acute thyroid deficiency," he admitted. "He cured hundreds of women with thyroid supplements. Incidentally, his grandson is achieving the same success today, as I learned not long ago while lecturing on thyroid to a group of physicians in Berkeley, California." The Hertoghe method spread to the United States in the early 1900s, bringing welcome relief to tens of thousands of women.

Early medical textbooks and journal articles mentioned the effectiveness of thyroid supplementation in problems peculiar to women. In Curtis and Huffman's *Textbook of Gynecology* (1950), the authors wrote that even medical conservatives accept that thyroid substance has definite value.[1] It is helpful in promoting conception, in stopping functional uterine bleeding from various causes, in improving gynecological disturbances in many patients with a low metabolic rate, in correcting delayed onset of menstruation in adolescents and, most especially, in adjusting disorders of menstrual flow.

In his *Essentials of Gynecology*, E. Stewart Taylor, MD, states that in myxedema (acutely subnormal thyroid function), premenopausal patients may show menstrual excesses, and this condition may be corrected with thyroid extract.[2] Dr. Taylor relates that one researcher (Lerman) discovered that the hypothyroid patient has a loss of normal follicle-stimulating hormone (the substance that spurs growth of cells surrounding the eggs in the ovaries) preceding menopause. In patients past menopause, Lerman found that follicle-stimulating hormone levels were lower than in normal patients of the same age. He also learned that treatment of hypothyroidism with thyroid hormones was accompanied by a rise in follicle-stimulating hormone.

"Occasionally, amenorrhea [interruption of normal menstrual periods] will be a complication of hypothyroidism," wrote Dr. Taylor. "With correction of the hypothyroidism, regular menstrual cycles will follow."

In a study of fatigued hypothyroid women with menstrual disorders, Mayo Clinic researchers administered thyroid hormone to bring their metabolism to normal range.[3] Numerous gynecological conditions improved: amenorrhea improved in 72 percent of the women; oligomenorrhea (deficient menstruation) in 55 percent, and menorrhagia (excessive blood flow) in 73 percent. A bonus value was an improvement in the health of 75 percent of the women, including higher energy levels.

An experiment reported in the *International Journal of Gynecological Obstetrics* illustrates that just one component of the thyroid hormone, thyroxin, helps restore menstruation in women with low-normal thyroid function. Regular menstrual cycles were restored in ten of seventeen test subjects.[4] An article published in another international journal, *Problems of Endocrinology*, revealed that in a study of twenty-three infertile female hypothyroids with amenorrhea and lactorrhea, most were returned to normal by thyroid therapy.[5]

Thyroid hormones, too, are essential to the proper development of the breast, as shown by animal experiments. They help to regulate the growth and development of the mammary gland. By decreasing the levels of thyroid hormone in the blood, researchers were able to retard the growth of key parts of the breast.[6]

Although hypothyroidism contributes to many kinds of female problems, the most widespread in my practice are menstrual. This was also true for Dr. Barnes, who scanned his office files on 2,051 adult female patients with a complete menstrual history and was amazed to find that 1,980 of them (80 percent) had some kind of female problem. Of these, 1,590 had had menstrual cramps; 883 had had irregular periods, usually accompanied by cramps; and the remainder had undergone occasional flooding or had had an early or late onset of menstruation.

Those with menstrual distress experienced moderate to severe pain (a day or two of school or work lost each month). Individuals whose menstrual periods started later than the average age of twelve numbered 438. The oldest was eighteen. Those whose periods started too early numbered 260, the youngest being a five-year-old who also developed mature breasts and pubic hair. Immediately recognized as hypothyroid, she was treated with low-potency natural desiccated thyroid and in a month menstruation stopped, the breasts started regressing, and pubic hair disappeared until puberty.

In most of Dr. Barnes's cases—and in mine, as well—painful menstruation, irregularity, too copious flow, and premature or delayed menses normalized with administration of thyroid supplementation. The type of uterine bleeding brought about by low thyroid function runs to opposite extremes—excessive flow to sparse flow. A word of caution: chronic abnormal blood flow may be a sign of uterine cancer, so it makes sense to be checked by a gynecologist.

If thyroid function is normal and menstrual irregularities continue, certain vitamin deficiencies may be the cause. A lack of vitamin B_{12} or folic acid has been found to bring on irregularity, sparse flow, or no flow, conditions that are corrected when the missing vitamins are supplied.

A heavy menstrual flow for three or four days has often been corrected if the patient takes 600 IU of vitamin E daily for thirty days. Sometimes a damaged liver—which cannot inactivate hormones that govern menstruation—may cause a too-copious flow. Liver damage can result from alcoholism, from a diet high in sugar or other refined carbohydrates or saturated fats, or from deficiencies of calcium, magnesium, or protein (particularly the amino acids cystine and methionine) or vitamins A and C, which, with choline, are protectors of the liver.

Like menstrual problems, female sexual dysfunction syndrome (once called frigidity, an insensitive, finger-pointing word) can arise from one or more factors: fatigue, illness, dyspareunia (pain during intercourse), guilt feelings, self-consciousness, and emotional tension with one's mate, to name some of the common ones.

A spectrum of supercharged emotional problems can contribute, too: indelicate treatment in the first sexual encounter, rape, a hangover from childhood conditioning to taboos of sex, or a lingering attachment to a parent. Some can be so traumatic and unyielding that they need psychological or psychiatric treatment.

Physical problems, some common and some not so common, can contribute, too: irritation or infection of the vulva or vagina, the injured remainder of the hymen, the bruised tissue from abortion, or crudely executed surgery in the mouth of the vagina to aid delivery in difficult childbirth.

Even seemingly insignificant factors can bring on discomfort in intercourse. A patient with a sinus infection complained of producing too little lubrication for enjoyable sex. Inasmuch as antihistamines are drying agents, I told her to stop taking them. Her sinus infection cleared up, and soon she was again producing ample lubrication.

Both physical and emotional obstacles to sexual enjoyment— fatigue, vague illnesses, and even childhood conditioning against sex—are often overcome by thyroid supplementation.

A patient we'll call Linda told me bitterly, "I don't feel a thing during lovemaking."

She showed a low temperature of 96.8°F on the Barnes Basal Temperature Test. Clinical symptoms and her medical history told me plainly that she was hypothyroid, and I prescribed the natural desiccated thyroid supplement.

"Thyroid? How can that possibly help?" she asked incredulously.

I explained that the electrocardiogram (EKG) of hypothyroid individuals shows reduced nerve stimulation of the heart muscle, causing blood to be pumped in lesser quantities and less forcefully. Reduced nerve conduction influences not only the heart but many other parts of the body, often desensitizing the sex organs.

This patient's response to thyroid supplementation was cheering: a temperature rise to normal and ecstatic reaction to lovemaking including, for the first time, sexual orgasim.

Another satisfying case was that of a young woman named Ardis.

"Doctor, I'm cold physically and sexually. I'm never spontaneous in bed," she confessed. "It's probably my puritanical upbringing. My husband wants to trade me in for a better model." She paused with a sigh. "Maybe I should be seeing a psychiatrist."

I shook my head. "No. You came to the right place."

Her underarm temperature test showed her to be markedly hypothyroid, so I prescribed a grain of thyroid daily. During her fourth visit, Ardis beamed.

"My hands, feet, and the rest of me are warm now," she bubbled. "How I enjoyed sex last night! I wasn't at all self-conscious."

Thyroid supplementation has fanned many fires, banishing bedroom headaches and guilt feelings. Aside from its values in heightening sexual urge and the enjoyment of sex, thyroid therapy helps marriage become more productive. One authority told the Section of Obstetrics and Gynecology of the American Medical Association that 30 percent of infertile women with low thyroid function conceived while on thyroid supplements.[7]

Before thyroid treatment was pushed into the background by the plethora of drugs from the arsenal of the pharmaceutical industry, a gynecology textbook by Emil Novak, of Johns Hopkins Medical School, stated that, in hypothyroids, thyroid therapy will usually correct menstrual disorders, infertility, and miscarriage.[8] In these times, however, less accent is put on sex for procreation. Most patients seem more interested in birth control—in finding the elusive, foolproof way of avoiding pregnancy. The Pill currently enjoys the greatest popularity because of its effectiveness and convenience.

The Pill distributes its two major ingredients—estrogen and progestin (synthetic female hormone)—throughout the body's cells, acting to prevent the ovaries from producing eggs. Among other things, it creates a hostile environment for pregnancy, thinning the endometrium (uterine lining) while decreasing its secretions.

I am unenthusiastic about the use of drugs that are not absolutely necessary, especially powerful ones with well-documented side effects, such as the Pill, which is contraindicated for women with asthma, cystic breast disease, a family history of breast cancer, diabetes, blood-clotting disorders, high blood pressure, heart, kidney, and liver disease, exposure to DES before birth, elevated blood serum cholesterol or triglycerides, epilepsy, fibroid uterine tumors, gallbladder disease, menstrual abnormalities, migraine headaches, and the habit of smoking.

In addition to women with these problems, I never prescribe the Pill for anyone older than age thirty-five. The momentum of risk gains dizzying speed with each year after that age. I prescribe it only if would-be users are safeguarded against blood-clotting disorders by adequate thyroid function or by thyroid supplementation. Of more than one hundred patients in my practice who took the Pill for less than five years, not one developed any of the wide range of common side effects: blood-clotting disorders, high blood pressure, strokes, heart attacks, migraine headaches, eye ailments, and liver tumors, among others.

I have been well guided by a report that Dr. Barnes wrote for Federation Proceedings (a copy of which he gave me for my patients' benefit and for use in this book) called "Making the Pill Safer with Thyroid."[9] In it he states:

> The most serious complication from oral contraceptives has been a seven- to tenfold increase in morbidity and mortality due to thromboembolic diseases reported in Great Britain. . . .
>
> Since these changes are characteristic of abnormalities found in thyroid deficiencies . . . it would appear that a careful scrutiny of thyroid function should be made in all cases before initiating the Pill. The Basal Temperature has been found to be the most satisfactory test. If a woman has any symptoms of thy-

roid deficiency and/or a subnormal Basal Temperature, adequate thyroid therapy is maintained as long as she is taking the Pill.

In my years of practicing preventive medicine, no case of thrombophlebitis has occurred, and few patients have complained of water retention. Thyroid is an excellent diuretic in hypothyroidism. A few cases have been seen by me in which thrombophlebitis occurred while taking the Pill prescribed by other physicians.

In each instance, evidence of thyroid deficiency was present before the contraceptive was started. Thyroid prophylaxis for thromboses in those taking the Pill seems to be as effective as it is for the prevention of coronary disease.

Obviously, there are hazards in almost every form of birth control. However, if the ground rules are adhered to with the Pill, this method seems to have many advantages. Most birth control methods are not fair, in that they place the responsibility entirely on the woman. But now there is a way that men can share responsibility— not just by the obvious means of vasectomy, a surgical procedure that some men live to regret. This will be discussed in the next chapter.

8

Thyroid and Sex— for Men

I THOUGHT I had heard everything when a new patient, twenty-six-year-old Clayton, sole owner of a small manufacturing company, admitted to using the headache alibi when his wife wanted sex more often than he could deliver. In this liberated society, bedroom headaches are no longer the sole prerogative of women!

Already a workaholic, Clayton avoided embarrassment over the test of his virility—"or lack of it," as he put it—by also taking refuge in long hours of work in his plant. As the story unfolded, the problem came into sharp focus. Within five years, Clayton had translated a patent into a thriving production firm through the usual entrepreneurial formula: a clear-cut goal—wishing to become a millionaire—little capital, and many long, grueling hours.

To Clayton, the first to arrive at the plant early each morning and the last to leave late at night, weekends were just two more workdays. Obviously, he had not only worked at a sprint but could have made the *Guinness Book of World Records* for rapid eating. He consumed two-minute meals from the lunchmobile, gulped eleven cups of coffee daily, and chomped endless glazed donuts, sweet rolls, and cookies "to get me through the day and night."

Fear of bedroom failure and embarrassment compounded Clayton's intermittent impotency. Diagnosis? Emotional causes compounded by physical ones: exhaustion (never calculated to enhance sexuality), little sleep and relaxation, junk foods—and subnormal thyroid function.

I advised Clayton to level with his wife—to tell her that he was under doctor's orders not to have sexual demands placed on him until his total recovery—and also to delegate tasks, to stop suicidal fourteen- to sixteen-hour workdays, to take weekends off, to get more sleep, and to cut out junk foods. I told him to improve his diet by adding more protein, fresh vegetables, and food supplements: a high-quality B complex supplement; vitamins C, D, and E; essential fatty acids; and the minerals selenium, calcium, magnesium, and potassium.

After finding that his basal temperature was 96.2°F, I put Clayton on a daily grain of natural thyroid. This regimen turned him around in three months. Then the power of his sex drive overcame his self-consciousness and fear of failure, and he recovered completely. Like Clayton, many men feel their masculinity tested, even threatened, by the increased aggressiveness of women—a good reason to make sure that their thyroid function is normal and that they are in peak condition otherwise.

Aside from wanting to feel equal to sexual demands, male patients appear to be assuming more responsibility for birth control, as evidenced by a growing number of vasectomies. Because of the difficulty of reversing vasectomy, many men want to know if there is an effective means of contributing to birth control without surgery.

I tell them that beta blockers serve as an efficient birth control product. Knowledge of this came about accidentally some years ago in Great Britain when men were treated with beta blockers for heart conditions and began to complain to their doctors that they couldn't make their wives pregnant. To investigate, researchers put a drop of the drug into vigorously swimming sperm. Within ten seconds, the sperm lay dead. After testing is done to determine if a man can use the drug safely, he can begin to assume the responsibility for birth control.

As interesting as this subject is, most men are mainly preoccupied with making sure that their sexual ability meets or exceeds demand. This fact did not come to light immediately relative to a new patient of mine, a bright, thirty-one-year-old insurance salesman called Jerry. His problem was irregular heartbeat.

I was perplexed. Jerry had no history of illness. The diet sheet he had filled out revealed no clue. My questions turned up nothing helpful except that occasionally he seemed hesitant, guarded. Obviously, he was holding out on me. Sometimes patients do that when asked about their sex lives.

"Look, Jerry, you came to me with a problem," I said bluntly. "You're not telling me things that could let me help you."

He flushed.

"Tell me, what have you been doing differently in the past month or so that might account for your problem?"

"I'm having trouble with my sex life," he admitted.

It turned out he was having a problem getting an erection, and he was humiliated.

"What did you do about it?" I asked.

"I began taking zinc. That's supposed to be the sexy mineral."

I agreed with him silently. The prostate gland and its secretions have a high content of zinc, as do the sperm cells. Potency and fertility disorders often yield to supplementation with zinc and its vitamin companion, B_6. Zinc is essential in the formation and function of a number of sex hormones, including gonadotrophin, which excites and stimulates the sex glands of males and females. One medical paper had shown that without zinc, no gonadotrophin could be produced.

"Zinc certainly contributes to sex drive, enjoyment, and fulfillment," I told him.

"I felt I couldn't get enough zinc from my diet," he said. "I read in an article that zinc content of grains—corn, oats, and wheat—has dropped 10 percent or more in recent years."

"True. Some studies show that zinc and other trace minerals are being taken out of the soil year after year and not returned. What is happening to farmland is similar to what is happening to money values through the invisible larceny of inflation."

"My zinc supplement helped me to a degree," he went on.

"How much zinc are you taking daily?"

"Just a small amount, about 100 milligrams."

This remark upset me.

"Just 100 milligrams a day? Jerry, that's a lot. You can't take trace minerals in the liberal amounts that you can many vitamins."

Then I remembered a talk given by Jeffrey Bland, PhD. He and I, along with Dr. Barnes, had been speakers at a symposium for medical doctors in Texas on the subject of hypothyroidism. Dr. Bland had done some original research on zinc and copper and their relationship to low thyroid function and had studied the literature on this subject for many years. Something Dr. Bland had said told me what Jerry's trouble was. He had probably upset the natural ratio of zinc to copper in his body.[1]

Quickly, I skimmed over Jerry's food chart to confirm my opinion.

"I don't find seafood on your chart."

"I don't eat it too often."

"How about organ meats—kidneys, brains, sweetbreads, liver?"

"Never."

"How about nuts?"

"Once in a while."

"Those are copper-containing foods. What I suspect is that you've disturbed your zinc-copper ratio. Many biochemists feel that we get all the copper we need from our foods and don't have to supplement. Therefore, if we increase our zinc intake as you have—and the ratio for most individuals is roughly eight parts of zinc to one of copper—we throw off the relationship."

I told him that Dr. Bland had found that irregular heartbeats, premature beats, and other EKG abnormalities were caused in animals by a diet deficient in copper and had been corrected by the addition of minute amounts of copper in their diet.[2] Dr. Bland had cited similar results in human test subjects.

I asked Jerry to reduce his zinc intake to no more than 15 to 20 mg daily and to add 4 mg of copper. Within two weeks his heart irregularity stopped. I found his thyroid function a bit low and added a grain of thyroid to his daily regimen.

Not long ago, Jerry told me, "My sex life is great again, and my heart is fine."

So many thanks that I get from patients should actually go to thyroid pioneers like Dr. Barnes and to biochemical pioneers like Dr. Bland.

Copper and zinc are important trace minerals, vital in a number of bodily functions including the sexual ones. I remembered clearly that Dr. Bland had mentioned that the list of symptoms for zinc and copper deficiencies was almost identical to that for hypothyroidism. He had also said that trace minerals within human beings act as coenzymes. Enzymes are molecules which cause biochemical changes without being changed themselves. They cause carbohydrates to be split into simple sugars, fats to be broken into fatty acids, and proteins into amino acids. There are, in addition, thousands of other enzymatic actions.

Some enzymes can't act on their own—metalloenzymes, for instance. They have to become bound to trace minerals such as zinc and copper to work.

So if there is not enough zinc or copper or any other trace mineral to go around, certain enzymes can't become attached to them and do their proper job. Metalloenzymes work in the brain, the liver, the heart, and every other body organ and tissue.

One kind of copper-containing molecule is necessary to oxidize iron and change it to a form acceptable in hemoglobin molecules—those that carry oxygen throughout the arterial system.

"There are many people in our population with an anemia that doesn't respond to iron supplementation," says Dr. Bland. "They are truly suffering from copper insufficiency."[3]

Without a copper-containing enzyme, the skin could not accept pigmentation. One of the first signs of copper deficiency is called *subtle albinism,* and extremely white skin, which tans poorly and sometimes develops white spots. Still another copper-containing enzyme concentrates heavily in the adrenal glands, which could not synthesize norepinephrine, one of its key hormones, without it.

Two more copper-dependent enzymes guard against body deterioration: superoxide dismutase (SOD), a compound well known for protecting individual cells from attack by free radicals (chemicals that cause our bodies to age), and a metalloenzyme that forms elastin, one of the integral parts of the artery walls.

Likewise, five zinc-bound enzymes make life-or-death contributions. One of them controls the rate of protein synthesis, cell growth, cell repair, hair growth, and white blood cell production. A second zinc-bound enzyme is an important part of the first step in metabolizing alcohol. A third zinc-containing enzyme contributes to the manufacture of retinaldehyde, a pigment that makes night vision possible. Still another one enables us to enjoy a full sense of smell and taste. Zinc-deficient people often lose the ability to smell, or objects give off a strange odor to them. The fifth zinc-attached enzyme helps to clear lactate from muscles and joints. In shortages of this trace element, muscle and joint pains are more acute.

On this subject, Dr. Bland mentioned a little-known fact based on an authoritative published paper that says that many symptoms of old age are really not the results of the aging process, but rather the results of malnutrition, including a deficiency of trace minerals.

A lack of these metalloenzymes creates many symptoms similar to those of hypothyroidism, but do they in fact have a direct influence on thyroid function? They do in several ways. Before going into detail, it is important to mention again that the thyroid gland is activated, first, by thyroid-releasing hormone (TRH) from the hypothalamus gland by way of the pituitary gland, which gives off thyroid-stimulating hormone (TSH) to signal the thyroid to release its hormones into the bloodstream.

According to Dr. Bland, "neurotransmitters in the brain and the TRH from the hypothalamus and the TSH from the pituitary are controlled by copper nutrition." How well the thyroid hormone thyroxine (T4) is metabolized in our trillions of cells depends on the proper ratio of zinc to copper in all these sites.[4]

"What does this mean?" asks Dr. Bland. "There are two direct relationships between zinc and copper nutrition and thyroid status. One is to the production of T4 and, potentially, to T3 and to the metabolism of these hormones in the cells where their activity will be used."

Dr. Bland reminds medical doctors that there are at least two ways to approach the patient with the symptoms of hypothyroidism:

"One way is the pharmacological approach, supplying larger doses of thyroid hormone through supplement. The second is normalizing the pituitary-thyroid and peripheral cell system by restoring the zinc-copper status in the individual deficient in these trace minerals."[5]

Such approaches often return the deficient male to full sexual potential, as many doctors who are experienced in thyroid hormone and trace mineral replacement are aware.

Hypothyroidism can diminish sexuality directly and indirectly. Fatigue and low endurance reduce both men and women to the survival level, where sexual activity plunges to the bottom of the priority list. Sex life automatically improves when general health is better.

Sex drive, potency, and sexual sensitivity and enjoyment rise with a normal thyroid or one that is adequately supplemented. In hypothyroidism, insufficient pituitary hormone is synthesized and, as a result, the level of the sex hormone testosterone is low. Brain levels of dopamine are also low, which further diminishes sexual desire. Animal experiments show that thyroid hormones administered to the hypothyroid raise dopamine to normal levels.

Sluggish blood flow to the sex organs in hypothyroidism also can lessen sexual performance, as it can in atherosclerosis (narrowing of the arteries), a condition encouraged by subnormal thyroid function. (Atherosclerosis and hypothyroidism will be covered extensively in several later chapters.)

Hypoglycemia, whose symptoms are similar to those of hypothyroidism, often is present in the latter condition, resulting in zero energy and not much interest in sex.

One cause of hypertension, or high blood pressure, is hypothyroidism. Males who take hypertensive drugs over a protracted period sometimes lose their sex drive. Addiction to alcohol, narcotics, and tobacco can also neutralize sex drive.

As in the case of Clayton, stress of various types can result in lower sex drive. An experiment with young male soldiers under the severe physical strain of a five-day combat course without sleep was reported in the *European Journal of Applied Physiology*.[6] After the first twenty-four hours, one of the thyroid hormones, thyroxine (T4), increased (apparently to compensate for stress). However, the other thyroid hormone, triiodothyronine (T3), did not. Within forty-eight hours, T4 had declined to normal, and T3 had gone lower.

The blood serum level of TSH went down throughout the experiment. Other hormones related to sexuality, prolactin and testosterone, also declined. Sleep helped reverse downtrends, particularly in prolactin and testosterone. Thyroid hormone production did not respond as readily. This experiment, in almost complete agreement with a previous study, points out the harmful effects of physical stress on general health and sexuality.

A less obvious stressor in many instances is low thyroid function. Sidney C. Werner, MD, coeditor of *The Thyroid*, one of the most respected books in its field, states that sexual urge and potency are definitely reduced in extreme hypothyroidism.[7]

Among authorities who claim that decreased sexual drive is the most common reproductive abnormality of hypothyroid men is Peter Singer, MD, associate clinical professor of medicine and director, Thyroid Disease Diagnosis Center, Hospital of the Good Samaritan, Los Angeles.[8]

This, too, has been my repeated experience with patients. In psychological circles, it has been the custom to say that impotence is "all in the mind." Don't you believe it. It is also in the glands, starting with the thyroid. That is also where overconcern and immobilizing fears about potency may originate, as well as a host of emotional problems in areas other than sex.

9

How to Enhance
Fertility and Pregnancy

A HUSBAND AND wife in their late thirties came to my offices, both dragging with fatigue—Amanda, a business consultant, and Mack, an attorney. Depressed, they each suspected they were suffering from hypothyroidism and proved to be right, as shown by their resting basal temperatures—just below 96°F—medical histories, symptoms, and blood tests.

A half grain of Armour desiccated thyroid hormone and a 100 mg vitamin B-complex tablet daily for four weeks began to increase their energy and lift their depression. After several months on a full grain of Armour desiccated thyroid hormone and the vitamin B complex, they turned around dramatically. One day when my waiting room was crowded and I was far behind schedule, Amanda phoned, insisting on speaking to me. She wouldn't accept that I would call her back within hours. I took the call, and Amanda shouted with enthusiasm:

"Doctor, I had to talk to you. There's a bonus benefit to your treatment. I'm pregnant. Mack and I had given up after trying for a baby for eleven years. Thanks! Thanks! Thanks!"

That phone call was the greatest news I had had in months.

However, this occurrence made me painfully aware of something that all frustrated and longing would-be parents should know, from the standpoint of therapy and dollars and sense.

As long as one hundred years ago, doctors coped successfully with menstrual problems, infertility, miscarriage, and menopause with natural desiccated thyroid hormone—even with marginally hypothyroid patients. However, now knowledge of this is left in dusty, unopened medical history books and unknown to most doctors indoctrinated to believe that modern fertility drugs are the only way to go.

Treatment for Amanda and Mack cost less than a dollar a day for Armour thyroid hormone. However, costs of fertility testing for women are out of sight—often tens of thousands of dollars. Seemingly endless appointments, time-consuming trips to and from the fertility clinic, interfering with work schedules and personal plans, sometimes extend over years with nothing to show but bills that are often too high to pay.

And the mechanized sex required to conform to ovulation times kills bedroom spontaneity and pleasure. As the months go by with no pregnancy, frustration and stress levels rise, one person blames the other, and, with the blame game, resentment accumulates, tempers flare, and what was once a peaceful home becomes a battle zone.

Ellen made an appointment with me, because she was weary of fertility clinic routines and no pregnancy. "My gynecologist refuses to order anything but a TSH test for my thyroid. That's inadequate from everything I've read. I've got all the symptoms of hypothyroidism— fatigue, depression, feeling cold, hair loss, and brain fog—yet I can't get complete testing for it."

Having read the previous edition of this book, Ellen and her husband Bart requested a thorough diagnosis and, if warranted, treatment with natural thyroid hormone.

"Doctor, we want a baby desperately," Ellen told me. "We're not getting any younger."

Symptoms, medical history, and the full panel of thyroid function tests indeed showed that Ellen was hypothyroid. (Bart's blood tests, medical history, and symptoms revealed that his thyroid gland was working well, and his sperm proved to be normal). A grain of Armour thyroid hormone daily, plus a 100 mg vitamin B-complex tablet, failed to bring Ellen expected instant results, but four months later she became pregnant, and delivered a healthy, full term, perfectly formed, seven-pound bundle of boy.

In many instances, fertility testing is warranted. However, first it's logical to be tested comprehensively for hypothyroidism and, if necessary, supplemented with thyroid hormone. When I say "comprehensively," I mean not just the TSH test ordered by many doctors as the conclusive diagnostic tool. Such superficiality is an injustice to the patient and to the medical profession.

Undiagnosed hypothyroidism often causes years of unnecessary pain and suffering, depression, fatigue, and weight gain—as well as infertility or miscarriage and, with this, a sense of deprivation, inferiority, unhappiness, and domestic discord. If there's no pregnancy after a year of regular unprotected sex, the woman is usually suspect. This isn't fair or necessarily accurate. Dr. Barnes practiced medicine for many decades when general practitioners still coached women through pregnancies and delivered babies. He shared many case studies with me. In about one-third of them, infertility was the man's failure. In another one-third, it was the woman's. In the remaining one-third, it was due to both—the reason he examined the man and the woman. Modern statistics break down to similar percentages.

For practical and budgetary reasons, the man's thyroid function and sperm cells should be tested first for their number in the multimillions, for vigor, shape, and agglutination, the unhealthy massing together of cells. As the old song goes, "It takes two to tango," but it takes only one sperm cell to contribute to a pregnancy.

Through high-powered lenses, a sperm cell may look familiar to you. Except for a tail twice as long as its head and body, it is shaped much like a tadpole with a somewhat pointed head to penetrate the egg and deposit its DNA there. Its body contains mitochondria, microscopic powerhouses, to energize the tail's whipping action that drives it through the woman's reproductive tract.

Deformed cells rarely reach the goal, because of their inefficient shape and sluggishness. Sperm cells that stick to one another are doomed. In union there may be strength, but there's no pregnancy. An abundance of sperm cells is essential to increase the odds that at least one will make it.

A lab test of sperm cells readily reveals whether or not the man's contribution is viable. Many factors can cause poor sperm: smoking, excessive alcohol or caffeine, some prescription drugs for ulcers and ulcerative colitis, environmental pollutants and—most prevalent— overheating of the testicles. Several researchers have indicated that sperm counts of men are 40 percent lower in summer than winter.

However, the reasons for failure extend far beyond the season to such things as hot tubs, showers, saunas, steam baths, too many blankets, tight-fitting jockey shorts, frequently worn athletic supporters, laptop computers used on the lap, torrid work environments (such as foundries where molten metals are cast), and labor under the blistering equatorial sun, as well as driving cars, trucks, or buses for a living.

It is no accident of nature that the testicles, where sperm is secreted, are in the scrotum, suspended from the body. The lower temperature there often makes the difference between fertility and infertility. Despite this, the testicular temperature of some men is still too high. Frequent wearing of shorts often corrects this. Generally cool weather in Scotland and air-conditioned kilts contribute to high male fertility there. Modern medicine offers a scrotal pouch that promotes evaporative cooling. In as few as twelve weeks, many men wearing the pouch are able to impregnate their partners. Your doctor can give you more details.

Our polluted environment undoubtedly is one of the greatest threats to male fertility, as demonstrated by a study of men in rural central Missouri compared with those in Minneapolis and New York City.[1]

Epidemiologist Shanna Swan, PhD, professor of family and community medicine at the University of Missouri in Columbia, was sure that men in the clean rural area of Boone County, Missouri, would have higher sperm counts than males in the cities. The findings shattered her preconception.

Men in rural Missouri had a 42 percent lower sperm count than those in Minneapolis and New York City. Further, the quality of their sperm was inferior—more misshapen, sluggish, and agglutinated—due to exposure to the herbicides alachlor and atrazine and the insecticide diazinon and twelve other commonly used farm chemicals.

"A conglomeration of pesticides, plastics, petrochemical byproducts, and synthetic estrogens and estrogen imitators fills our world. Add to that the excess hormones and hormonelike compounds we consume in everyday food, and humankind is suddenly on estrogen overload," comments William Wong, PhD, a Texas naturopathic doctor and health writer.[2]

"This estrogen dominance can affect ovulation in women and can lower sperm count, sperm viability, and the amount of seminal fluid produced in men."

Like environmental factors, deficiencies of certain vitamins and minerals, also needed to support normal thyroid gland efficiency, cause much male infertility. Earl B. Dawson, PhD, of the University of Texas Medical School, Galveston, conducted a double-blind study on twenty-seven infertile men, totally incapable of impregnating their wives.[3]

Twenty men took 500 mg of vitamin C every twelve hours for sixty days. The remaining seven took a look-alike placebo. At experiment's end, sperm of the twenty vitamin-takers showed negligible agglutination, a 57 percent increased count, proper shape, and more aggressive movement. All of these men impregnated their wives. Sperm of the placebo-takers stayed the same and failed to bring their wives to pregnancy.

Like vitamin C, vitamin E, the trace minerals selenium and zinc, and the amino acid L-arginine enhance the secretion, population, shape, and vigor of sperm cells, as shown by many authorities. Along with all other cells, sperm cells are ceaselessly attacked by free radicals, caused by many factors—metabolizing of food, exercise, emotional crises, pollutants, radiation, stress, and, among others, illness. These molecular muggers destroy cell walls, mitochondria, and DNA—the matrix for cell replication—and cause sperm abnormalities and deficiencies.

Vitamin C quenches free radicals and, when Vitamin E loses power in the battle against free radicals, vitamin C restores it to fight another day. Vitamin E protects sperm cells' delicate, unsaturated fatty acid walls from free radical attack and helps to increase the thyroid gland's iodine absorption for making its hormones.

As various studies show, vitamin E also boosts the number, quality, and aggressiveness of sperm cells. However, I recommend that my patients never exceed 800 IU of natural vitamin E daily—including the full complex of tocopherols. And those with high blood pressure are urged to take no more than 400 IU daily.

Patients with hyperthyroidism, overactive thyroid gland, high blood pressure, anemia, bleeding disorders, and liver disease should always consult with a health professional before supplementing with vitamin E.

Vitamin E and selenium work closely together as antioxidants. Selenium helps to produce testosterone and thyroid hormones and helps to assure the sperm cell a strong and properly shaped tail.

Nearly 50 percent of the body's selenium is concentrated in the testicles and seminal ducts. In a double-blind study, infertile men took 200 mcg of selenium daily and supercharged the mobility of their sperm cells by 100 percent.[4] I warn my patients not to take more than 200 mcg of selenium daily, because it can be toxic to some individuals at higher levels. The trace mineral zinc is often called "the sexy mineral"—with good reason. Without it, there would be no testosterone, erections, seminal fluid, sperm, or ejaculation.

Thirty-seven men who had been infertile for five-plus years and whose sperm counts were less than 25 million per milliliter—low for insemination—were given 60 mg of elemental zinc sulfate daily for forty-five to sixty days.[5] Twenty-two of them, initially low in testosterone, showed significant increases in testosterone levels and sperm count, ranging from 8 to 20 million/ml. During the study, nine of the twenty-two wives got a surprise pregnancy!

However, the fifteen men normal in testosterone showed only a slight sperm count increase, and no change in their testosterone levels, and none of their wives became pregnant. The researchers concluded that zinc is effective in enhancing male fertility when testosterone levels are low.

Much study shows that the amino acid L-arginine increases sperm count and motility, stimulates the immune system, acclerates wound healing and, along with L-lysine, increases blood levels of human growth hormone.

I don't recommend taking individual amino acids for a long period. There's too much danger of upsetting the body's total amino acid balance. Instead, I suggest eating foods rich in L-arginine for specific cases: eggs, pumpkin seeds, split peas, and nuts.

When correcting male deficiency fails to solve fertility, it's time to check the woman. A specific chain of events leads to pregnancy. An egg must be released from an ovary—a process called ovulation—and migrate through a fallopian tube to the uterus. A sperm cell must fertilize the egg en route. Then the fertilized egg must become attached to the endometrium, the uterus inner lining. It all seems simple, but problems often occur.

If the woman is even marginally hypothyroid, she can't produce and regulate the sex hormones estrogen and progesterone necessary for ovulation of a mature egg and provide the endometrium with the mucus necessary to accept and hold the implanted embryo. Scar tissue or cysts there can also block this implantation. Infection-caused damage to the fallopian tubes can prevent the egg from moving to the uterus.

Fertility authorities in the United Kingdom warn women against smoking.[6] "In women, there is unequivocal evidence that smoking negatively impacts virtually all aspects of fertility. This includes effects on follicle/ovulation, oocyte pickup from the ovary and its transport down the fallopian tubes, fertilization and early embryo development," writes fertility researcher Richard Sharpe, PhD.

"Such effects have been demonstrated by numerous studies in a variety of countries. . . . When pregnancy occurs in a woman who smokes, the future fertility of the foetus (as well as its general health and wellbeing), whether male or female, is also put at risk. A wealth of documentation shows that smoking depletes vitamin C and that thiocyanate in tobacco suppresses thyroid function."

Both obesity and severe underweight contribute to infertility in women. A key study indicates that women need at least 17 to 21 percent body fat in order to menstruate and ovulate.[7]

Female athletes in rigorous training and others below this level of body fat often menstruate irregularly, if at all, and fail to ovulate. It is as if the body says, "There aren't enough nutritional reserves to sustain a pregnancy."

Another study found obesity reduced a woman's chances of conception, especially, if the weight was carried mainly around the waist.[8]

"However, even a small amount of weight loss (5 percent) may improve fertility. An Australian investigation of the effects of weight loss in overweight women with anovular infertility found that 60 of the 67 women ovulated spontaneously after losing an average of 10 kilograms (approximately 22 pounds)."[9]

A major cause of infertility for women that's rarely recognized is the army of stressors that upsets glandular balance:

"Researchers at the Mind/Body Program for Infertility at the New England Deaconess Hospital in Massachusetts found that one-third of previously infertile women became pregnant after they learned relaxation techniques."[10]

The pregnancy-impeding stressors range from life-threatening to milder forms—loss of a job or a lifetime's savings, death of a spouse or family member, serious illness, divorce, or a prison sentence, among other violent disrupters, to little-considered forms such as a job you hate, demanding deadlines, incessant minor ailments, polluted air and water, crash diets, fasting, feelings of inferiority, and a lack of friends or other support groups.

These and negative thinking trigger the adrenal glands to release the "fight-or-flight" hormones adrenaline and cortisol. When stress persists, this emergency system keeps drawing away nutrients from glands and body systems not directly involved in the crisis.

Thyroid hormones can't be made without the amino acid tyrosine. Neither can antistress hormones. The adrenal glands have first priority on available tyrosine, so incessant stress often reduces the body's ability to make enough thyroid hormones, accounting for much unsuspected and, therefore, undiagnosed hypothyroidism.

The answers? Dealing with stressors by avoidance, when possible, or by use of relaxation, meditation, yoga, and tension-breaking physical exercises—especially in the early evening—to relieve the day's stress. Walking for twenty to thirty minutes daily stimulates more efficient function of every body cell, and increases secretion of thyroid hormones and tissue sensitivity to these hormones.

A little-considered complication to fertility is celiac disease, which is intolerance to gluten in grains such as barley, oats, rye, spelt, and wheat and, therefore, inability to digest them fully. An article in a respected European medical journal states that "fertility problems are often found in women with celiac disease."[11]

Gluten attacks the stomach lining and may cause diarrhea, gas, cramping, gray or tan, fatty stools, weakness, and poor food absorption. Celiac disease occurs twice as often in women as men, mainly those of northwestern European ancestry. It is rare to nonexistent in African, Asian, or Mediterranean-born people and in Jews. Those with celiac disease often become undernourished. Unfortunately, this disorder doesn't always produce readily noted symptoms, and, so, often escapes diagnosis. Celiac disease stealthily steals essential nutrients. Many patients I've treated for celiac disease, initially say, "But, doctor, I don't eat wheat or rye bread."

No? Gluten is often a hidden ingredient in processed foods: pasta, barley malt, luncheon meats and sausage (some have wheat fillers), processed cheese (this sometimes contains wheat flour and oat gum), gravy, mixes, dips, salad dressings, soups, and sandwich spreads, among others.

Although you rarely overcome celiac disease without divine intervention, you may be able to compensate for it by taking nutrients that it characteristically steals: iron; vitamins A, D, E, and K; and various trace minerals. Inasmuch as iron diminishes the effectiveness of thyroid supplements, it is best to separate their intakes by twelve hours. Tests can determine your exact deficiencies.

My celiac patients enhance their digestion with a pancreatic or vegetable enzyme—one before each meal. A formula containing acidophilus and many other probiotics implants friendly organisms in the digestive tract and promotes better digestion and assimilation of nutrients.

One of the best probiotics is Kyo-Dophilus 9, which contains three billion cells per capsule. Unlike most other products in this category, it is not milk-based and, therefore, is helpful even to the milk-intolerant. I suggest taking one capsule before each meal.

Certain foods interfere with thyroid hormone synthesis and may contribute to developing goiters, early stage hypothyroidism: broccoli, brussels sprouts, cabbage, cassava root (from which tapioca is derived), cauliflower, kale, kohlrabi, lima beans, maize, millet, peaches, pears, pine nuts, radishes, rutabaga, soy, spinach, sweet potatoes, and turnips.

It is best to eliminate them during pregnancy and through the nursing period. Likewise, avoid fluoride in tap water, toothpastes, and processed foods and beverages.

Many reports show that fluoride, chemically related to iodine, which is essential to thyroid gland hormone synthesis, impairs the thyroid gland's iodine receptors. (For more detailed information on this and other environmental pollutants, see Chapter 29, "How to Thrive in a Polluted World.")

Even if untreated hypothyroid women become pregnant, they often suffer miscarriages. Marva, a young woman referred to me by an obstetrician friend, had miscarried three times and was deeply depressed.

Over and above depression, she had the most obvious symptoms of hypothyroidism—exhaustion, cold extremities, hair loss, dry skin, mental sluggishness, weight gain, and muscle cramps. Her history of illnesses and blood tests confirmed the diagnosis. I started her on a 50 mg vitamin B-complex tablet and a grain of Armour desiccated thyroid and told her that, although overnight miracles of recovery do occur, it would probably take at least six to eight weeks before she began feeling well enough to consider another pregnancy.

"Pregnancy and sustaining a pregnancy make extra demands on the body that often cause hypothyroidism," I told her. "The vitamin B-complex tablet helps metabolize food and boost positivism."

Actually it took almost three months. "I feel like a human being again," Marva enthusiastically told me. "I haven't had this much bounce since I was a cheerleader in college."

The only news better than this came much later. Marva conceived, carried her baby to full term, and delivered a healthy seven-pound girl. She was so grateful that she named her baby Stephanie, a female version of my given name.

This success caused her obstetrician to refer another patient to me. Kay had had a history of miscarriages. However, this time the thyroid supplementation and vitamin B complex prolonged the pregnancy beyond her previous ones, but not to term.

Saddened, I recalled a possible solution to Kay's problem, based on old research that had produced excellent results. Some years ago two doctors, Carl Javert, MD, of Cornell University, and Robert Greenblatt, MD, of the Medical College of Georgia, independently found that habitual miscarriers were deficient in vitamin C and a nutrient that accompanies it in most produce: bioflavonoids.[12]

Now called *flavonoids*, these more than four thousand nutrients are the coloring matter in fruits and vegetables—citrus, apples, broccoli, green peppers, among many others—and buckwheat, red wine, green tea, and grapeseed.

A great deal of scientific investigation shows that they strengthen capillaries and help in treating circulatory ailments, bleeding gums, heavy menstrual flow, and easy bruising.

Testing 1,334 women who had had a number of miscarriages, Dr. Javert discovered that 45 percent were vitamin C–deficient. He recommended foods that supplied 350 mg of vitamin C and added a pill with 150 mg of vitamin C and bioflavonoids. (Some brands of vitamin C contain flavonoids and are your best bet). Ninety-one percent experienced full-term pregnancies!

Dr. Greenblatt administered a similar dietary regimen to 13 multiple-miscarriage women, and 11 who had endured two miscarriages gave birth to healthy infants.

Kay told me that she bruised easily. Red blotches on her legs and arms revealed her capillary fragility. She seemed an ideal candidate for this treatment. When I mentioned these studies, Kay eagerly went on my special diet: ten different raw fruits and vegetables daily and, with each meal, a supplement containing 500 mg of vitamin C, 200 mg of lemon flavonoid complex, and 50 mg of rutin (flavonoid derived from buckwheat), as well as a grain of natural desiccated thyroid and a 50 mg tablet of vitamin B complex.

Less than a year later Kay, her husband, her obstetrician, and I were elated with Kay's delivery of a very vocal, healthy, 7½-pound boy! My analysis of the case was that miscarriages often result from fragility of capillaries and other blood vessels in the uterus lining. Unless capillaries are sound and resilient, they can't be healthy supply lines for food and oxygen and physically support a fetus. When they rupture, the placenta becomes detached, slides off, and the pregnancy is over.

It is inconceivable that any woman longing for a child would follow a lifestyle that might harm her fetus by drinking alcohol, smoking, or eating junk food. Yet a minute percentage does just that, despite the fact that their guest within—sometimes it's more than one—merits special consideration.

This reminds me of something I experienced at a party recently. A woman in her late thirties who learned that I'm a physician said to me:

"Doctor, thanks to my son, I quit smoking cold turkey."

"I'd like to congratulate him," I responded.

"He wouldn't understand. He's just a year old."

Then *I* understood. She had given up a harmful habit to help assure her baby's good health and had also helped her own.

"Now I have no craving for cigarettes that would pollute my milk for breast-feeding and his, my husband's, and my environment!"

Critically important as nonsmoking is to mothers-to-be and to giving birth to and nurturing a healthy baby, are a diet of wholesome and fresh foods and normal thyroid function. Among many required nutrients in pregnancy, three stand especially tall: folic acid, a B-family vitamin, and the trace minerals selenium and zinc.

It has been well publicized that a woman's folic acid deficiency in the first few weeks of pregnancy can increase the fetus' risk of spina bifida (failure of the spinal cord to close fully) leading to paralysis and often death. Other possible consequences are an incomplete brain, a hairlip, or a consequent speech defect.

What hasn't been emphasized enough is that a 400 mcg daily supplement of folic acid or foods enriched with an equal amount are assimilated far better than folic acid in fruits and vegetables, as shown in research by Irish biochemists.[13]

This is not to diminish the great value of fresh produce that's rich in many vitamins, minerals, and also enzymes needed for proper digestion and assimilation of food. The supplement folic acid is better absorbed and vitally needed for egg production, as are vitamin B_{12} and the trace minerals selenium and zinc. It is no coincidence that these nutrients also support normal thyroid gland function.

One of those "too bad" items is that pregnancy catches some women unaware and unprepared emotionally and physically to develop and support a healthy fetus to full term. Although obstetrics is not my specialty, I urge all premenopausal women to stay in the best of health with regular aerobic exercise, wholesome and fresh food, and the security of knowing that their thyroid function is normal. Physical demands of pregnancy often bring on hypothyroidism or a need to increase the amount of thyroid hormone already being taken.

"Untreated hypothyroidism in a pregnant woman, particularly in the first trimester, may have adverse neurologic effects on the unborn child," states a report from the University of Maryland Medical Center. "All pregnant women should be tested for thyroid function."

Women with mild hypothyroidism before pregnancy almost invariably develop more severe hypothyroidism in pregnancy. This sometimes endangers the mother-to-be with high blood pressure, sluggishness, and super-fatigue and the fetus with possible low birth weight, developmental delays, subnormal brain development, and lower than normal IQ. Babies from hypothyroid mothers are four times more likely to have low IQ scores than normal, according to an in-depth study.[14]

These are good reasons for a young woman to take a home pregnancy test immediately if she suspects she's pregnant. If so, she can have this verified by her gynecologist and be checked for thyroid function to establish normality or the need for thyroid hormone treatment. This should be done within six weeks of pregnancy.

During pregnancies of patients, I ask obstetricians to test them for thyroid function at least every eight weeks and, when necessary, supplement them with thyroid hormone, preferably a natural form containing both thyroxine (T4) and triiodothyronine (T3). It is not a given that T4 always converts to enough of the more bioavailable T3.

Although rare, hypothyroidism does occur in infants, one of the reasons that all babies born in the United States have their heels pricked to obtain a few drops of blood for thorough testing. It's a good idea to make sure that the test includes a check for thyroid function and that your baby's thyroid is normal. Have your obstetrician verify this and report your infant's thyroid status to you and to establish that she or he is being given thyroid hormone, if required.

Symptoms of hypothyroidism in the newly born are high birth weight, quietness, lack of interest in sights and sounds, indifference to breast or bottle, slow heartbeat, low blood pressure, cold hands and feet, and goiter. If hypothyroid, the baby should receive treatment without delay.

Many women who have never had a thyroid insufficiency frequently develop postpartum thyroiditis or full-blown hypothyrodism that's often temporary or long-term along with postpartum depression. This should be treated immediately, particularly if the mother is breastfeeding.

Jessie Anne had never had a thyroid problem until her first baby was born, although her father had been on a thyroid supplement for most of his adult life. Midway in her pregnancy, she felt so weak and depressed that she cried much of the day. Her obstetrician put her on a synthetic thyroid hormone containing only T4. However, her condition remained the same.

The obstetrician phoned me to see if I thought natural thyroid would work better. I suggested a grain of Armour desiccated thyroid hormone daily and a 50 mg B-complex tablet, and he agreed to try it. Nothing positive happened for two weeks.

Then at the start of the third week, Jessie Anne felt a surge of energy. Her emotional darkness began to give way. A few weeks later, she was excited about the prospect of having a baby and, later, experienced a relatively painless delivery. Her problems and those of many others accent the need for diagnosing and, if necessary, treating hypothyroidism from prepregnancy through the postpartum period for the health and well-being of the mother and infant.

It is not uncommon for young pregnant women to experience the thyroid disorder at the opposite pole: hyperthyroidism. There's a definite danger of mistaking this condition's main symptoms—palpitations, excessive warmth, nervousness, irritability and sleeplessness—as common to pregnancy and not treating the condition.

Untreated hyperthyroidism can result in a high incidence of miscarriages or birth defects, due to an excess of thyroid hormones. One conventional and effective treatment is Tapazole, an antithyroid medication. If administered by a specialist, this treatment often rapidly controls hyperthyroidism. Naturally, thyroid hormone levels and thyroid-stimulating hormone (TSH) should be monitored frequently for the duration of the pregnancy to assure that the medication doesn't overcompensate and make the person hypothyroid.

A little preparation and precaution before, during, and after pregnancy can eliminate unwanted complications and do much to assure a healthy baby and mother.

Why depend on the luck of the draw when you can stack the deck in your favor?

10

Thyroiditis:
A Growing Menace

ONE OF THE great mysteries to solve is an inflammatory condition known as *Hashimoto's thyroiditis* or *Hashimoto's autoimmune thyroiditis* (HAIT). In this autoimmune illness, the body produces antibodies that attack the thyroid gland as if it were a threatening invader such as bacteria, viruses, or fungi (yeast). Why? We don't know conclusively. However, there are clues as well as a workable means of coping with this disorder. More about that later.

Hashimoto's thyroiditis appears to be hereditary, because often not only a parent has it but also one or more of the children. Unfortunately, it is not suspected in children and, therefore, they may go on suffering untreated. In my practice, it is not uncommon for me to treat an entire family.

Way back in 1935, Hashimoto's thyroiditis was almost too rare to be a statistic, occurring in probably six individuals in one hundred thousand. Today approximately two out of one hundred are afflicted with Hashimoto's thyroiditis, according to an article in *Medical Clinics of America*. More recent estimates boost that figure to about 3 percent of the population—as it is among my patients.

Inasmuch as Hashimoto's thyroiditis is a diagnosis that is often not suspected and, therefore, not treated, we decided to devote a full chapter to it. We particularly alert women to this condition, because statistics show that 95 percent of patients turn out to be women.

Do these figures agree with my medical findings?

No. Among my patients, almost an equal number of men have Hashimoto's thyroiditis. However, because it is a condition not generally suspected in men, Hashimoto's thyroiditis is often a diagnosis that should be made but isn't.

In different stages of this serious illness, a person can manifest symptoms of either under- or overactive thyroid function (hypo- or hyperthyroidism).

What are Hashimoto's thyroiditis's classic symptoms?

1. Deep fatigue, often written off as chronic fatigue syndrome. Such patients go to sleep exhausted and wake up even more so. Their endurance is often low to nonexistent. Usually performing their day-to-day activities is beyond them.
2. Depression. Patients' exhaustion and inability to function normally bring on feelings of futility. In any acute onset of depression—especially in adult women—thyroiditis should be suspected and ruled out by proper testing for antibodies to the thyroid. Thyroiditis is frequently a common cause of postpartum depression.
3. Memory loss, characterized by severe problems with recent memory and ability to concentrate, is often a disaster for working adults and students.
4. Nervousness ranges from mild anxiety to full-blown panic attacks—some of which are true psychiatric emergencies. These are puzzling to Hashimoto's thyroiditis patients and, often, to their physicians who, in desperation, usually recommend psychotherapy or prescribe powerful tranquilizers. Most patients with psychiatric symptoms brought on by thyroiditis tell me, "I have no reason I know of to feel this way. Something's wrong physically, yet all my medical exams are normal." (However, at this point, they haven't had autoimmune antibodies to their thyroid gland checked.)
5. Allergies, food and environmental.

6. Heartbeat irregularity and palpitations.
7. Muscle and joint pains.
8. Sleep disturbances and insomnia.
9. Reduced sex drive.
10. Menstrual problems.
11. Suicidal tendencies.
12. Digestive disorders.
13. Headaches and ear pain.
14. Lumps in the throat.
15. Difficulty swallowing.

Many new patients who come to me with Hashimoto's thyroiditis are baffled. Recently a woman told me: "I don't understand any of it, mainly the depression. I have a husband who loves me, a good position, and caring relatives and friends. Something's wrong physically, but no one's able to figure out what it is."

A few of my new patients have admitted becoming so desperate that they have voluntarily signed into a psychiatric hospital because they feared harming themselves. Unfortunately, the typical treatment for patients with chronic depression in whom thyroiditis goes undiagnosed is a powerful antidepressant, which, quite frequently, makes them worse.

Inasmuch as exhaustion, depression, and other psychological problems are the most common complaints of Hashimoto's thyroiditis patients, they often eat to feel better and gain weight that's difficult to lose. Inability to curb their intake of food and added weight make them even more depressed.

Hashimoto's thyroiditis is often a missed diagnosis because the routine thyroid hormone blood levels test used to rule out thyroid disease is frequently normal, and no additional testing is then performed. If you suspect Hashimoto's thyroiditis is your condition, share that suspicion with your doctor and ask him or her to order a specialized blood test known as an antithyroid antibody panel consisting of antithyroglobulin and anti-TPO (thyroid peroxidone) antibodies. These tests can be performed by any physician or authorized by him at a clinical laboratory. They will corroborate a presumptive diagnosis of Hashimoto's thyroiditis.

Often the signs of thyroiditis are contradictory. *Usually any elevation of antithyroid antibodies is significant.* Yet, in severe cases, there may be a reading of low antithyroid antibodies and, in a mild case, markedly elevated antibodies.

My policy is to treat patients medically for thyroiditis even when they have just a small elevation of antithyroid antibodies, if they also present symptoms of this disorder. I emphasize this point, because many doctors become interested in this condition only if the antibody level is sky high.

D.M., a forty-seven-year-old woman, is just one example of the hundreds of patients I've treated for Hashimoto's thyroiditis over the years. She came to me complaining of a two-year history of chronic fatigue and severe depression, alternating with bouts of anxiety and heart palpitations.

During this trying period, she had been hospitalized for six months in a psychiatric unit and treated with lithium, a major antidepressant, and had had numerous rounds of shock therapy. In the year that I first saw her, her weight had ballooned up by fifty pounds with no real change in her food intake.

Noting that her thyroid levels were normal but that she had an elevation of antithyroid antibodies, I treated her with thyroid medication, starting with a quarter grain of Armour desiccated thyroid, increasing that dosage by a quarter grain every several weeks.

Within ninety days, all of the major symptoms were under control, and she was on the road to recovery. Along with this treatment, I upgraded her diet with liberal amounts of vitamins, minerals, and essential fatty acids—particularly gamma-linolenic acid (GLA), eicosapentaenoic acid (EPA), vitamin B complex, and vitamin C. Within months, she had lost all of her excess weight and felt as if she had been reborn.

Although thyroiditis can affect any age group, most patients are in the age range from thirteen to forty years. If either parent of a patient is diagnosed with Hashimoto's thyroiditis or is experiencing symptoms mentioned above, I urge him or her to have other bloodline family members checked for antithyroid antibodies elevation—particularly if no other medical cause has been detected.

Many of my patients ask if they have to stay on thyroid supplementation indefinitely. My answer is, "A person with diagnosed Hashimoto's thyroiditis may not have to remain on prescription thyroid forever when careful attention is paid to eating a well-balanced diet of natural foods and taking proper supplements."

What causes Hashimoto's thyroiditis? I have no evidence from published research. However, my clinical experience leads me to believe that Hashimoto's thyroiditis is caused, in part, by viral infections such as chronic Epstein-Barr virus or other chronic/systemic infections that may trigger the body's autoimmune response to the thyroid.

Supernutrition with accent on fresh fruit, protein, and low carbs often strengthens the immune system enough for it to control these microorganisms, resulting in a sharp decrease in the body's autoimmune response to the thyroid.

Many patients with Hashimoto's thyroiditis may improve as well if they eliminate glutenous items from their diet.

11

How to
Beat Hyperthyroidism

It DIDN'T HAPPEN suddenly to thirty-nine-year-old Dave!

While watching TV, he began to feel uncomfortably warm, removed his yellow cardigan sweater, and noted that his T-shirt was damp with perspiration. Now he found it hard to breathe, as if he were in a steam bath. He began to be anxious. Then he became dizzy, nauseated, on the verge of passing out, and felt a slight pain in his chest. His heart started racing. All of his body functions seemed to be running wild. Dave panicked. "My God! A heart attack!" he shouted. Alice, his wife, heard him, and, dish towel in hand, ran into the family room, took one look at him and, frightened, phoned 911. Twenty-two minutes later, a sweat-soaked Dave, his face ruddy, was in a hospital emergency room bed. A battery of exams revealed that his heart was all right, but he was hospitalized overnight and part of the next day for observation. Tests disclosed that he had survived what is called "a thyroid storm," something that occurs only infrequently even in much older hyperthyroid individuals. He was given medication to slow down his thyroid function. After his referral to me, he asked, "Doctor, what brings on an attack like this?" "Usually, a physical, psychological, or emotional crisis." Dave pressed the palms of his hands to the sides of his head. "A few days ago, I was fired from my job!"

Assuredly, this could have started the thyroid storm. However, Dave, who had never before experienced full-blown hyperthyroid symptoms, had probably developed this disorder much earlier without knowing it. This proved to be the case. He revealed that, periodically, he had felt waves of excessive heat but had laughingly attributed them to an "early male menopause." Dave had also experienced occasional nervousness, impatience, irritability, sleeplessness, and a ravenous appetite without gaining weight. Noting on his medical forms that his father was hyperthyroid, I told him that the most probable cause for his condition was heredity. However, other possibilities existed, including the defective working of his immune system in which autoimmume antibodies attack the thyroid gland as if it were an enemy. This is what happens in Graves' disease and Hashimoto's thyroiditis. As a result, the thyroid gland reacts by releasing too much hormone. Another likely cause could have been a growth that enlarged the thyroid gland and made it overproduce thyroid hormone.

Unlike hypothyroidism, hyperthyroidism is usually easy to diagnose by common signs and symptoms, including a family history, a goiter, exaggerated body heat, stepped up appetite, pronounced weight loss, accelerated or irregular heart rate, high blood pressure, shortness of breath, disturbed sleep, fatigue, muscle weakness, tremors, vision problems, anxiety, or impatience and irritability. Free-floating anxiety attacks resulting from an overproduction of thyroid hormone, when undiagnosed, often cause panic. I've known of patients whose palpitations, heightened by anxiety, increased their heart symptoms to the extent that they wound up in a hospital emergency room only to be told, "There's nothing wrong with your heart. It's all in your head."

To avoid the danger of not diagnosing a hyperthyroid condition, I give every new patient a thorough medical workup along with testing for thyroid stimulating hormone (TSH), free and total T3 and T4, along with antithyroglobulin and anti-TPO antibodies.

Hyperthyroidism should be treated at once to prevent or minimize its damage. Severe and untreated hyperthyroidism may result in heart arrythmias, hypertension, delirium, and heart failure. Graves' disease, which accounts for from 60 to 80 percent of hyperthyroidism, is an autoimmune disorder often caused by antibodies attacking the TSH receptors. This autoimmune onslaught causes the gland to synthesize and release excess hormone. In almost 50 percent of the cases, Graves' disease may result in an infiltrative eye disease that can cause visual changes and, in rare cases, even blindness.

There are three main and effective therapies for Graves' disease and non-Graves hyperthyroidism: drugs, radioactive iodine, and surgery. I prescribed Tapazole (methimazole) for Dave. This is an antithyroid medicine that has brought my patients excellent results through the years. Like Tapazole, Propylthiouracil limits the amount of iodine that reaches the thyroid gland, restricts the synthesizing of thyroid hormones, and makes it difficult for them to enter the bloodstream. When too much thyroid hormone persists in the bloodstream, along with this therapy, I may prescribe a beta blocker to treat the symptoms of the disease.

Perhaps the most frequently prescribed treatment for hyperthyroidism is radioactive iodine. The patient swallows a capsule or drinks a glass of water containing radioactive iodine. This effectively destroys the overactive thyroid tissue, causing permanent hypothyroidism. The patient must therefore be maintained on thyroid medication for the rest of her or his life. The body eliminates most of this radioactive iodine in urine, saliva, and feces within forty-eight hours. Hyperthyroid patients treated with radioactive iodine are well advised to double flush the toilet, wash their hands frequently for a few weeks, and avoid close contact with children and pregnant women for from twenty-four to seventy-two hours.

The third treatment is surgery. Fortunately, this is rarely performed. There's a risk that the parathyroid glands may be damaged, resulting in calcium metabolic disorders, or the laryngeal nerve may be nicked, causing problems with voice intonations and speech. Patients who require surgery are often those who experience problems with breathing or swallowing. Large thyroid glands are far more numerous than generally believed. Research by Roger J. Williams, PhD, an authority on human physical variation, shows that thyroid glands in normal people can differ in size by six times.[1]

Thyroid surgery can involve removing an overproducing thyroid nodule or the whole gland and then replacing the lost thyroid hormone with prescription medication. Prior to surgery, ice packs applied to the throat will often reduce inflammation and ease breathing.

Hyperthyroid patients should avoid any food or beverage that revs up their metabolism such as coffee, tea, or soft drinks containing caffeine. The same applies to using tobacco, antihistamines, ephedrine, and Novocain.

It would be ideal if one could manage hyperthyroidism with nutritional supplements or herbs. However, only occasionally have they worked for my patients, although test tube and animal experiments indicate that the herb bugleweed may reduce hyperthyroid symptoms.

The German Commission E, a world authority on the use of herbs, issued a monograph claiming that bugleweed helps to control mild hyperthyroidism.[2] This commission recommends 1 to 2 grams of the whole herb per day or the tincture of 1 to 2 ml three times daily.[3] The theory behind bugleweed's claimed effectiveness is that it blocks antibodies from binding with the thyroid gland and attacking it, and, by this means, reduces the amount of thyroid stimulating hormone that regulates thyroid hormone release.

At the insistence of some patients, I have tried bugleweed in the past with marginal success. I warn patients not to medicate with bugleweed without monitoring by a health care professional—preferably a medical doctor or naturopathic physician who is expert in herbology. Further, this herb should not be taken during pregnancy or breast feeding.

Even when thyroid function is restored to normal, by whatever means, there can still be health complications. This is because insufficient thyroid hormone has caused stress and consequent free radicals, molecular muggers that damage sensitive cellular membranes, and, on occasion, even DNA, the blueprint for cellular replication.

When oxidation takes place for this and other reasons, such as for metabolizing food in your trillions of cells, it causes the loss of one of a pair of electrons. This imbalance turns a normal cell into a free radical, which forcibly steals an electron from a neighboring cell, turning it into a free radical. This destructive process continues until antioxidants such as vitamins A, C, E, and beta carotene and lycopene stop it by supplying missing electrons.

High magnification microscopes have verified such a process for researchers. If continued over a long period, this stress causes degenerative changes all over the body.

Severe free radical damage indicates that there are too few antioxidants to control oxidative stress. In the free radical chapter, we introduce the new, innovative, and noninvasive Wellness Index, a test that measures your isoprostane level. Isoprostane is a recently discovered biomarker that measures your oxidative stress level, serving as a precise guideline for the need and efficacy of antioxidant therapy.

Some of the antioxidants my patients find most helpful are vitamin C—the old standby—natural vitamin E, pycnogenol, grapeseed extract, green tea and its extract, coenzyme Q10, and alpha-lipoic acid, among the most prominent and effective. (Be sure to check with your treating physician before starting any new supplementary regimen!) Often patients ask if foods known to interfere with thyroid functioning—when eaten in large quantities—help to control symptoms of an overactive thyroid. I'm talking about cassava root—the basic ingredient for tapioca—millet, peaches, pears, peanuts, pine nuts, and soybeans, plus the cruciferous vegetables, so named because their molecules are shaped like a cross: broccoli, brussels sprouts, cabbage, cauliflower, kale, mustard greens, rutabagas, and turnips and radishes.

The best of these is the radish, claims medical anthropologist John Heinerman, PhD. Russian doctors use them often for diminishing hyperthyroidism.[4]

In treating thousands of thyroid cases, I have observed that, in some instances, eating these foods in quantity has helped to correct hyperthyroidism. I have also found that omitting them has occasionally alleviated hypothyroidism. Relative to hyperthyroidism, one of my patients told me, "The cruciferous vegetables are so boring to eat that I can't stay on them long enough to control my condition." At any rate, it is important for hyperthyroid patients to eat a wide range of nourishing foods to satisfy their increased need for nutrition—fresh fruits and vegetables, nuts, poultry, lean meat, and dairy products. Yogurt with friendly bacteria cultures (probiotics) added after pasteurization has proved especially helpful to my hyperthyroid patients. It's interesting to note that pasteurization makes milk's tyrosine less available, an assist in tempering high thyroid function, inasmuch as thyroid hormone cannot be synthesized without sufficient tyrosine.[5]

The accelerated metabolism, nervousness, difficulty relaxing, and sleeplessness of hyperthyroids often respond to a heavy intake of the B-family of vitamins in almonds, liver, and protein-rich sardines. In addition, I often recommend a 50 or 100 mg tablet of B-complex daily.

Perhaps the most glaring health problem for hyperthyroids is loss of bone mass, a condition that, if untreated, may lead to serious osteoporosis. The tendency of such patients is to drink a lot of milk. Surely, milk is rich in calcium and other nutrients that help to build strong bones and teeth. However, milk doesn't supply all the nutrients required to compensate for bone loss. Further, its calcium-to-phosphorus ratio may preclude optimal calcium absorption. Magnesium intake should usually be kept at a one-to-two ratio with calcium. Manganese, copper, silica, boron, and vitamins C and K are necessary, too. You'll find these essential minerals in the soft bones of sardines and canned salmon and in anchovies—the latter are great in Caesar salad—and also to some degree in almonds, broccoli, beans, and green leafy vegetables.

I usually advise my patients to abstain from canned foods, but canned sardines and salmon supply the world's richest and most easily assimilable minerals. In past times, children used to fight to get the thighs and drumsticks of baked or broiled chicken, so they could chew on the mineral-rich soft ends of their bones.

Only North Americans, dependent mainly on dairy products as sources of calcium, consume such high amounts of calcium daily— 1,200 to 1,500 mg. Other cultures get along with far less calcium and, yet, have strong bones and teeth. Bantu women of Africa ingest only about 350 mg of calcium daily, bear as many as nine children, and breast-feed them for an average of two years. Deteriorating bones and teeth are virtually unknown to them.

How come? They do much outdoor physical work that is weight-bearing, a proved assist for strong bones. Further, they get more sun exposure, insuring the adequate production of vitamin D.

A low-cost bone mineral density measurement will tell you what you need to know about the state of your bones. It's a good idea to have one every year for comparison. Your height should also be checked yearly. Even a small loss of height may indicate softening of the bones or osteoporosis. Sometimes the scarcity or lack of one trace mineral can undermine the nutrition that supports our bones. A star professional basketball player, now a TV basketball commentator, had incessant and excruciating pain in his ankle bones, as well as other bones, and had to sit out key games.[6] Doctors advised him to increase his calcium intake to 1,500 mg daily. He did. However, he continued to be intermittently disabled.

After many months in and out of the lineup, he was advised by someone who understood nutrition to take in enough trace minerals. A diet analysis showed the star to be deficient in manganese, essential to human growth and healthy bone formation. Increasing his daily intake of vegetables, fruit, grains, nuts, and seeds containing manganese —avocados, buckwheat, oats, barley, pecans, hazelnuts, whole grain cereals, sunflower seeds, bananas, and grapefruit—and adding a 10 mg tablet of manganese solved his problem.

University of Louisville researchers write that "nutritional supplementation with L-carnitine has been shown to benefit the symptoms of hyperthyroidism, and may help prevent bone demineralization."[7]

I usually recommend 500 to 1,000 mg of L-carnitine daily for my hyperthyroid patients, even though it is unclear whether taking L-carnitine plays a significant role in treating hyperthyroidism. Studies about this nutritional supplement are anecdotal. However, conventional medical treatments are well proved for their effectiveness. Fortunately, hyperthyroidism gives ample warnings by symptoms, so you can visit your doctor for diagnosis and, if necessary, therapy, and avoid a 911 crisis!

12

Selenium Deficiency and Hypothyroidism

MUCH HAS BEEN written about the trace mineral selenium as a part of the enzyme/antioxidant glutathione peroxidase that protects cell membranes and DNA and helps to prevent cancer, heart disease, and premature aging. Selenium is also a key ingredient in the enzyme that converts thyroxine (T4) into triiodothyronine (T3), the major hormone that makes cell metabolism of nutrients possible. This explains why selenium-deficient individuals usually turn out to be hypothyroid.

To correct selenium deficiencies, it's best to supplement with selenium yeast; this type of selenium is far more body-available than the inorganic form. Biochemist Richard Passwater, PhD, writes that 150 mcg daily of selenium yeast raises the blood levels of selenium of healthy adults.[1]

The safe range of intake of selenium is 50 to 200 mcg daily. Dr. Passwater also reports that vitamin C increases the absorption of organic selenium-containing yeasts. (I recommend that my patients take at least 500 mg or more of vitamin C, three times daily.)

However, there's more to the story as to how selenium intake relates to thyroid function. Deficiency of the hormone T4 is often associated with dietary iodine inadequacy, commonly worsened by goitrogens in water and food.

In a letter to the *Journal of Orthomolecular Medicine*, Harold D. Foster, PhD, a biochemist at the University of British Columbia, Victoria, B.C., Canada, writes:[2]

Depressed serum T4 levels, however, are not necessarily accompanied by below normal serum T3 . . . When severe iodine inadequacy is present, serum T3 tends to remain stable or even rise as T4 levels drop . . . . This relationship occurs because T3 contains less iodine, weight for weight, than does T4 . . . . It is more metabolically active, and, hence, is produced by the thyroid when iodine is scarce . . . . Only in extreme iodine deficiency, when there is inadequate iodine even to produce T3, does its level decline. However, the T4 to T3 conversion requires the catalytic selenoenzyme iodothyroninedeiodinase. As a consequence, T4 and T3 deficiencies together are commonest in individuals living in environments depleted in both iodine and selenium. In contrast, depressed T3, without unusually low serum T4 is characteristic of populations in regions where diets contain adequate iodine but lack selenium. Furthermore, animal studies suggest that, just as excess iodine consumption results in lowered serum T4 levels, an elevated intake of selenium may depress serum T3.

In addition to its role in thyroid function, selenium, like iodine, also appears to protect against breast cancer and various other types of cancer. In his book *Healing Nutrients*, Patrick Quillin, PhD, writes that researchers determined soil levels of selenium throughout the United States. Next, they studied distribution of cancer cases across the United States. When they laid the selenium map over that of the cancer map, they found an astonishing correlation. States most deficient in soil and water selenium showed the highest incidence of cancer. Ohio, poorest in soil selenium, reported the highest incidence of cancer—a frightening 200 percent above that of South Dakota. South Dakota, richest in soil selenium, reported the fewest cancer cases.[3]

Women have to make special considerations before taking selenium, particularly those women who are considering becoming pregnant. "A decline in serum T4 is likely to be most significant during pregnancy, since this hormone is of major importance to the developing fetal brain," writes Dr. Foster. "Shortages are known to result in mental retardation and even in neurological cretinism."

However, pregnant women—or those likely to become so—should not be given selenium supplements unless they know for certain that their iodine intake is adequate. Therefore, it's advisable to treat premenopausal hypothyroid patients whose hypothyroidism is not due to excess dietary iodine or selenium with desiccated thyroid tablets.

13

A New Look
at Iodine

WE EXAMINED THE role of iodine deficiency in hypothyroidism in Chapter 2. Iodine deficiency has also been long known to reduce the capacity to learn and remember. Now, we find that an iodine deficiency can undermine the desire to succeed, as demonstrated in a study conducted in India.[1]

Banarasi D. Tiwari and associates at the Sanjay Gandhi Post Graduate Institute of Medical Sciences in Lucknow, India, compared 100 boys, aged nine to fifteen years old, from two villages in eastern India. Iodine was deficient in the soil and water of one village: consequently, fifty boys from that area had goiters, a symptom of low thyroid function. Iodine was adequate in the soil and water of the other village, so fifty boys from there showed no symptoms of hypothyroidism.

All the boys attended school. Testing revealed that boys from the iodine-deficient area were slower learners than those from the iodine-sufficient area (with one exception: in recall of verbally relayed information). Boys with goiters improved less after practice drills than did the others. Researchers concluded that, in their earlier development, they had probably suffered nerve damage that affected their ability to learn and retain information. Invariably the older goitrous children's performances were inferior to those of the younger children, suggesting that their impairment was cumulative. Most surprising was the finding that childhood iodine deficiency not only impaired the boys' ability to learn, but their motivation to learn as well.

"These abnormalities may prevent millions of children from achieving their full potential, even if learning opportunities are available," Tawari told *Science News*.

The goiter belts we mention in Chapter 2 are no longer as important a health issue in the United States and in other developed nations as they once were, for two reasons: first, because food now comes from all parts of the world, and second, because many people eat heavily salted (and iodized) processed foods. In fact, some authorities now oppose supplementing with iodine, because most individuals—especially children and youths—eat so many fast foods heavily seasoned with iodized salt: french fries, potato chips, potato skins, hamburgers, and other junk foods. Even sugary processed products contain hidden sodium.

In a report titled "Minerals: Iodine" that appeared on Health World Online, Elson Haas, MD, writes that a gram of salt ($\frac{1}{28}$th of an ounce) contains roughly 76 mcg of iodine.[2] The average person uses 3 grams of salt daily that contain 228 mcg of iodine, far exceeding the RDA of 150 mg. Despite this, the incidence of goiters is again rising. Can factors other than iodine be involved?

"There is no significant danger of toxicity of iodine from the natural diet, though some care must be taken when supplementing iodine or using it in drug therapy," he indicates. A regular excessive intake of iodine—too much iodized salt or too many kelp tablets—may exacerbate Hashimoto's thyroiditis and reduce thyroxine production and thyroid function.

In addition to the threat of iodine toxicity, one must be aware of the danger of insufficient iodine intake, which still exists for certain population groups, including dieters on super-low caloric intake, anorexics and bulimics, and individuals on low-sodium diets so prevalent among heart disease patients. Numerous studies show that the low-sodium diet does little to prevent heart disease. Assuring enough potassium to balance the sodium intake is far more important.

Only infinitesimal amounts of iodine are needed daily for the following age groups: 35 mcg for newborns to six months; 45 mcg for those six months to a year old; 60 mcg for one- to three-year-olds; 60 mcg for those four to six years of age; 80 mcg for seven- to ten-year-olds, and 110 to 150 mcg for those age eleven and older. Pregnant women require 125 mcg, and lactating women 150 mcg.

Nursing women—any individuals, for that matter—can usually fulfill their iodine quota by eating ocean fish such as cod, haddock, halibut, or sea bass twice weekly. (The problem there is finding uncontaminated fish.) The supplement cod liver oil contains a lot of iodine, and health food stores sell unpolluted products. Kelp, a brown seaweed, is the supplement richest in iodine.

I'm often asked, "If sufficient iodine intake can help to prevent mental retardation, can it also reverse learning disabilities and elevate IQ caused by such a deficiency?" In the few such efforts that I've witnessed, iodine supplementation contributed to small gains, but not enough to warrant recommending it. Apparently, the neurological damage was too great. All the more reason to prevent such damage in the first place!

For more than a generation, it has been known that a pregnant woman's extreme hypothyroidism can cause her infant to be mentally retarded—a condition called *cretinism*. Deficiency of thyroid hormone during the fetal stage or early life may cause the infant's thyroid gland to be a fraction of normal size. It may even be missing. Typically, the cretinous baby has thick, sallow, and wrinkled skin, thickened lips, an enlarged tongue, an open mouth that drools, a broad face, and a flat nose. Cretins are dull, unresponsive to stimulus, and apathetic. Large at birth, they fail to grow normally and become dwarfs in adulthood, if they live that long.

Although reversal of this condition is impossible, improvement is possible. Dr. Broda Barnes told us about several such cases referred to him. Early thyroid supplementation normalized growth and improved the mental ability to some extent. "Total reversal can't happen in such cases, except by divine intervention," Dr. Barnes told us. Fortunately, the odds of this happening today are quite long. However long the odds are, they don't comfort the woman to whom it happens.

In our book *Raise Your IQ!*, Jim Scheer and I stress the importance of couples—not just women—preparing for pregnancy with proper food, supplements, and exercise, because they don't always know when conception will take place.[3]

In his classic book *Nutrition and Physical Degeneration*, Dr. Weston Price, a Cleveland dentist who circled the world observing, interviewing, and photographing natives of primitive cultures, compared the superhealthy cultures in isolated areas of their lands who thrive on native food with those hooked on modern civilization's fractional foods.[4] His comparison showed that refined sugar, flour, and other processed food causes rampant tooth decay and every one of our degenerative diseases, including chronic conditions that date back to the womb.

For instance, even though they knew nothing about iodine and the thyroid gland, Eskimos of the Arctic Circle prepared women for pregnancy with iodine-rich fish eggs.

Fathers consumed milt, the sperm-containing fluid of salmon, to assure them the highest degree of fertility. During pregnancy and nursing as well, women followed a highly nutritious diet to assure the baby a sound body and brain.

One of Dr. Price's most fascinating discoveries was a tribe in the South Pacific that—with no understanding of the biochemistry—provided an iodine- and nutrient-rich diet for pregnant women. Dr. Price was shown a species of spider crab that the islanders fed mothers-to-be "so that their children will be physically excellent and mentally bright."

A young woman of the tribe is required to tell her chief as soon as she knows she's pregnant. The chief then arranges a feast to celebrate the "new person" who will soon join the colony. During the feast, the chief has one or two young men bring the pregnant woman special seafood to give her and her fetus the most nourishing fare to assure the baby a strong body and a good mind.

Newer information supports the need for all women intending to become pregnant not only to get sufficient iodine, but to be tested for hypothyroidism as well. An article in the *New England Journal of Medicine* warned that untreated hypothyroidism during pregnancy could cause baby to have a substantially lower IQ, diminished motor skills, and attention deficit disorder, as well as problems in mastering language and reading.[5]

Researchers found that women with underactive thyroid function during pregnancy are almost four times more prone to have babies with lower IQ scores. Nineteen percent of children born to thyroid-deficient mothers had IQ scores of 85 or lower, compared with only 5 percent of infants born to mothers with normal thyroid function. An IQ level this low can seriously impair a child's chances for an education and success in life.

James E. Haddow, MD, who led the study, wrote, "The children whose scores are in this range may face lifelong developmental challenges. It might be possible to prevent these problems through early diagnosis and treatment of thyroid disease in their mothers."

The researchers reported that the mothers found to be hypothyroid had been that way for five years before their doctors diagnosed the condition. Women who have had their thyroid glands removed or those found to have Hashimoto's thyroiditis are well aware of the need for thyroid supplementation; the greatest danger lies in women whose hypothyroidism or subclinical hypothyroidism is undiagnosed, or those with normal thyroid levels but a high level of antibodies, indicative of autoimmune thyroiditis.

Baby IQ problems result because the mother supplies all thyroid hormones for growth and development of the fetus for the first twelve weeks of pregnancy. After twelve weeks, the fetus develops its own thyroid gland; however, the mother-to-be is still the source of thyroid hormone. During those first twelve weeks, a hypothyroid mother can't always assure enough thyroid hormone for proper brain development. In some cases, miscarriage occurs at this point.

The *New England Journal of Medicine* study shows how important it is to plan and act well in advance for pregnancy and nursing. Women should cooperate closely with a doctor schooled and experienced in identifying and treating hypothyroidism properly. As it is, there's too little preparation and too much Las Vegas-style risk taking in conception for many American couples—a sad fact, because most people don't win in Las Vegas!

14

Better Skin, Better Living

WHETHER TO MAKE yourself more desirable for sexual, social, or career purposes, it is critically important to put your best face forward. And that means presenting a complexion that's appealing.

In her early twenties, auburn-haired Melissa would have been a striking and lovely young woman, if her face hadn't been covered with acne. Hers was as severe a case as I had ever seen. Her first words shocked me:

"Dr. Langer, when I look in the mirror, I want to cry." She nervously clasped and unclasped the pale hands in her lap.

I had never before met Melissa, but I had met her condition on the faces and necks of dozens of other patients in my years as a medical doctor. Many of them had responded to treatment with natural thyroid.

Before her next office visit, I checked results of her Basal Body Temperature Test and thyroid function tests and saw that my suspicion was correct.

Melissa was definitely hypothyroid. I started her with a half grain of natural thyroid a day and a 50 mg vitamin B-complex tablet and 500 mg of vitamin C after each meal. Within three weeks, her skin appeared to be better.

"Look at the improvement!" she exclaimed during her next office visit. "My depression has lifted, too," she continued. "For the first time in years, I feel there's hope."

Indeed there was. I increased her thyroid medication gradually over the subsequent months until she was taking two grains daily, her skin condition improving with each office visit.

As with many such disorders, Melissa's took almost seven months to clear up, and her skin was so clean, smooth, and healthy looking that she refused to wear makeup. She didn't have to.

One of my unusual cases was a six-month-old baby boy, named Zack, who suffered severe eczema. From birth, he had endured incessant itching and soreness from eczema all over his body.

"No matter where I've taken Zack—clinics, hospitals, offices of dermatologists—no treatment has helped," his mother, one of my patients, told me.

I explained that I don't usually treat infants or children, but Zack's mother pleaded:

"I can't stand by and let him suffer."

Neither could I. Inasmuch as many abnormal skin conditions result from low thyroid function, I consented to see Zack at once. His tests indicated a hypothyroid condition, so I prescribed thyroid. As with Melissa, improvement started immediately, but it took almost eight months to clear up the skin lesions, bleeding, and itching. It was a great relief to Zack, and a joy to his mother and me.

Even more extraordinary than this case was that of Jo, a thirty-year-old hair stylist. She had dry, scaly skin (called *ichthyosis* or *fish skin*), brittle, pitted nails, and patches of baldness, which she hid with a brunette wig.

"Doctor, I'm sick with embarrassment. I can't stand the sight of myself. My skin itches like fire and, of course, I can't scratch myself in the beauty salon." She sighed deeply. "Starting today, I'm taking a month's leave of absence, because I can't try to beautify someone else when I can't beautify myself."

Ichthyosis, poor nails, and hair loss are not uncommon in hypothyroid individuals, as I told her. I rushed her lab tests through and made a special appointment for her on the day I received her test results, which indicated severe hypothyroidism.

On thyroid hormone supplementation, her turnaround was remarkable within two weeks! Her skin had begun to soften and the scaliness was less visible.

"Jo, in time, your hair will fill in, too," I promised.

There was no miracle within the month, but her appearance had improved enough for her to return to work.

Several months later, the fish scales were replaced by soft, clean, pliable, and pink skin. Her nails were coming in smooth and hard. And a stubble of new, healthy, black hair had begun filling in the bald spots.

Within a half year, Jo looked so stunning that I hardly recognized her. Supplementing a weak thyroid function had worked again!

Throughout my practice, I have seen astonishing reversals in the skin of patients through supplementation with desiccated thyroid. Sometimes various other skin abnormalities clear up with this form of treatment: acne, eczema, fish skin—as indicated—and cellulitis, erysipelas, impetigo, lupus erythematosus, and psoriasis.

Rarely is an acne patient suspected of thyroid deficiency. Yet, hypothyroidism is at the root of many acne cases. When hair follicles on the skin surface become filled with dirt, makeup, or oil from the sebaceous gland, skin eruptions soon appear—blackheads, whiteheads, pimples, and boils.

Infection then sets in, and cysts may form, some leaving unsightly scars. A change of diet, scrupulous facial hygiene, and frequent washings with antibacterial soap are often recommended by dermatologists. They help, but not enough. Thyroid hormone supplementation usually clears up the condition.

This is no surprise. Two factors are responsible for correcting all the serious skin ailments: improved blood circulation and return to normal metabolism due to thyroid supplementation.

Electronic equipment monitors the efficiency with which blood circulates to our trillions of cells. Hypothyroidism causes low readings, meaning that the heart isn't pumping forcefully enough, so, consequently, circulation is reduced. In advanced cases of low thyroid function, sensitive measurements show that extremities such as the skin may get delivery of only 20 to 25 percent of their required blood supply.

That is only part of the story. With reduced blood supply, the skin cells are oxygen and fuel deprived. Further, waste products of skin cells are not entirely removed—a sort of skin constipation.

Such an unhealthy skin cannot resist invading enemy bacteria that multiply and cause infection. Result? Pimples and boils erupt and refuse to leave. Bacteria such as staphylococci establish beachheads in sebaceous glands and at the bottom of hair follicles. Then come unsightly skin blemishes and merciless itching.

Treatment with antibiotics brings temporary relief and skin improvement, but soon the negative condition returns, because the cause—low thyroid condition—has not been corrected. Many such cases I have treated respond to natural thyroid, a B-complex supplement, and a reduction or elimination of junk foods.

Like acne, eczema is one of the most torturing skin conditions. It can involve any part of the body, causing itching that can bring on emotional trauma in some patients. Further, the skin becomes scaly, often swelling, blistering, and oozing. Scratching may cause excessive bleeding and infection.

Use of thyroid supplementation to correct eczema is not new. In fact, an English doctor discovered it in the 1890s when he treated a sixty-five-year-old woman with eczema for her major complaints: low energy and cold extremities.[1]

The eczema disappeared. Now the doctor's curiosity was aroused. He stopped the thyroid, and, sure enough, the eczema returned. After renewed treatment, this disorder again disappeared.

Almost any skin ailment can have its basis in hypothyroidism, although this isn't always the main cause.

Cellulitis is a swelling of the skin and tissues under the skin, which brings on redness and pain. These symptoms are accompanied by chills, fever, headache, and low energy. Cellulitis is caused by streptococci, staphylococci, or other unfriendly bacteria, which take advantage of the skin's inability to defend itself and the body it encloses against invaders.

This condition is not taken lightly by physicians or knowledgeable patients. In its most deep-seated and advanced form, it can cause tissue-destroying abscesses to form. Cellulitis is particularly dangerous when it breaks out in the scalp, because it can cause brain damage and serious complications.

One of the worst complications I have seen is cellulitis of the mouth. Sometimes surgery is required. However, antibiotic treatment saved my patient until his condition could be managed with thyroid hormone.

Erysipelas, with a frightening name that sounds somewhat like a social disease, is a streptococcal infection that brings on hot, red skin blotches—as well as a fever, fatigue, and an often depressed state. Unless this ailment is checked, it can poison the system through invading bacteria and the toxins they introduce into the blood (septicemia), kidney inflammation, pneumonia, and even rheumatic fever. Before we had sulfa drugs and antibiotics, erysipelas often killed the patient. Today, it is again dangerous, because there is so much new antibiotic resistance. In many instances, erysipelas indicates hypothyroidism.

Like erysipelas, impetigo also can kill. It seems just a superficial skin disorder at the start, brought about by the invasion of streptococcal or staphylococcal microorganisms. Its symptoms are pustules half an inch in diameter to small, hotcake-sized, crusty, pus-swollen blisters that often break. These are localized in a small area or cover the entire face, neck, and body and may evolve into ulcers or boils.

Toxins can spread throughout the whole system to poison vital organs and cause death. Antibiotics usually control the condition, but, again, hypothyroidism should be suspected and, if present, treated. Otherwise, this condition can return.

Lupus erythematosus, too, is a serious disorder, most frequently affecting the skin only. However, it can also attack the internal organs. In its initial stage, it causes butterfly-shaped, red flushing on the nose and cheeks. Sometimes it manifests as hard, red lesions covering the ears, scalp, and mucous membranes of the mouth and/or throat.

When this condition seizes upon internal organs or joints, it becomes especially critical. Lupus erythematosus is characterized by deposits of mucopolysaccharides in connective tissue and elsewhere. As mentioned in previous chapters, such depositions are caused by a deficiency of thyroid hormone. So lupus has much in common with rheumatic arthritis, rheumatic fever, amyloiditis (deposits in internal organs, which undermine their function), and necrotizing arteritis (inflamed arteries), among other connective tissue ailments. Lupus usually responds to thyroid supplementation.

One of the most difficult skin disorders to control by conventional methods is psoriasis, recognizable by bright red outbreaks laced with silvery scales. Although the red patches can appear anywhere on the body, they usually manifest on the arms, legs, palms of the hands, elbows, knees, buttocks, and scalp.

Often psoriasis accompanies rheumatoid arthritis, an added misery. As with lupus, mucopolysaccharides invade connective tissue. One of the most successful treatments for psoriasis is thyroid supplementation, but it is not consistently effective.

In the history of thyroid supplementation, sometimes psoriasis responds well. Sometimes there's no improvement of the condition. My experience with psoriasis is somewhat limited. However, with thyroid supplementation, a large number of my patients with this disorder eventually showed a dramatic reduction of this condition or total disappearance.

The remainder showed slight or no improvement, indicating the possibility that their psoriasis had one or more other causes. These are some alternative modalities that have worked: a gluten-free diet, avoiding food allergens such as corn, citrus fruits, nuts, milk, acidic beverages (coffee and soft drinks), and acid-containing pineapple and tomatoes.

S. S. Bleehan, MD, Professor of Dermatology at the Royal Hallamshire Hospital in Sheffield, England, demonstrated that the omega-3 oil in 5½ ounces of mackerel, salmon, or sardines taken daily significantly improved this disorder's itching, redness, and scaling.[2] Elsewhere in this book, we have warned against eating large fish such as mackerel and salmon due to possible mercury pollution, but small fish like sardines do not pose this risk.

Dr. Bleehan achieved comparable results by feeding patients ten omega-3 capsules daily for twelve weeks. Several other researchers have reported similar improvement with this regimen. Labels of some fish oil products in health food stores offer the assurance that the omega-3 was derived from small, mercury-free fish.

It is sensible insurance for a healthy and youthful-appearing skin to have your thyroid function checked and, if needed, supplemented. Otherwise, as illustrated by case studies in this chapter, a poor complexion can contribute to many emotional, social, and career problems, an added burden that none of us needs.

15

Mind and Emotions: The Thyroid Connection

SKIN PROBLEMS, EXHAUSTION and lack of endurance are not the only handicaps of many untreated hypothyroids grimly trying to compete in the real world. To these must be added emotional problems. Some are so subtle that those who have them may not even be aware of them.

The late Roy G. Hoskins, MD, an eminent endocrinologist, found that even in seemingly mild cases of myxedema (acutely subnormal thyroid function), there is an underlying irritability and hostility, in addition to mental and physical sluggishness.[1] In another common type of hypothyroidism, Dr. Hoskins noted a chip-on-the-shoulder attitude, an abnormal responsiveness to petty annoyances, but not necessarily the usual overweight or sluggishness. A state of general fatigue exists, along with "general poor health and, particularly, lack of endurance often designated chronic nervous exhaustion—and inability to endure physical or mental strain."

Dr. Hoskins referred to findings of endocrinologist H. F. Stoll, who discovered the following characteristics in "chronic hypothyroid invalidism": irritability, lying, suspiciousness, delusions, retarded ability to think, inability to concentrate, introversion, and failing memory. Even mild to moderate stress can tilt the delicate balance of the low-thyroid person and cause acute anxiety or depression. Such events as marriage, birth of a first child, a financial reversal, and new job responsibilities can bring on greater energy depletion, headaches, temper tantrums, diarrhea, or constipation, according to Dr. Stoll.

A study of twenty untreated hypothyroids by Martha Schon, MD, a researcher at the Neuropsychiatric Service at Memorial Hospital in New York City, revealed such emotional traits as fatigue, nervousness, irritability, contrariness, and temper explosions, which made it easy to mistake them for neurotics. She noted a major difference, however. Genuine neurotics blame others or circumstances for their problems. Low-thyroid persons will generally accept responsibility for their emotional conduct.[2]

Dr. Schon found that with thyroid supplementation, almost all physical and emotional symptoms lessened or disappeared. Patients developed a sense of well-being and integration of personality. Apparently, subclinical hypothyroidism can remain latent for years and not show itself in emotional or mental symptoms until after severe stress. A number of my patients have had this experience. Dr. Schon made the same discovery, observing that mental pressures with which patients could not cope brought on hypothyroidism.

Postpartum depression (the "blues" experienced by some women after delivery of a baby) may be attributable to a low-thyroid condition. That hypothyroidism can be a causative factor in mild to severe neuroses and psychoses is not a new discovery.

Let us remember that Sigmund Freud, the father of psychoanalysis, predicted that some day a biological or physiological therapy would prove more effective in coping with emotional illness than psychotherapy.

Carl Jung agreed.[3]

In the 1920s, Karl Mayer, MD, a German scientist, demonstrated the power of thyroid extract to act as a biochemical psychiatrist on a patient no livelier than a block of ice—and equally silent—and normalize him.

More recently, successful use of thyroid hormone and vitamin therapy on psychiatric "rejects"—patients virtually unimproved with psychoanalysis—convinced Nathan Masor, MD, that conventional psychiatry needed biochemical backing.

Edward R. Pinckney, MD, and Cathey Pinckney, authors of *The Fallacy of Freud and Psychoanalysis*, agree that unless the physical requirements for thyroid hormone are satisfied, psychiatric techniques will not help.

According to the Pinckneys,

All too often, thyroid disease will manifest itself through nothing but behavioral symptoms. Neurotic actions may be the sole result of too little or too much thyroid, and the taking of a few inexpensive pills each day can produce instant normality in someone who seems to have a mental illness. Compare this type of treatment with years and years of costly lying on a couch, trying to uncover some infantile sexual frustration.

But thyroid disease is not the only illness that indicates neurotic behavior. Patients with lung cancer repeatedly show marked hostility reaction. Infectious diseases, pelvic inflammations, and even enlarged arteries have produced the very symptoms the psychoanalysts claim are due to unresolved sexual problems that began in childhood. What is contradictory to the Freudian doctrine is the fact that once an organic diagnosis is made and treated, there is an immediate disappearance of all neurotic behavior.[4]

While at the University of North Carolina, P. C. Whybrow, MD—now at the UCLA Neuropsychiatric Institute—studied a group of patients with severe mental disturbances who seemed excellent candidates for typical psychiatric treatment.[5] One of them was a woman whose son had been killed in a head-on car collision many years before and who constantly said that it would have been better if she had been the one killed. She had recurring dreams of reclaiming him from his grave by digging him up with her bare hands. All day long she heard her son calling to her. Considering herself a heavy burden for her family, she often entertained thoughts of suicide.

Another woman, plagued with insomnia, experienced vivid, horrifying dreams when she did sleep—the death of her son and the mutilation of other family members. "I'm losing my mind," she insisted to family and doctors.

Both serious cases were quickly cleared up and the patients returned to normal behavior after thyroid treatment, thanks to enlightened psychiatrists.

Dr. Whybrow also found that hypothyroidism often manifests itself in two mental symptoms that are severe handicaps in daily living: poor recent memory and difficulty in concentrating. A Georgetown University study discovered these very symptoms in more than half of 109 cases of hypothyroidism.[6]

The most extreme form of hypothyroidism, myxedema, which is four to five times more common in women than in men, exaggerates mental shortcomings. Thinking, remembering, and reacting occur in slow motion, if at all. A need to concentrate often puts the person to sleep. As one recovered patient told me, "In myxedema, thinking results in nonthinking. Mental effort is next to impossible. One is just a super vegetable."

Dr. Masor reports that in even less extreme hypothyroidism, thinking is slow and memory impaired, often compounding emotional conditions such as listlessness, restlessness, irritability, a paranoid tendency, easy fatigue, and miscellaneous body pains.[7] The fact that these symptoms melt away with appropriate daily thyroid therapy indicates that, in most cases, they are probably due to hypothyroidism.

In addition to supplementation with thyroid hormone, the diet should supply all essential nutrients. Lack of any B vitamins—particularly thiamine (B_1) and cyanocobalamin (B_{12})—can slow thinking and cause memory lapses and irritability, as studies of semistarved prisoners of war have revealed. On the other hand, supplying subjects in starvation experiments with missing B-complex vitamins, with an accent on B, and B_{12}, brought about enhanced thinking and remembering, among other positive results.

In a double-blind experiment with matched-ability children, Dr. Ruth Flinn Herrell added just 2 mg of vitamin B to the daily diet of one group and a placebo to that of the second group. At the end of the study, the first group's mental and physical abilities had risen from 7 to 87 percent. Those of the other group remained almost the same.[8]

An article in the *British Medical Journal* by J. MacDonald Holmes, MD, that cited various experiments revealed that a deficiency of vitamin B_{12} brought on devastating mental and emotional symptoms, such as difficulty in thinking and remembering, confusion, mood disorders, agitated depression, paranoia, delusions, visual and auditory hallucinations, maniacal behavior, and epilepsy.[9]

Along with good nutrition, aerobic exercise encourages brain and memory function, says Professor Robert Rivera, a memory expert and speech teacher at Los Angeles Valley College in Van Nuys, California. Professor Rivera has found that more efficient blood and oxygen circulation to the brain can cause a significant increase in a person's IQ—as much as thirty points.

You may be able to validate Professor Rivera's findings by trying these simple exercises. First, you inhale for eight counts, hold your breath for twelve counts, then exhale for ten counts. He recommends repeating this exercise ten times. (*Warning:* If you feel dizzy, stop exercising at once!)

Second, you practice sitting up erectly at work and improve your posture by standing and flattening yourself against a wall, then stretching. If the experiment is successful, you should observe a new sense of vigor, well-being, and clarity of thinking.

The importance of oxygen to brain function is underscored by the fact that the gray matter, where thinking is done, uses one-quarter of our oxygen intake. Arterial blood of the brain must have an oxygen saturation of 90 percent for efficient thinking, according to Dr. Masor.

If it is reduced to 85 percent, the ability for fine concentration and fine muscular coordination decreases. Reduce it to 74 percent, and faulty judgment results.[10] Such oxygen deprivation may also lead to emotional instability. Further oxygen reduction causes the nervous system to be depressed. Complete oxygen starvation for more than four minutes will often contribute to irreversible brain damage.

Hypothyroidism can cause oxygen deprivation in the brain in numerous ways: by impeding blood circulation (slowing the delivery of oxygen and nutrients); by slowing the rate of oxidation (burning) of food (glucose) to nourish brain cells; by depressing production of blood cells; by contributing to atherosclerosis (narrowing of arteries); and by limiting the amount of blood that reaches the brain. Dr. Masor points out that narrowing of vital brain arterioles by even one-sixteenth of their caliber can limit oxygen supply and bring about mental and emotional disturbances.

How hypothyroidism depresses blood cell production (and can actually contribute to a form of anemia) has been covered in detail in Chapter 5. How subnormal thyroid function encourages atherosclerosis will be explained in later chapters on heart and artery diseases.

Over and above contributing to disturbances of thought and memory processes, hypothyroidism may cause severe emotional changes, which, unfortunately, may be misdiagnosed as psychiatric disorders and treated unnecessarily with powerful drugs (some of them habit forming) and hospitalization. One of its most serious, persistent, and widespread consequences is depression, the subject of the next chapter.

16

Reversing Depression

DEPRESSED PERSONS ARE more likely to get relief from thyroid supplementation than from warmed-over psychotherapy.

New evidence that thyroid insufficiency is at the root of much depression and fatigue was announced by Mark Gold, MD, and associates at a conference on affective illness at Friends Hospital in Philadelphia.[1] In examining 350 inpatients and 44 outpatients at Fair Oaks Hospital in Summit, New Jersey, Dr. Gold found a "significant incidence of low-level hypothyroidism," convincing him that depression is often the first sign of low-level thyroid failure not always detectable by the usual thyroid function tests. Traditional blood tests for thyroid function in depressed patients revealed only 10 percent hypothyroids. Ninety percent of the depressed who were clinically hypothyroid showed normal thyroid blood tests.

Dr. Gold discovered that, when untreated, hypothyroidism became increasingly severe in a very short time. Early diagnosis and treatment led to a desirable reduction in depression. It is imperative to evaluate all psychiatric patients for hypothyroidism, Dr. Gold feels, because new data show that if thyroid function is reduced by 10 percent, brain thyroid function is diminished by a corresponding amount. A slowdown of the thyroid, even if we remain normal, will cause some changes in the brain. It doesn't surprise Dr. Gold that hypothyroids appear to be psychiatric patients.

He also explained that more than 10 percent of patients who visit psychiatrists with depression have the condition called *Hashimoto's thyroditis*, an ailment in which the immune system attacks the thyroid gland tissue, causing inflammation and underfunctioning of the organ. This disorder was discussed in greater detail in Chapter 10.

However, most cases of thyroid-induced depression are caused by simple hypothyroidism. A letter to me from a patient who had suffered from depression of unsuspected origin for decades expresses the anguish that many such persons have in common:

My depression started when I was sixteen. The doctor ordered a basal metabolism test, which turned out to be low. He prescribed one grain of thyroid. I took it for a year and felt better.

Then I discontinued thyroid; I don't remember why. When I was thirty-five, the depression came back, along with low energy, but I never sought help. I didn't realize what was wrong.

I'm married and have three children but never seem to have enough energy to do anything except take care of the children. In my late forties, I lost interest in everything, just dragging around, feeling low and blue. I was little more than a vegetable. I couldn't have cared less if I woke up the next day.

Finally, a doctor diagnosed me as having depression. I had a series of shock treatments and several mood-elevating drugs. Then, when my doctor relocated, I couldn't find another doctor to help me. I struggled along with periods of mild depression and very low energy.

About five years ago, I heard Dr. Broda Barnes on a radio talk show, discussing hypothyroidism and his test. Later, I asked my new doctor for a thyroid function test, which proved negative. He refused to prescribe thyroid.

All my life, I had noticed that I ran a subnormal temperature but hadn't thought much about it. One day I took my early-morning temperature and found it low. My cousin, who was visiting, had some thyroid pills, and I started taking a small dose. Almost immediately my depression lifted and my energy rose, too.

Then I heard Dr. Barnes on the air again, this time as your guest, and I decided to see you. I'm so glad I did. As you know, my basal temperature was low and you gave me thyroid. Many, many thanks for seeing through my problems, for realizing I was not a mental patient who needed more shock treatments, mood-elevating drugs, or psychoanalysis. I feel great now!

Within a month, her fifteen-year-long depression was eliminated. It saddened me that this well-meaning person could not get simple, safe, low-cost thyroid to help her and instead was subjected to two series of arduous, expensive, and unnecessary shock treatments, which could do nothing to compensate for her shortage of thyroid hormones.

I wish I could say that this is a rare case. However, many of my patients are over age fifty and, as children, teenagers, or even adults, had had thyroid supplementation that was cut off when they or their doctors moved. During the 1950s, blood tests came into vogue and were not always positive for hypothyroidism. Patients were told that they no longer needed thyroid, and most of them suffered decades of unnecessary depression, anxiety, and physical discomfort and limitation.

In fairness to the doctors of the 1950s and 1960s, the Barnes Basal Temperature Test was not then widely known, although Dr. Barnes's landmark paper on this test had already been published in the *Journal of the American Medical Association*. Today, however, there is little excuse for being unaware of it and its validity.

Despite the Basal Temperature Test's accuracy in revealing hypothyroidism, there is a minute percentage of cases that are too subtle to be detectable by this method. Not long ago, a patient in her early thirties, whom I'll call Phyllis, took the Barnes test and registered 97.8°F degrees the first day and 97.7°F the second day. She tried again on the third day and showed a temperature of 97.7°F. This averaged out to less than a tenth of a point below normal. Yet this woman had a serious problem with depression. She admitted that frequently, in the electronic assembly department that she supervised, she almost burst into tears at the slightest frustration, something she couldn't afford to do without reducing her stature and jeopardizing her position, which she had worked hard for fifteen years to attain.

I asked all the right questions. Had she gone through severe stresses—the death of a spouse, relative, or close friend, a revolutionary change on the job, the breakup of a love affair?

"No, doctor. Nothing like that," she responded.

"Anything seem radically wrong physically?" I asked.

"No. I'm a little more tired than usual. That's all."

"Are you always depressed, or is it intermittent?"

"I do have good days and weeks, sometimes months. But it's worse this winter than last."

I glanced at the calendar (sometimes you need a calendar to determine the season, because winters in northern California are quite mild) and realized that Phyllis had given me the clue I needed. She was definitely hypothyroid, despite her body temperature reading. Her deepest depression was in the winter season, when temperatures were 10 to 15 degrees cooler than in fall or summer.

Colder weather makes it necessary for the thyroid to step up the burning of fuel. This slight change accented her hypothyroidism, mild as it was.

I explained the problem to Phyllis, who agreed to take a grain of thyroid daily. She never regretted it. Within three weeks, her depression began to recede, and two months later she said, "It's hard for me to remember not feeling okay. My energy level is great. It's wonderful to be a human being again."

Like Phyllis's case, Benton's had certain mystifying aspects at first. A certified public accountant who owned his own firm, Benton plunged into deep depression near the middle of April—the end of income tax season. That was understandable, because of the extreme stress he was under at tax deadline time. However, it was now the end of May, and the depression had grown worse. Certainly a person in good health would have recovered already.

Benton's basal temperature was just a shade under the normal 97.8°F. A complete medical history and physical examination done at that time were inconclusive. Because of his symptoms, however, I started him on a half grain of desiccated thyroid. Even this small amount of natural thyroid medication worked wonders.

Thyroid hormone has been studied intensively in depressed patients. In one double-blind controlled study, just 25 mcg of thyroid daily enhanced the antidepressant action of the drug imipramine by 50 percent. Forty mcg was even more effective with imipramine.[2]

Of course, not all depression is caused by hypothyroidism.[3] Poor nutrition is another major unsuspected cause. In such cases, dietary counseling and nutritional supplements banish depression almost miraculously.

An unsuspected cause of depression in women is taking oral contraceptive pills. When a patient is depressed and on the Pill, I have her change to another form of contraception as soon as possible and treat her immediately for B-complex deficiency, particularly vitamin B_6, known to be depleted in chronic users of oral contraceptives. If there is, in fact, a B-complex deficiency, a B-complex vitamin including at least 50 mg of vitamin B_6 usually helps to dispel depression.

Sometimes when the lack of B complex is caused by the use of birth control pills, severe depression follows childbirth (postpartum depression). This condition usually responds to B-complex vitamins.

The trace mineral lithium is often thought to be an excellent treatment for depression. Actually, it may worsen depression, because it interferes with thyroid function. On the basis of a thorough study, P. L. Rabin, MD, and D. C. Evans, MD, of Vanderbilt University School of Medicine, verify this fact in the *Journal of Clinical Psychiatry*: "... goiter formation and hypothyroidism are not infrequent following lithium therapy...."[4]

Unfortunately, hypothyroidism is still not widely enough recognized as a major cause of depression. It would be a mistake, however, to consider subnormal thyroid function and nutritional deficiencies as the *only* causes.

17

Medical Look-Alikes: Hypoglycemia and Hypothyroidism

ANOTHER HEAVYWEIGHT CONTRIBUTOR to depression is hypoglycemia (low blood sugar), an insidious disorder with many emotional and physical symptoms, the best known of which is deep fatigue. It is also known as hyperinsulinism.[1]

In a survey of 600 hypoglycemia patients, Stephen Gyland, MD, found that depression ranked fifth among their complaints and was experienced by 77 percent of them. It is understandable why hypoglycemia causes a long list of additional emotional ailments: forgetfulness, insomnia, anxiety, confusion, antisocial behavior, crying jags, lack of concentration, and assorted phobias. When our blood sugar is too low, our brains are deprived of glucose, the only fuel they can use. This starvation brings on the symptoms that are often misdiagnosed as neuroses.

Hypoglycemia results mainly from how the body handles—or mishandles—sugar, rather than from the amount of sugar in the blood at a given time. When a normal person takes in a simple refined carbohydrate, such as table sugar, the blood level of sugar rises. Then the hormone insulin, secreted by the pancreas, soon brings down blood sugar to the fasting level.

When the hypoglycemic ingests sugar, however, the pancreas suffers shock and overreacts, discharging so much insulin into the blood that sugar is removed too rapidly, creating a glucose deficit. Secondary results from prolonged hyperinsulinism are an off-balance nervous system, overstimulated adrenal glands often stressed in the process of elevating blood sugar level, and an eventual shortage of blood sugar–elevating hormones—adrenaline, glucagon, and a pituitary gland hormone.

From the standpoint of symptoms, hypoglycemia is like hypothyroidism. Dr. Broda Barnes felt that these disorders are almost as closely related as Siamese twins, and his reasons make good sense.

He told me how he happened to stumble onto this connection. A legal secretary, prior to being treated by Dr. Barnes, passed out in her office, apparently from a heart attack, and was rushed to a hospital's intensive care unit. Three days of comprehensive, sophisticated tests revealed nothing organically wrong. She had other blackouts, more siren-screaming races to intensive care, more tests, more medical costs, and still no diagnosis firm enough to support a therapy program. Then she found a physician who understood the biochemical basis for hypoglycemia and put her on a high-protein, low-carbohydrate diet, which brought about some improvement. However, she wasn't completely satisfied. She was referred to Dr. Barnes, who observed that she showed many symptoms of hypothyroidism, including a subnormal basal temperature.

With natural thyroid therapy, she recovered rapidly and never again experienced a blackout. As Dr. Barnes put it, "The light suddenly dawned. If she were hypothyroid and hypoglycemic, might not the two ailments occur together in many individuals?"

He explained his theory in the following terms: "A sluggish liver results from subnormal thyroid activity. During periods of stress, the liver can't produce enough sugar from protein. Then hypoglycemia occurs. Thyroid therapy stimulates the liver to normal function, and hypoglycemia usually disappears."

Dr. Barnes cited three bits of evidence of sluggish liver in hypothyroidism. For more than one hundred years, researchers have noted that myxedema patients (those with extremely low thyroid function) have a yellowish skin color, caused by too much carotene in the blood. A liver low in thyroid hormone has difficulty converting carotene to vitamin A, which is colorless. Thyroid therapy stimulates liver function, and the yellowish skin color vanishes.

Another piece of evidence is that blood cholesterol is usually high in hypothyroidism. Thyroid supplementation lowers cholesterol, because the liver is once again working normally, turning excess cholesterol into bile salts, which are discharged in the bile.

The third piece of evidence is that the sluggish liver of the hypothyroid stores glucose more slowly than a normal organ. Therefore, the blood level of sugar may register high during a fasting glucose tolerance test. The patient may also spill glucose in the urine and, for these reasons, will probably be labeled a "prediabetic."

"When such an individual is put on thyroid therapy, the liver begins to function properly and the glucose tolerance test is normal," said Dr. Barnes. "Many so-called prediabetics are really hypothyroids. This accounts for the fact that so few of them ever become diabetics."

Blood sugar levels are also closely associated with correct functioning of the adrenals, two ductless glands that perch on top of the kidneys and produce antistress hormones. Most of us are familiar with one essential function of the adrenals: triggering the discharge of liver glucose (stored as glycogen) into the bloodstream to give us instant energy in the face of stress. These key glands also secrete and release other essential hormones—the major ones are cortisol (hydrocortisone) and cortisone, both glucocorticoids related to liver sugar.

A study included in perhaps the most prestigious textbook on the thyroid gland, *The Thyroid*, edited by Sidney C. Werner, MD, and Sidney H. Ingbar, MD, gives a clue as to how hypothyroidism influences at least one important function of the adrenal glands related to blood sugar.

One of cortisol's most significant functions is stimulating the liver's production of glycogen. An experiment cited in *The Thyroid* shows that hypothyroids secrete cortisol at a reduced rate. This means that liver sugar is produced more slowly. Treatment with thyroid hormone normalizes cortisol metabolism.

The Werner-Ingbar book states that hypothyroidism in animals sometimes causes adrenal atrophy (wasting away), which could undermine every function of this gland. The findings in human beings have not been so conclusive. What is well established, however, is that the thyroid gland is closely associated with blood sugar levels, although all the reasons for this are not as yet known.

Dr. Barnes added a footnote in regard to hypothyroidism and hypoglycemia. In more than four decades as a medical doctor, he treated more than five thousand patients for the symptoms of subnormal thyroid function and did not see one case of hypoglycemia develop. He admitted, however, that only in the last several decades had this disorder become well enough known for him and other medical doctors to be alert to it.

Patients who went to Dr. Barnes with hypoglycemia usually responded to thyroid therapy with no change in diet. My experience in this regard varies slightly. In many instances, my patients have overcome low blood sugar with thyroid hormones. However, I have also had excellent response from diet.

My dietary approach to this disorder is purposely uncomplicated. First, I explain to patients that a simple carbohydrate wastes no time going through the digestive process and into the bloodstream—foods such as sugar, corn syrup, and glucose, for example. Complex unrefined carbohydrates—legumes, nuts, seeds, vegetables, whole grains, whole-grain cereals—are slower, followed by proteins and then fats, the slowest.

A mixed diet—some complex carbohydrates, protein, and a little fat—assures gradual release of sugar into the bloodstream. The pancreas is protected from sugar shock. Ample protein from meat, fish, poultry, eggs, or dairy products and low-carbohydrate vegetables and fruits make an ideal diet for the hypoglycemic. Most fruits and vegetables can be included, although I usually eliminate those in the

20 percent carbohydrate bracket: bananas, sweet cherries, fresh figs, grape juice, and prunes, as well as kidney, lima, and navy beans, corn, and hominy. Fruits and vegetables to be eaten sparingly are the following in the 15 percent carbohydrate group: apples, apricots, blueberries, sour cherries, grapes, loganberries, pears, pineapple, plums, and raspberries, as well as artichokes, parsnips, and peas.

Some authorities on hypoglycemia recommend from five to seven small meals daily, rather than the traditional three. By mixing food groups, I find that most patients can manage hypoglycemia well with three meals, but I suggest that they experiment. If more small meals work for them, I urge them to follow such a routine.

So much for low blood sugar. Next we will deal with high blood sugar.

18

Diabetes:
A Preventable Illness

A LITTLE KNOWLEDGE about diabetes, a blood sugar disorder that plagues almost eleven million Americans, will go a long way to prevent it and—for those already diabetic—to lessen this ailment's health-destroying effects, reduce dependency on insulin, and dramatically decrease the chances of sometimes fatal diabetic complications.

Telltale symptoms of diabetes are excessive thirst, frequent and copious urination, constant hunger, rapid weight loss, severe itching, fatigue, weakness, and, above all, high sugar level in the blood and urine.

Elevated blood sugar is due to a breakdown of the body's energy use system. Glucose, a simple sugar derived from food, is our major fuel for heat and energy. Although blood circulation carries glucose to all of our body cells, it cannot penetrate the cell membranes unless it is attached to molecules of the pancreatic hormone insulin. In an insulin shortage, much blood sugar accumulates and circulates helplessly, finally passing into the kidneys for excretion in the urine.

On its way into the stomach, food triggers the release of insulin into the bloodstream. Although most blood sugar is used for energy, some enters the liver to be changed into glycogen and is stored there and in the muscles for use according to the body's needs. If we overeat and underexercise, the excess calories are converted into fat deposits.

Insulin is secreted by the pancreas, a yellowish glandular organ lying horizontally under the stomach. This hormone is formed in a part of the pancreas called the *islets of Langerhans*, which contain the all-important alpha and beta cells. Alpha cells secrete a hormone called glucagon, which, when called upon, raises the blood sugar level by activating the conversion of stored glycogen into glucose. The beta cells secrete the hormone insulin, which lowers blood sugar level. The outputs of the alpha and beta cells are supposed to be in balance. In the diabetic, however, insulin is often in short supply, for reasons which will be discussed later.

In addition to these secretions, the pancreas excretes proteolytic enzymes, molecules that help create the proper pH (acid-base) environment in the digestive system for these proteolytic enzymes to function. They break down proteins into body-usable amino acids.

How does a person become diabetic? In several ways. First, by heredity. Children born of at least one diabetic parent are more likely to be diabetic than those from non-diabetic parents. The islets of Langerhans in their pancreas secrete too little insulin or receptors of their trillions of cells fail to take in glucose efficiently.

In some instances, they may secrete pre-insulin, rather than biologically usable insulin. This "not quite" form of the hormone never completes its final cycle.

Another cause appears to be repeated and heavy intakes of sugar that exhaust the insulin-making capacity. Sugar entering the bloodstream signals the beta cells to secrete more insulin, keeping them in production until the glucose level drops to normal. Repeated assaults by large amounts of sugar force the pancreas to work overtime. Eventually, it becomes exhausted and insulin production slumps.

In some instances, however, insulin shortage may not be the problem. Experiments by Walter Mertz, MD, former chief of the U.S. Department of Agriculture's Vitamin and Mineral Research Division, indicate that a shortage of chromium can bring on diabetes.[1]

To escort glucose through cell walls, insulin needs the close cooperation of infinitesimal amounts of chromium as a catalyst. Most maturity-onset diabetes (also known as Type 2 diabetes) results from a diet of chromium-poor processed foods and could probably be prevented by use of chromium-rich foods such as brewer's yeast, beef liver, chicken, various meats, and whole grains.

Innumerable environmental factors, including food selection, preparation, consumption, and repetition, as well as stresses, are important causatives. Some authorities hold that heredity is given more weight than it deserves, because researchers gather their statistics without considering that poor diet and other negative environmental conditions passed down from generation to generation are also a key part of physical ailments that appear to be strictly hereditary.

It is now well known that one of the adrenal gland hormones, epinephrine, released into the bloodstream in fight-or-flight situations, increases free fatty acids in the blood and turns off the release of insulin. Unresolved and continued stress can, therefore, upset the balance of pancreas hormones and bring on diabetes.

Another kind of stress, obesity, invites diabetes. At a conference on diabetes mellitus and obesity, W. John H. Butterfield, MD, Professor of Medicine at Guys Hospital in London, revealed an amazing similarity in how the body handles carbohydrates in diabetes and in gross overweight.[2]

Dr. Butterfield described his experiment on comparative cell glucose uptake of three groups of test subjects: juvenile diabetics, maturity-onset diabetics, and normal controls.

Juvenile diabetics absorbed no sugar in their cells, a strong indication that they were short on internally secreted insulin. Glucose uptake of older diabetic patients and obese normal subjects was similar. Lean controls took up more sugar than plump ones.

Obese subjects handled carbohydrates almost like diabetics, said Dr. Butterfield. As obesity progresses, less and less insulin reaches the insulin-responsive muscles, so less and less glucose uptake occurs there, making it necessary for more and more insulin to be formed. When obesity increases to certain proportions, the pancreas can't keep up production of insulin to meet demand, and hyperglycemia results.

Reversible-obesity diabetes, then, adds up to a breakdown of the body's insulin-glucose economy.

Another significant insight of Dr. Butterfield's about the proneness of obese people to diabetes is that body fat competes with muscle for insulin, and fat wins. Then carbohydrates are changed into more fat.

Both obese and lean diabetics usually reduce blood fats and the need for insulin on a high-fiber diet. This is the conclusion reached by James Anderson, MD, of the University of Kentucky, a long-time researcher in high-fiber diets—those containing large amounts of raw foods, fruits, vegetables, whole-grain breads, bran, nuts, and seeds. The most marked improvement was in obese patients who lost the greatest amount of weight. Excellent high-fiber foods are spinach, prunes, corn, fresh peas, blackberries, sweet potatoes, apples, whole-wheat bread, potatoes, broccoli, almonds, raisins, zucchini, plums, and kidney beans.[3]

Associate Professor Somasundaram Addanki, of the Ohio State University College of Medicine, agrees with the need for a high-fiber diet in managing and preventing diabetes. However, he goes further. Ninety percent of diabetes-prone individuals can avoid this disorder by not eating "the typical high-fat, high-sugar, and low-fiber diet consumed in Western countries," he writes in the journal *Preventive Medicine*.[4]

Professor Addanki speaks from personal experience as well as in-depth research on this subject. A diabetic who married a diabetic, he says that he and his wife did not develop diabetes until they left their native India and started eating American foods. He does not agree that heredity is a primary factor.

Only 8 percent of cases can be attributed to heredity, as comparative studies in Africa and Japan indicate. These findings relieved Addanki about the future of his children.

Further data that the typical American diet exerts the most powerful influence on the development of diabetes emerge from a comparison of Japanese living in Japan and others who moved to Hawaii. After eating Western food in Hawaii, they invariably developed diabetes in greater numbers.

A biochemist and nutritionist, Addanki explains why the poor American diet turns healthy individuals into diabetics. Fatty, sugary, low-fiber foods stimulate certain intestinal bacteria to produce excessive estrogen, a female hormone. It is also probable that an enzyme in fatty tissues unites with testosterone, the male hormone, to synthesize more estrogen. Estrogen desensitizes skeletal muscles to insulin action. As more weight is added, more estrogen is produced, more insulin is required to be effective, and there is greater stress on the pancreas, the insulin producer, which wears out too soon.

The excess estrogen theory explains why obese adult men are often impotent, while women frequently experience a more powerful sexual drive. In a United Press International story explaining his theory, Professor Addanki admitted to six years of "diabetic impotence" before a change of diet brought him control over his disease. He advises all overweight people to give up sugar, white flour, and fatty foods if they want to avoid the risk of developing diabetes.

Another authority who has evidence that exhaustion of the pancreas underlies the development of diabetes is William H. Philpott, MD. A prominent specialist in environmental medicine, he has a different explanation as to how this happens, and he elaborates in an illuminating book, *Victory over Diabetes*, written with Dwight K. Kalita, PhD.[5] He observes that the pancreas secretes a substance called *somastatin*, which acts as a balancing mechanism between the organ's other hormones, glucagon (blood sugar raising) and insulin (blood sugar lowering).

> "Obviously, a proper harmony must exist between these various functions of the pancreas to avoid diabetes," he writes. "If we were to stop at this point with our examination of the pancreas, we might conclude, as has been done by many physicians, that diabetes is a simple matter of controlling high blood sugar levels by the daily injection of insulin.
>
> "However, as we have already seen, although high blood sugar levels may indeed be controlled by insulin, the associ-

ated killing complications of diabetes are not easily dealt with. There is, in fact, medical evidence . . . that daily injections of insulin may, in part, actually be responsible for some of the many severe cardiovascular and cerebro vascular complicatios associated with this disease." (Complications of this disorder will be dealt with in detail in Chapters 19 and 20.)

Dr. Philpott explains that pancreas-made insulin travels through the bloodstream to the liver, where at least half of it is used. The rest of the body needs only a small amount.

Insulin injected under the skin of the arm, leg, or buttocks travels the entire peripheral circulatory system before reaching the liver, and much more insulin than is needed in the vascular system remains there. Compounding this problem is the fact that unless sufficient insulin is injected to satisfy the liver's requirements, a serious condition, ketoacidosis, will develop. Dr. Philpott feels that, under these conditions, hyperinsulinism is almost unavoidable and contributes to severe complications of diabetes.

Why should a natural substance such as insulin create problems? Dr. Philpott answers in the following terms: ". . . R. W. Stout, MD, of Hammersmith Hospital in London, actually showed that when laboratory rats were given insulin intravenously, the insulin stimulated the synthesis of cholesterol in blood vessel walls.

"Other investigators have shown that when too much insulin is present in the blood, all kinds of metabolic debris can be found, including certain chemicals that are deposited on the insides of blood vessels that have been partly occluded [closed], as in arteriosclerosis."

No part of the body, including the pancreas, is necessarily exempt from this condition. Over and above injected insulin, other outside factors can undermine the pancreas, including chemicals in the environment and foods to which we may be allergic or hypersensitive.

The first organ to be influenced by exposure to ingested foods and chemicals, the pancreas has the key task of turning these substances into forms usable by the body and also of protecting the body from negative reaction to them. Food allergens and harmful chemicals cause the pancreas to be overstimulated and overworked, and thus weaken it.

"All addictions, of course, whether they are foods, chemicals, tobacco, and/or alcohol, eventually lead to pancreatic insufficiency of varying degrees," Dr. Philpott explains, "but what is important to realize is that most affected in pancreatic insufficiency of these types are the bicarbonate and enzyme productions of the organ. . . ."

Let's look at what happens in pancreatic insufficiency. Added to a lessening ability to secrete insulin and glucagon, the pancreas produces inadequate amounts of pancreatic enzymes and bicarbonate, which threatens the proper functioning of the entire organ.

Unless the pancreas can make sufficient proteolytic enzymes to secrete into the intestines, proteins cannot be properly broken down into amino acids for body use. This leads to a deficiency of amino acids and a disastrous chain reaction. Proteolytic enzymes are made from amino acids. In a deficiency of amino acids, these enzymes will soon be deficient.

"With an amino acid deficiency, there is more than just a reduced enzyme production from the pancreas. . . . Insulin is composed of fifty-one amino acids. When these all-important building blocks of hormones are in short supply, the quality and quantity of insulin production actually begin to diminish. This, of course, can lead to a deficiency of insulin with the resulting effect of high blood sugar or diabetes," writes Dr. Philpott.

Subnormal pancreas function also causes diminished production of lipase, an enzyme essential to proper metabolism of fats. This causes a rise in free fatty acids in the bloodstream, which is encouragement for arteriosclerosis.

Still another complication from reduced production of proteolytic enzymes is that proteins are not properly digested into amino acids, and large particles in the bloodstream lodge in the tissues. The body's immune system is immediately activated and attacks these particles as undesirable aliens, causing inflammation and injury in the arteries or wherever else they lodge.

Dr. Philpott warns that cooking foods above 118°F destroys digestive enzymes, putting an added burden on the pancreas, salivary glands, stomach, and intestines to come "to the rescue and furnish digestive enzymes (protease for the proteins, lipase for fats, and amylase for carbohydrates) to break down these substances.

"To do this repeatedly, the body must rob . . . enzymes from other glands, muscles, nerves, and the blood to help in its demanding digestive process. Eventually, the glands—and this includes the pancreas—develop deficiencies of enzymes, because they have been forced to work harder, due to the low level of enzymes in cooked food."

An experiment in the University of Minnesota's Department of Anatomy showed that rats fed an 80 percent cooked food diet for 155 days had an increase of pancreatic weight by 20 to 30 percent "with a corresponding decrease in digestive enzyme secretions. And what is true of animals is also true of man," writes Dr. Philpott.

Although the pancreas can manufacture enzymes, we must not overdraw on our enzyme potential.

"The more we use our enzyme potential, the faster it is going to run out," he maintains. "When you eat food that is raw, the enzymes contained in the food immediately start breaking down the food ingested."

In other words, if you eat as much raw food as possible, you put less burden on your pancreas and extend its healthy life. When pancreas function is diminished, production of bicarbonate is also reduced. This is a vital secretion needed to increase the alkalinity of the small intestine.

"In pancreatic deficiencies, acute metabolic acidosis after the meal occurs," writes Dr. Philpott, "since the pancreatic bicarbonate, now undersupplied, has not neutralized acid from the stomach as it empties into the duodenum plus the small intestine.

"This reduction of proper bicarbonate levels in the pancreas results in a chain reaction whereby the pancreatic proteolytic enzymes, which are also secreted into the small intestine, and which need an alkaline medium in which to function best, are destroyed."

There is a wealth of additional helpful information in Dr. Philpott's *Victory over Diabetes*, which is a book that every diabetic should have for ready reference.

Another stress on the pancreas not mentioned by Dr. Philpott is subnormal body temperature caused by hypothyroidism, particularly myxedema, and by less extreme subnormal thyroid function. This may be the reason why so many diabetics are also hypothyroid.

Some years ago, C. D. Eaton, MD, of Detroit, published a revealing report, "Co-Existence of Hypothyroidism with Diabetes Mellitus," in the *Journal of the Michigan Medical Society*.[6] In studying hundreds of his diabetic patients, he found symptoms of hypothyroidism and diabetes to be similar—all but the carbohydrate metabolism disturbance in the latter.

Symptoms in common were low energy, weakness, constipation, itching, sleepiness, high levels of blood fat, muscle pains, high susceptibility to infection, poor wound healing, early atherosclerosis, and gangrene. He discovered that hypothyroidism was far more frequent in diabetics than in nondiabetics.

Dr. Eaton observed that insulin controlled the blood sugar level in diabetics but did nothing to correct the other symptoms. Administration of small doses of natural thyroid did, however, as I will explain in a later chapter.

To summarize and accentuate the key points in this chapter, here are the principal ways to prevent diabetes or to lessen its effects and the chances of diabetic complications:

1. Refrain from eating refined sugar and other refined carbohydrates. (Remember that processed food products often contain hidden sugars. Read labels carefully.)

2. Make sure your diet includes some chromium-rich foods—brewer's yeast, beef liver, chicken, meat, and whole grains—because without chromium, insulin cannot carry nutrients through the walls of your trillions of cells.
3. Try to avoid unnecessary stress, and make practical adjustments to that which is unavoidable. Stress slows down insulin production.
4. Exercise regularly.
5. Eat a high-fiber diet for reasons of general health but particularly to reduce chances of developing diabetes or of lessening the need for insulin.
6. Avoid becoming obese. Overweight individuals are prime candidates for diabetes. (The next chapter deals with weight loss.)
7. Keep your pancreas healthy, not only by avoiding assaults of refined sugar, which overwork this organ, but also by avoiding chemicals, tobacco, and alcohol, and by eating more raw vegetables for their live enzymes. A steady diet of cooked foods can deplete the existing bank of digestive enzymes and harm the pancreas.
8. Be certain that your body temperature is normal and that you are not hypothyroid, a condition that places stress on the pancreas.
9. Remember that insulin can control blood sugar levels but does nothing to prevent complications of diabetes. Thyroid hormone can help in this regard.

19

How to Prevent a
Heart Attack—Your Own!

HIDDEN IN THE throats of unsuspecting millions is the reason for many—if not most—heart attacks: a subnormal thyroid gland.

Unfortunately, many medical doctors still don't recognize this fact and instead continue to urge us to avoid many wholesome, nourishing, cholesterol-containing foods to prevent or diminish cardiovascular ailments. It's hard to understand how they can overlook a mountain of evidence that places the guilt on hypothyroidism—a mountain whose base was formed in England more than a century ago.

It all began with a case mentioned earlier—Dr. William M. Ord's severely atherosclerotic female patient with the grossly enlarged, fibrous, nonworking thyroid gland; mucin-logged, swollen tissues; and a tight-skinned, masklike face.

Reports of similar cases by contemporaries of Dr. Ord made the medical community aware that this new ailment was widespread and required special study. In 1883 the London Clinical Society formed a task force, including elite Harley Street physicians, for this purpose. Within five years, the medical researchers identified and investigated one hundred cases of myxedema.

Experiments, observations of patients, and analyses of autopsies, reported in a hefty 300-page volume, revealed unequivocally that myxedema was caused by decreased function of the thyroid gland. Atherosclerosis, commonly found in these cases, received no more attention than other symptoms, inasmuch as cardiovascular ailments were a rarity then. Epidemics of contagious diseases finished off most people before they could live long enough to develop cardiovascular disease.

Then, in 1890, Viennese pathologists discovered that thyroid deficiency helps bring on heart attacks, thanks to the wisdom and foresight demonstrated one hundred years earlier by Austrian Empress Maria Theresa. The Empress had passed a national law making it mandatory that the body of each patient who had died in a hospital had to be autopsied. This law actually turned Austrian hospitals into laboratories of learning so that, in a real sense, Maria Theresa accelerated medical progress for the world.

Unfortunately, knowledge of heart attack prevention seemed of little value in the 1890s, because heart attacks were rare. An idea had been born before its time—a solution for which there was no problem.

Yet for the sake of science, researchers pursued further experiments. They found that after the thyroid gland was removed from test animals, they always developed atherosclerosis and mucin-logged tissues. Professor Theodor Kocher, MD, of Berne, Switzerland, a surgeon practicing in a known goiter belt, had to remove patients' massive goiters to keep them from compressing the windpipe and causing them to suffocate. After this life-saving surgery on 101 patients, the same thing happened. They developed symptoms like those in Dr. Ord's classic case and died. To assure continued thyroid hormone production in other goitrous patients, Professor Kocher developed a novel surgical technique, removing only the part of the thyroid gland that threatened the windpipe.

During the same period, Professor Theodor Billroth, MD, Vienna's most eminent surgeon, noted for perfecting the stomach ulcer operation still in use, totally removed gigantic goiters and, like Kocher, lost the lives he was trying to save. Over and over, Austrian pathologists observed and reported that thyroidectomy invariably brought on exaggerated hardening of the arteries. Despite journal articles on the findings of Drs. Kocher and Billroth, surgeons in some enlightened nations persisted in total thyroid removal until the 1950s.

Eager to learn reasons for deterioration of arteries and heart after thyroidectomy, Dr. Billroth's brilliant protégé, von Eilsberg, in 1895, performed this surgery on animals and noted the same results: myxedema and gross deterioration of arteries throughout the body.

Several years later, two other leading Viennese surgeons, E. P. Pick, MD, and F. Pineless, MD, used their heads as well as their scalpels in performing thyroidectomies on patients with massive goiters. They supplemented their diets with fresh animal thyroid extract and kept them alive and well without symptoms of hypothyroidism and damage to their circulatory system.

Supplementation with animal thyroid was new in Vienna and throughout most of the world. However, it was old in China. Two thousand years before Christ, Chinese doctors rejuvenated aging patients with failing faculties by means of an animal thyroid soup. Patients became younger looking, developed more energy, and often regained their ability to think and remember.

Many centuries later, during Queen Victoria's reign, London's most prominent Harley Street doctors took a cue from the Chinese and served elderly and failing patients special sandwiches of raw animal thyroid. Ugh!

Many patients became squeamish about these sandwiches, so doctors looked for alternatives. G. R. Murray, a British medical doctor, found one. He concocted a glycerine extract of fresh thyroid tissue, injecting the juice into patients. Although it achieved desired results, Dr. Murray found that his preparation rapidly oxidized and molded. Then he struck upon the idea of removing fat from the fresh animal glands and drying them. This process preserved the active thyroid principle.

Now he needed a patient to try his desiccated thyroid. A middle-aged woman with acute myxedema, not many heartbeats from death, volunteered. She never regretted her decision, because all of her symptoms disappeared, and she remained in excellent health for nineteen years, when she died of natural causes at age seventy-two. Several times she stopped taking thyroid supplements and, in each instance, her former symptoms returned until she renewed her thyroid regimen.

Although Dr. Murray's natural desiccated thyroid formula is still used—it has been improved upon through the years—much research on its importance in preventing and treating cardiovascular ailments has been forgotten. The result is millions of unnecessary and premature deaths. Meanwhile, the international pharmaceutical giants are churning out new, expensive drugs that always come with frightening side effects—products promising a new solution to an already solved problem.

For better or for worse, most of today's physicians are wedded to their medicines and the theory that a diet low in cholesterol and saturated fat will reduce serum cholesterol levels and the hazards of serious cardiovascular ailments. There have been so many tidal waves of official warnings about the harm of cholesterol and the need for everyone to eliminate dietary fats and cholesterol that all opposition was swamped.

One hardly heard opponent, Rockefeller University biochemist Edward Ahrens, MD, who had conducted cholesterol research for over forty years, told *Time* magazine that only a small minority of Americans is threatened by cholesterol. One in five hundred individuals afflicted with severe familial hypercholesterolemia have super-high levels of blood cholesterol.[1]

Dr. Ahrens claimed that denying everyone red meat, eggs, and dairy products, when only a small fraction of the population has hypercholesterolemia, is unnecessarily reducing the joy of life.

John Story, MD, a Purdue University cardiologist, scoffed at what he calls "cholesterolphobia." In the same issue of *Time*, he indicated that we should not treat everyone with diet, just as we wouldn't give insulin to everyone for fear of their developing diabetes.

Many other authorities echoed these sentiments, among them Michael F. Oliver, MD, president of the British Cardiac Society, George V. Mann, MD, then an associate professor of medicine and biochemistry at Vanderbilt University's School of Medicine, and Edward R. Pinckney, MD, author with Cathey Pinckney of *The Cholesterol Controversy*.[2]

My experience with many patients is that elevated cholesterol is often caused by hypothyroidism, even subclinical hypothyroidism. These elevated levels are always reduced by thyroid gland therapy.

The reasons for inordinate fear of cholesterol had their roots in 1913, when the Russian physiologist Nikolai Anitschkov drew an erroneous conclusion from one of the faultiest experiments ever designed by a scientist. To gain information of use to human beings, the experimenter usually selects a member of the animal kingdom whose physiological processes closely resemble those of human beings.

Anitschkov's history-changing work was performed in rabbits fed huge doses of cholesterol. Rabbits are vegetarians. No self-respecting rabbit would ever eat cholesterol-containing foods. Their livers are not equipped to handle them chemically. As a result of this unnatural diet, the cholesterol content of their blood skyrocketed by several hundred percent and, in the end, these high concentrations of cholesterol proved toxic. This severe biochemical stress caused some atherosclerosis and the appearance of cholesterol in arterial lesions.

To Anitschkov's credit, he realized that his research results did not necessarily apply to human beings, and he never suggested a low-cholesterol diet to control atherosclerosis.

Many decades later, an explanation of the rabbit findings emerged from Anitschkov's laboratory through one of his protégés, L. V. Malysheva, MD, who, in a published paper, reported that huge doses of cholesterol suppressed rabbit thyroid function as thoroughly as surgical removal of the thyroid gland.[3]

However subnormal thyroid function comes about, the result is the same: the development of atherosclerosis. Malysheva explained that deteriorated arteries in the rabbits were due to low thyroid function, not to cholesterol itself.

Researchers in Anitschkov's lab, Malysheva included, rejected the cholesterol theory, as American physicians embraced it. Another biochemist, I. B. Friedland, a student of Anitschkov, did much research on cholesterol and fats and published a comprehensive report, representing five years of study. He made a significant discovery. When he fed rabbits large amounts of cholesterol, he was able to prevent high levels of blood cholesterol and atherosclerosis by administering thyroid hormone to them. He concluded that thyroid hormone controls blood fat and cholesterol levels and recommended thyroid therapy in human beings with elevated fats in the blood serum.[4]

Dr. Barnes once told me that "if the Friedland recommendation had been followed, cardiovascular diseases would have been conquered decades ago and much time and many lives would have been saved."

In the cholesterol controversy, a key question is whether this fatty substance plays a major role in the deterioration of arteries. More than 125 years ago, Rudolph Virchow, MD, professor of pathology and the father of what was then a new science, performed many autopsies and concluded that cholesterol has only a minor influence on arteries. In a paper published in Berlin, he revealed that degeneration of the blood vessels' connective tissue had started before cholesterol appeared in the lesions. Next, drops of fat accumulated there and then, finally, came cholesterol. Dr. Virchow considered cholesterol a belated sign of fatty degeneration.[5]

Another research finding that deflated the cholesterol balloon was that of a German physician, Hermann Zondek, MD, during World War I.[6] With Germany isolated from the rest of the world and supplies of protein foods running low, military personnel and civilians were, of necessity, eating mainly grains and vegetables—a low-cholesterol, low-fat diet.

Dr. Zondek, who was in charge of a ward of cardiac patients, made the astute observation that these soldiers had all the symptoms of myxedema, the most dominant of which was heart failure. The usual treatment for heart disorders at that time was digitalis, which had already failed to help his other patients, many of whom were bedridden. Inasmuch as they had swollen tissues, no energy, shortness of breath, and enlarged hearts, he decided to try thyroid therapy. Much to his surprise and delight, his patients soon recovered and were able to return to military duty or civilian life. He gave the name "myxedema heart" to their former ailment.

Soon after the war, Dr. Zondek wrote *Diseases of the Endocrine Glands*, a book translated into English, featuring illustrations of electrocardiograms of some of his patients. Individuals with "myxedema heart" showed low voltage, because of weak heartbeats. After thyroid therapy, when the heart contracted with more power, the voltage on the EKG returned to normal. A low voltage reading on the EKG reveals the status of the thyroid gland more accurately than many common blood tests for thyroid function, as many doctors have discovered.

Have we been unduly alarmed about intake of cholesterol in relation to blood serum levels of this compound? Numerous studies in various nations indicate that we have. The much-publicized Framingham study of thousands of individuals, aimed at revealing the major risk factors for heart attack, failed to zero in on dietary cholesterol as the enemy within, despite the prestudy assertion by William B. Kannel, MD, the project's director, that the blood test for cholesterol levels was perhaps the most useful method for determining present or impending heart disease. Results of the study changed his opinion.[7] Half the people who died of heart attacks failed to show the high cholesterol levels he believed warned of impending danger. As a matter of fact, Dr. Kannel saw "no discernable association between the amount of cholesterol in the diet and the level of cholesterol in the blood." Regardless of how much or how little animal fat is in the diet, some people will have low blood cholesterol levels, while others will have moderate levels, and others high levels, he stated.

Some time ago, researchers at the University of California School of Medicine, Berkeley, fed 1,934 men and women anywhere from zero to fourteen eggs each week. Although one large egg contains about 250 mg of cholesterol, researchers were surprised to find no statistically significant relationship between number of eggs consumed and the blood serum cholesterol level.

A few years earlier, experimenters at the University of California at Los Angeles under nutritionist Roslyn Alfin-Slater, PhD, found no increase in cholesterol levels on normal diets when egg intake was increased.[8]

"We, like everyone else, had been convinced that when you eat cholesterol, you get cholesterol," she told the *Los Angeles Times*. "But when we stopped to think that all the studies in the past never tested the normal diet in relation to egg eating . . . we decided to see what happened to blood cholesterol levels on normal diets when egg intake was increased. Our finding surprised us. . . . "

The research of Professor A. H. Ismail, an anti-aging authority at Purdue University, confirmed the results of the UCLA group.[9]

Eggs are not really saboteurs of health. Researchers at Massachusetts Institute of Technology found that by eating two eggs per day, subjects benefited from the 5 grams of lecithin in the yolks.[10] They learned that within twenty-one days, such a regimen increased the brain's plasma choline content by 500 percent, enhancing the synthesis of acetylcholine, a key neurotransmitter of the brain. Results of this study indicate that lecithin can be helpful in restoring short-term memory loss.

Does a high-polyunsaturated-fat diet actually prevent or cure cardiovascular ailments? A six-year study in England is typical of research undertaken to establish the facts.[11] Four hundred elderly men were divided into two groups. Half of them were fed a diet high in polyunsaturated fats—no less than 3 ounces of polyunsaturated oil daily, plus polyunsaturated margarine. Whole milk, butter, cheese, egg yolks, and saturated cooking fats were forbidden. The other half stayed on their usual diet, which contained six times as much saturated fat as polyunsaturated fat.

At first, cholesterol levels came down in the first group, a common occurrence with this sort of diet. Then, after the initial year, they began to rise. Following conclusion of the study, the cholesterol levels of the first group were about the same as when they started. Blood cholesterol of the saturated-fat eaters stayed virtually the same, too.

However, the death rate from cardiovascular disease was slightly higher in the group that ate polyunsaturates—twenty-seven patients to twenty-five. Results of a study conducted in Oslo, Norway, under similar conditions, were almost the same.

If the low-cholesterol diet is so effective, how can one account for the study results of Somali camel herdsmen, the Masai tribe of Tanzania, and the natives of the Cook Islands?[12] Dr. Pinckney related that Somali camel herdsmen drink an average of five quarts of high-fat camel milk daily. Shouldn't their blood cholesterol levels rocket out of sight? Actually, the highest blood serum cholesterol reading among them was 153. The Masai tribe lives almost entirely on meat and milk (whose fat content is almost twice that of ours) and shows a cholesterol level around 125 and negligible heart disease. Those over age sixty-five autopsied after accidental death revealed only negligible signs of atherosclerosis. Comparisons have been made between two groups of Cook Islands Polynesians, one of which eats twelve times as much saturated fat as the other. Heart attacks were almost nonexistent in both groups.[13]

Because some authorities claim that low-cholesterol diets work, and others claim the opposite and have statistics to back them, Stewart Wolf, MD, of the University of Texas and John Bruhn, MD, of the University of Oklahoma Medical School, analyzed more than one hundred articles from all over the world to isolate a dietary common denominator that might be considered a risk factor. They could find no consistent pattern about a certain kind of fat or a particular cholesterol level that seemed to cause heart disease.[14]

One of the more recently cited causes for heart disease is homocysteine, formed from a breakdown of the essential amino acid methionine found in fish, meat, liver, eggs, dairy products, nuts, brewer's yeast, onions, and garlic. Even moderately high blood levels of homocysteine are associated with heart disease.

"In the 1993 Physicians' study, men with very high levels of homocysteine had a risk of heart attack three times that of men with normal homocysteine levels. In fact, elevated homocysteine was such a dominant factor that it indicated risk even in men who had no other cardiovascular risk factors."[15]

Some authorities claim that homocysteine is only a marker of heart disease, rather than a cause. However it is categorized, homocysteine is a warning signal if present at elevated levels. So how can a high concentration be lowered? In two ways. One is taking the B vitamins folic acid, B_6, and B_{12}.

Due to the fact that taking individual B vitamins can often cause an imbalance, I suggest that my homocysteine high patients take a 50 mg B-complex pill containing all B-family members in proper ratio.

However, many biochemists believe that coping with homocysteine in this way is dealing with a surface condition, rather than the basic underlying cause. Cleveland Clinic Foundation researchers discovered that when hypothyroids with elevated homocysteine supplemented with thyroid hormone, their homocysteine levels dropped to normal.[16]

This is not all that thyroid hormone can do to reduce heart hazards. It can also lower total cholesterol and low-density lipoprotein (LDL, the "bad guy" cholesterol), claims a report from The Thyroid Foundation of America.[17]

Hypothyroidism tenses the smooth muscles of blood vessels, raises total cholesterol, bad cholesterol, and triglycerides, slows the heart rate to less than sixty beats per minute, reduces the heart's pumping ability, and stiffens walls of arteries, often leading to high blood pressure, states a University of Maryland report.[18]

Hypothyroid patients have three times the risk of high blood pressure as individuals with normal thyroid function. Triiodothyronine (T3) relaxes smooth muscles of the heart. Some experts suggest "that patients with high cholesterol should be assessed for thyroid function before they are given cholesterol-lowering agents," continues the report.

All of these observations and recommendations were made to us thirty years ago by thyroidologist Dr. Broda Barnes. It is reassuring to know that present-day medicine is catching up with the past.

A way of predicting heart disorders other than through cholesterol levels is by means of C-reactive protein, a biochemical produced
in response to inflammation. A comparative study of women with
overt hypothyroidism and clinical hypothyroidism and women without a thyroid problem disclosed that overt hypothyroids have a
slightly higher C-reactive protein and concentration of homocysteine
than normal women. Subclinical hypothyroids show high homocysteine levels compared with those with normal thyroid function.

While C-reactive protein and homocysteine are easily measurable,
the amount of a biomarker called *isoprostane* has been difficult to determine. Isoprostane appears when fatty acids anywhere in the body
come into contact with oxygen. Oxidation upsets the stability of molecules. Before this happens, a molecule has a pair of electrons orbiting around it. Oxidation causes an electron to be pulled away
abruptly. This converts the molecule into an unstable free radical that
forcibly seizes an electron from a neighboring molecule, turning it into
a free radical. This repeated free radical activity starts a chain reaction of molecular destabilization which if left unchecked, over time,
will result in serious illness.

If antioxidants—vitamins C and E, and lycopene, for example—
are supplied in greater numbers than free radicals, they can control
free radicals. Any stressor can trigger free radicals.

Faulty food metabolism in hypothyroidism, for example, often
creates a firestorm of free radicals.

How many antioxidants do you have to take to keep them under
control?

Until recently, it has been guesswork. However, now, for the first
time in medical history, there's a noninvasive, inexpensive test that
provides a precise measurement of the isoprostane, a by-product of
free radical activity. Such information will catapult medicine into the
next century.

You can know with nanometric precision whether or not you
need more antioxidants and which ones are best for you.

Only a few drops of urine on a test strip are required for this patented test called the *Wellness Index*. If the isoprostane level is high, every cell in your body is under siege from destructive free radicals. You should therefore take suitable nutritional countermeasures, because free radical generation continues until it is quenched by an optimal amount of antioxidants. Isoprostane is the gold standard for measuring oxidative stress. Isoprostane research has been highlighted in nearly two thousand papers in scientific and medical journals. This is perhaps the most important biomarker in your body. Thanks to the Wellness Index, you can now assess free radical threat to all your cells, as well as the cellular threat from smoking and other environmental pollutants.

You can find out more about the Wellness Index on the Internet at www.thyroidmd.com.

This chapter featured many aspects of preserving your heart and arteries. The next will clear up many misunderstandings about cardiovascular disorders.

20

Be Kind to Your Arteries!

ONE OF THE prime arguments of those who favor the low-cholesterol diet is that heart attacks in Europe decreased drastically during World War II because of the scarcity of high-cholesterol foods.

Dr. Broda Barnes investigated this matter in depth, spending many summers in Graz, Austria, examining some of the world's most complete and definitive autopsy records.

"It is true that cholesterol-containing foods were scarce in Europe during World War II," he told me. "And, yes, heart attacks did decrease, but the interpretation of these facts led many investigators to the wrong conclusion.

"They failed to probe deeply enough. Instead of checking records of autopsies, they only counted the number of persons who had died of heart attacks."

So, in order to learn the truth for protecting the living, Dr. Barnes went to the dead, checking 70,000 autopsies recorded between 1930 and 1970.

Heart attacks had dropped sharply in the war years between 1939 and 1945, but he discovered unexpected evidence that astonished him. *The low-fat diet had not protected arteries from atherosclerosis!* The number of individuals under age fifty with atherosclerosis had doubled between 1939 and 1954. Further, the degree of injury to their arteries was approximately twice as great on a scale of zero to four. Not only had the low-cholesterol diet failed to guard the arteries, but atherosclerosis had increased fourfold.

Why?

"We found that tuberculosis had risen far faster than heart attacks as the cause of death," said Dr. Barnes. "Tuberculosis victims rarely live beyond forty years—not quite long enough to have heart attacks.

"In most instances, those who died of tuberculosis showed extreme damage to coronary arteries. It is clear that if the patients had not died of tuberculosis, they soon would have been cut down by a heart attack. Wartime conditions had substituted tuberculosis for heart attacks as the major cause of death. Low-cholesterol diets had had nothing to do with protecting the people from heart attacks.

"A few years later, conditions were reversed," said Dr. Barnes. "The antibiotics for tuberculosis had become available, and deaths from heart attacks started to rise. The autopsies told us why: the adult dying from a heart attack had healing tuberculosis in his or her lungs. The antibiotics had stopped immediate death from tuberculosis, giving the advanced arterial damage a chance to become the killer."[1]

Dr. Barnes is not the only researcher who discovered that a low-fat diet often fails to prevent heart attacks and that a high-fat diet doesn't necessarily bring on heart attacks. One of the most comprehensive projects, the Tecumseh study conducted by Allen B. Nichols, MD, and colleagues at the University of Michigan School of Medicine, reported similar findings and additional insight into causes for high serum cholesterol and triglycerides, a blood fat believed to contribute to cardiovascular ailments.

The researchers checked almost the entire adult population of Tecumseh, Michigan, to determine the effect diet and overweight might have on blood cholesterol and triglyceride levels. The influence on 4,057 persons of one hundred different foods—high or low in fats and sugar—was tabulated.

An article in the *Journal of the American Medical Association* reported these findings: There was no significant relationship between how frequently fat, sugar, starch, alcohol, and tea were consumed and the blood serum level of fats. Serum cholesterol and triglyceride concentrations were significantly higher in markedly overweight men and women. High fat levels in the bloodstream have long been associated with increased risk of heart disease and other health problems.

Dr. Nichols warns that these findings do not mean that diet and blood fat levels are not at all related, only that obesity more obviously raises serum cholesterol and triglyceride levels than any particular dietary regimen.

"Other factors besides fat intake determine cholesterol levels among the general public," he says. "From this study's findings, one may infer that weight reduction should be the initial course for control of hyperlipidemia, in the general population."[2]

Other studies indicate that more than the intake of fats is involved in elevated cholesterol levels. It is ancient history—and forgotten history—that low thyroid function encourages high blood cholesterol. As long as seventy-five years ago, experiments by the physiologist L. M. Hurxthal, MD, a thyroid authority at the Lahey Clinic, Boston, revealed that blood cholesterol levels were high in hypothyroids and low in hyperthyroids.[3]

During the same period, the book *The Biochemistry of Disease*, by Meyer Bodansky, MD, and Oscar Bodansky, MD, went a step further, stating that elevated cholesterol in hypothyroidism is just a part of the total pattern of increased blood fats. They claimed a close relationship between appropriate thyroid supplementation and a decline in these symptoms.

The relationship between low thyroid function and high serum cholesterol level found by three researchers, E. F. Gildea, C. B. Mann, and J. P. Peters, indicates that a serum cholesterol level below 275 mg/al practically excludes the diagnosis of hypothyroidism. Gildea discovered that two grains of thyroid would reduce cholesterol and triglyceride levels.

Drs. Bodansky and Bodansky made the interesting point that hypothyroidism can be diagnosed by high blood cholesterol, and effectiveness of treatment can be determined by the decline in blood serum level of cholesterol. A give-and-take relationship apparently exists between the decrease in basal metabolism in thyroid deficiency and the rise in blood cholesterol: *"On the average, the rise in cholesterol is approximately four times as great as the drop in metabolism."*[4] (Emphasis added.)

It remains a mystery to me why modern medicine fails to make use of this information. Perhaps it's because, during those times, some physicians started patients on too high dosages of thyroid and brought on heart attacks and, in several instances, death. The customary treatment for heart failure in that period was digitalis, administered in large dosages during this time. Large to massive dosages of thyroid medications were often used—anywhere from four to thirty grains daily—causing the heart to race beyond its ability. Because of this flagrant misuse, thyroid developed a bad name, one it is still having difficulty overcoming. It is perhaps for this reason that a prime way to lower critical blood fats, including cholesterol, is often denied to patients who need it.

Like the word *thyroid*, the word *cholesterol* has a negative connotation. Cholesterol physiology is misunderstood and a great deal of misinformation has been spread about this waxy, gray-yellow, fatlike alcohol, which does not readily dissolve in water or blood.

If we and the rest of the animal kingdom had no cholesterol, we would be vegetables (which contain no cholesterol). Without a steady supply of cholesterol, we would probably not be around to complain about it.

Cholesterol is so vital to our lives that we have a built-in mechanism in the liver and in each body cell to manufacture it. Ideally, when cholesterol intake is high, the liver and the cells slow down production. When intake is low, they increase production.

If you eat a lot of high cholesterol foods, your body, if healthy, will get rid of the excess. The amount of cholesterol you eat, therefore, doesn't automatically have a real relationship to its level in your blood serum. If you literally stuff yourself with cholesterol-rich foods, the small intestine provides the built-in protection of limiting absorption. Excess cholesterol does not make it through the intestinal wall and into the bloodstream. It simply is eliminated from the body through the bowel.

Contrary to the opinion of some, cholesterol can be synthesized from carbohydrates and proteins, as well as from fats. Therefore, no matter what kind of diet you eat, your body will have plenty of raw material for making cholesterol. If eaters of eggs, milk products, and meat happen to have a slightly higher blood cholesterol level than vegetarians, the reason may be simple, says one observer. When animal fats are digested, they are not soluble in water or blood serum. Therefore, intestinal tract cells must synthesize cholesterol to unite with them so that they can be transported through the bloodstream to be metabolized or stored. It is this synthesized cholesterol—not dietary cholesterol—that may raise the blood serum level of animal-fat eaters.[5] Vegetable fats are more soluble in water and thus require less cholesterol to be produced in the intestinal tract to promote their utilization.

Why do we need cholesterol? For many reasons.

It is a *must* for the creation of new life. When the male sperm cells fuse with the egg of a woman to create a new human being, they bring along their own supply of cholesterol. In a short time the mother-to-be's blood serum level of cholesterol rises by about 50 percent, the liberal amount necessary to supply the cholesterol needed by the fetus's trillions of cells until birth. Dr. Broda Barnes made the wry comment that if cholesterol were harmful to arteries, as so many have stated, "the fetus would have a heart attack before the baby saw the light of day."

The newborn baby comes fully equipped with the right enzymes to make possible the production of cholesterol in each cell, a necessity for the growth of tissue and for development of the brain. As adults, we no longer can synthesize cholesterol in the brain for a very good reason: we don't need to. Cholesterol already there and in the spinal cord (about 23 percent of the total in the body) is used and reused. Some authorities believe that brain cholesterol serves as part of the insulation for myriad nerve fibers there and as a nonconducting separator to prevent short-circuiting.

Cholesterol has other uses. It helps make fats soluble to be burned as fuel for muscles and connective tissue, the supporting members for various organs. About 10 percent of body cholesterol is in the skin, where it has a well-known use. Through a chemical reaction to sunlight, skin cholesterol produces vitamin D, which makes possible the assimilation of calcium and phosphorus essential to forming and sustaining strong bones and teeth. It also helps the growth of new skin to replace that which is scratched, cut, or burned.

You may not be aware of the contribution cholesterol makes to your body in emergencies: it serves as the basic building blocks for hormones produced by the adrenal glands. Without cholesterol, you couldn't survive stress-filled situations.

Despite cholesterol's all-important role in the body, it is still regarded by many as the enemy within. But does eating high-cholesterol foods really elevate our serum cholesterol? Not necessarily. Individuals from families with a pronounced record of early heart disease sometimes develop elevated cholesterol levels from a high-cholesterol diet. Other than that, the evidence that food intake causes this condition is inconclusive at best. Then what causes high blood cholesterol levels?

Heredity is a major contributing factor. Our anxiety and stress levels are also causes. Students before critical exams, athletes prior to key games, military men and women before combat (flyers, particularly), and accountants at tax time may have elevated cholesterol. High blood pressure, obesity, smoking, high blood uric acid levels, little or no exercise, and being male have all been associated with increased cholesterol levels.

One of the most dramatic and promising ways to reduce elevated cholesterol involves increasing the ratio of high-density lipoproteins (HDL) to low-density lipoproteins (LDL). If you have more HDL than LDL, your chances of escaping a heart attack are far more favorable.

Earlier we mentioned that fats and water don't mix well—usually not at all. The way that fats (including cholesterol) can be transported in the watery medium of the bloodstream is by becoming attached to lipoproteins, a combination of fat and protein. The best information today holds that LDL carries fats and cholesterol to the cells, including those in the arteries, and deposits them there. HDL units are like mini–dump trucks that haul off excess cholesterol (some think they even remove cholesterol from cells) and carry it to the liver for elimination.

There are five effective ways of increasing the ratio of HDL to LDL: (1) refrain from smoking; (2) exercise vigorously (check with your doctor first); (3) slash your intake of calories (become or stay fairly lean); (4) substitute some unsaturated fats (for instance, those in fish and fowl) for saturated; and (5) eat certain foods and food supplements, such as unpolluted cold-water fish, brewer's yeast, garlic, and lecithin.[6]

Instant results are not guaranteed. The program must be pursued for a period, particularly if you are middle-aged or older.

Now, finally, through the HDL theory, scientists are beginning to understand what they have known for many years—that regular and vigorous exercise helps to prevent cardiovascular disease. A team of researchers led by Josef Patsch, MD, at Baylor College of Medicine, found that jogging actually clears fats from the blood. Markedly higher levels of HDL were discovered in physically active individuals. How does this come about, according to the Patsch theory?

Within several hours after a meal, fat particles in the bloodstream (chylomicrons) encounter a blood enzyme that digests part of their cores. The remains are carried to the liver for digestion. Surfaces of the fat particles are then released by a blood enzyme and unite with other blood chemicals to become HDL.

Patsch's research indicates that vigorous exercise must be pursued regularly for at least several months to increase HDL to a pronounced degree. HDL declines rapidly if you become inactive. In other words, quick-fix exercise is not going to help much. You have to exercise vigorously for a lifetime to improve your health and extend your longevity.

Let's take a close look at how and why cholesterol affects the body.

Arteries are lifelines for channeling blood from the heart to living cells in constant need of nourishment and oxygen for energy, warmth, and tissue building. They must be kept clear, or trouble results.

A cross-section of human blood vessels reveals three layers of tissue. The innermost is an ingenious, smooth, and slippery lining that permits a near-frictionless flow of blood. Enclosing the inner layer is a circle of muscle fibers that permits the blood vessels to expand and contract as the heart expands and contracts. On the outside is the third layer, coarse and stout connective tissue to reinforce the blood vessels or the arteries.

Blockages occur where there has been wear and tear on the artery wall. An irregular area is the starting point for a buildup of cholesterol, which, in time, can slow or stop the blood flow.

Nature will not overlook such a defect, so she attempts to cope with it. Fibrin, a blood component essential to clotting, seals the stress point and begins a buildup on it. In performing autopsies, pathologist Rudolph Virchow, MD, discovered that arterial deterioration started long before blood fat began to cling to the fibrin, and that this was followed by the accumulation of cholesterol. He also discovered that a person's circulation almost shut itself off before cholesterol attached itself to the plaque on the artery walls.

Numerous pathologists have since come to the same conclusion: cholesterol buildup in the wall of arteries occurs only after arterial degeneration is far advanced. It seems strange, then, that cholesterol is singled out when arterial plaque is composed not only of cholesterol but also of fibrin, calcium, triglycerides, ceroids, and sometimes blood platelets.

In a monograph, *Thyroid Function and Its Possible Role in Vascular Degeneration,* William B. Kountz, MD, reviewed earlier experiments linking low thyroid and deteriorating arteries and studied 288 hypothyroid patients with elevated blood cholesterol—his own and those at the infirmary of Washington University, St. Louis. These included (1) businessmen averaging fifty-five years of age, (2) infirmary outpatients whose ages averaged sixty-one, and (3) infirmary inpatients averaging sixty-seven years of age.[7]

Few in the first group had atherosclerosis. Many in the second group were found to have moderate cardiovascular degeneration. Everyone in the third group showed evidence of advanced blood vessel disease.

Dr. Kountz administered thyroid to some in each group and kept others as controls. After five years of observation, he compared those on thyroid therapy with controls on the basis of number of deaths from heart attacks and strokes.

In the first group—the youngest men—no one on thyroid therapy died, compared with 15 percent of the controls. Only 3 percent of the second group died, compared with 19 percent of the controls. Gains from thyroid treatment were most marked in the older men in the third group. Their fatality rate was half as high as that of controls.

While assuring proper thyroid gland function or adequate supplementation seems the most basic approach to protecting or regaining a healthy cardiovascular system, sometimes other measures help, too, such as proper intake of vitamins, particularly vitamins C, B_6, and E.

An article in *The Lancet* stated that 1,000 mg of vitamin C daily lowered cholesterol levels of healthy individuals and that long-term shortage of this vitamin contributed to arterial diseases, which invite heart attacks and strokes.

In a revealing publication of the Linus Pauling Heart Foundation, *How Vitamin C Prevents Heart Attack and Stroke*, Matthias Rath, MD, who completed significant research with the late Linus Pauling, PhD, states:

"Heart attack and stroke are essentially unknown in most animals producing vitamin C in their own bodies. In human beings dependent on dietary vitamin C and frequently having a low intake of this vitamin, heart disease is a leading cause of death and disability.

". . . Vitamin C stimulates the production of collagen molecules, which play the same role in the human body that iron reinforcement plays in a skyscraper building.

"Heart disease is a form of prescurvy. . . . Heart attack and stroke are a direct result of low vitamin C intake over the years."[8]

Rabbit experiments conducted by Anthony J. Verlangieri, PhD, while at Rutgers University, prior to joining the University of Mississippi, revealed that lack of vitamin C in the daily diet brought about the loss of certain chemical compounds in the artery linings, creating roughness and irregularities where harmful plaques could readily form. High levels of vitamin C increased the amount of these chemicals, helping assure that artery linings stay smooth.[9]

In an article in the *Journal of the American Geriatric Society,* M. L. Riccitelli, MD, of the Yale School of Medicine, reported various experiments over twenty-two years that paralleled Dr. Verlangieri's findings.[10]

Several investigators have discovered that vitamin C–deprived animals developed atherosclerotic lesions like those in human beings and were cured by administration of vitamin C over a long period. Vitamin C not only reduced blood cholesterol levels but prevented cholesterol accumulation on artery linings.

Research done by Constance Spittle Leslie, MD, a pathologist at Pinderfields Hospital in Wakefield, Yorkshire, England, convinced her that atherosclerosis is a deficiency disease similar to beriberi, scurvy, rickets, and pellagra, caused by poor diet and reversible by corrective nutrition. Many of her findings have been published by the prestigious medical journal *The Lancet.*

Dr. Leslie conducted an important vitamin C experiment on herself. Noting that her cholesterol count dropped sharply when she ingested what some consider to be a large daily dose—1,000 mg—she reduced her cholesterol count from 230 to 140. She then brought her cholesterol levels right up by restricting her vitamin C intake.[11]

Another vitamin, too, seems to influence cholesterol levels and atherosclerosis, vitamin B_6. Roger Williams, PhD, cites a Russian experiment, which revealed low blood plasma levels of vitamin B_6 in coenzyme form in 31 of 48 patients with atherosclerosis and high cholesterol counts, and he theorizes that vitamin B_6 contributes to body production of lecithin, a dissolver of cholesterol.[12] On the basis of this and other experiments, Williams advises that daily intake of sufficient vitamin B_6 is one of the best guarantees against harm from fat and cholesterol combined with proteins.

Although many claims of early experimenters with vitamin E relative to cardiovascular ailments have not been substantiated, more recently this vitamin has been found to monitor and regulate magnesium and manganese penetration into heart cells, to enhance microcirculation, and to reduce arterial deterioration in the legs.

One theory of how arteries deteriorate is that they are attacked at their weak points by free radicals, highly reactive molecules. Any irregular site invites deposits of fats, cholesterol, and calcium. Vitamin E is a known neutralizer of free radicals and, as such, protects the integrity of arteries. Vitamin E also normalizes clotting time of blood, minimizing or eliminating the chance of clots that can block arteries and take lives.

Additionally, vitamin E has a proven track record in managing intermittent claudication, leg pain caused by obstructed circulation. Probably the most impressive performance relative to this condition was revealed in a seven-year study by Sweden's Knut Haeger, MD, a vascular surgeon.[13]

Those who suffer from intermittent claudication can walk only a short distance before the pain becomes unbearable. Once they stop, the pain slowly recedes. Dr. Haeger found that as little as 300 to 400 IU a day of vitamin E and daily walking brought about two results within several months: the ability of patients to walk longer distances before experiencing pain and increased blood circulation to the lower leg.

His 220 age-matched subjects (including some diabetics) had limited flow of blood to the feet. Such patients are subject to gangrene, a decaying of the flesh that follows choking off of the blood supply. The subjects were divided into two groups. Half received 300 IU of vitamin E daily; the other half were given placebos. During the seven-year period, only one of the patients on vitamin E had to have a leg amputated because of gangrene, compared with eleven on the placebo.

Dr. Haeger's experiment and those cited earlier offer convincing evidence that vitamins are valuable in efforts to manage vascular disorders.

It is customary to think of artery ailments in terms of extremes—gangrene, deadly heart attacks, and strokes. Yet there is a whole range of illnesses in various parts of the body that arise from imperfect arteries—conditions that can be prevented and, in many instances, reversed, if the proper measures are taken. That is the subject of the next chapter.

21

Dramatic Treatment for Circulatory Problems

SO FAR AS circulatory ailments are concerned, headlines and millions of words are devoted to strokes and heart attacks, but little helpful information is offered about preventing other related disabling complaints.

The major disorders of this kind are neuropathies (nerve deterioration, which often limits leg, arm, or eye function), kidney failure, detached retina, blindness, and—perhaps most frightening—gangrene. These often painful and handicapping conditions can limit the lifespan of anyone, particularly diabetics and the elderly. The good news is that something tangible can be done about them.

As matters now stand, almost 98 percent of some eleven million diabetics in the United States will suffer one or more of these complaints, the nightmarish complications of diabetes. Unfortunately, some of them don't know that with preventive health maintenance they can very likely be spared from them.

A specific example will illustrate this point. At a party a number of years ago, I heard a woman say, "My eyesight is beginning to fail as a result of my diabetes, and my doctor tells me he can't do a thing about it." The dismal prospect offered was "just to wait around to go blind."

Turning abruptly, I said, "I just overheard your remark. I'm a medical doctor and I may be able to help you."

I made an appointment for her to visit my office five days later, after she had taken her underarm temperature on two consecutive days.

Sure enough, she was hypothyroid. I put her on one-half grain of thyroid and, after a month, increased it to one grain.

Within nine weeks, she was feeling better than she had since the age of twenty-five and, even more satisfying to her, her eyesight remained 20/40 without glasses. Even after five years her eyes still test 20/40. Not long ago when I saw her, she gave me an undeserved compliment.

"Doctor, I owe my eyesight to you."

"Thanks for the compliment," I responded. "I helped, but you actually owe your eyesight to Broda Barnes, a medical doctor who made the discovery concerning diabetic complications that I used in your case and others."

As far as I am concerned, Dr. Barnes is worthy of a Nobel Prize in medicine for many solid reasons, one of the most important of which is his discovery that thyroid supplementation in diabetics who are hypothyroids can stop diabetic complications and, in some instances, even reverse them. I know this is true from my own practice and from that of others who follow Dr. Barnes's methods.

In my opinion, Dr. Barnes's contribution is the most noteworthy breakthrough for diabetics since the discovery of insulin. It all began when he suddenly realized that twelve diabetic patients whom he had treated for fifteen years showed no signs of diabetic complications.

Then came additional surprises.

His new diabetic patients with atherosclerosis, very high blood cholesterol levels, nerve deterioration, and impaired eye or leg movement experienced what modern medicine thought impossible: an arresting of these conditions and, sometimes, reversals and complete cures. Over the next fifteen years, forty-three diabetic patients who came to him were put on thyroid supplementation, and none manifested the slightest sign of typical diabetic complications.

A clear picture began to emerge. Dr. Barnes went to the medical literature and learned that several other medical doctors had independently discovered what he had and had published papers on the subject in important medical journals. These illuminating, lifesaving articles had been overlooked or ignored by most physicians and eventually forgotten.

Dr. Barnes was appalled. In the years between the publication of these articles, hundreds of thousands—even millions—of diabetics had unnecessarily gone through pain, disability, depression, and early death.

Among significant studies yellowing in medical libraries was the research of Dr. Elliott P. Joslin, MD, founder of Boston's Joslin Clinic. Before Sir Frederick G. Banting, MD, and Charles H. Best, MD, had extracted a safe and effective preparation of insulin, diabetics usually lived only four years after their illnesses were diagnosed. Now their life spans were extended. Instead of dying in a coma, diabetics were living seven years longer and then dying of different causes, among them heart attacks. Insulin was unable to prevent these devastating complications.

One of the few persons to understand the basic reason for complications of diabetics, Dr. Joslin published his findings in the best medical journals and predicted that some day atherosclerosis would be conquered and that subsequently the diabetic would live a normal life span.

Most diabetologists snubbed his findings and the heretical notion that insulin wasn't the final solution. They maintained that all physicians had to do was diagnose diabetes early enough and treat it vigorously enough.

"So they diagnosed it early and treated it vigorously, and, judging from their results, not early or vigorously enough," according to Dr. Barnes. Because of the longer life of diabetics, more complications of this ailment had time to appear. Foremost among them was hardening of the arteries.

"I find articles and books making the nonsensical statement that diabetes aggravates or accelerates hardening of the arteries," Dr. Barnes said. "No way! Hypothyroidism is perhaps the leading cause of this condition."

In Dr. Barnes's nearly half a century as a family doctor and thyroidologist, none of his five thousand patients (either with a normal thyroid gland or on thyroid hormone) showed a sign of diabetic complications. Further, only five of his patients developed diabetes in this period. The national average is 200 per 5,000 individuals—forty times higher.

On two occasions, Dr. Barnes told me something that I have subsequently observed in my practice; namely, that the same kinds of complications observed in the diabetic also appear in the nondiabetic, low-thyroid patient and that, when thyroid is administered, some of these complications, particularly neuropathies, disappear.

All diabetic and hypothyroid complications arise from the same basic cause: clogged arteries, which prevent the blood from bringing in food and oxygen and carrying off wastes.

Let's look at all the complications, starting with kidney failure. Kidney function is lost. Toxic wastes cannot be eliminated in the urine and accumulate in the bloodstream. Unless dialysis comes to the rescue, the patient dies of uremia.

A less common but even more devastating result of diabetic arteriosclerosis is gangrene. Gangrene occurs mainly in the legs, because their circulation is less efficient. The blood has to be forced against gravity back to the heart. In the fingers or arms, blood flows to the heart more easily.

Gangrene became much more prevalent after the discovery of insulin. Before this time, people generally did not live long enough to develop it. As critical as this condition is—and as difficult to treat—some patients have been spared the agony of developing it, thanks to Dr. Barnes's methods.

A new patient, Walter, a gray-haired sixty-year-old man who was paralyzed on one side from a recent stroke, was brought to Dr. Barnes for treatment. As he lay on the examination table, a remote part of his anatomy caught Dr. Barnes's attention—the big toe of the right foot. It looked abnormally red and misshapen, like a moderate-size, rotten, mashed tomato. The paralysis and stroke suddenly became less important. Walter had gangrene! His poor circulation had been worsened because of his paralyzed side.

"Many a knife-happy surgeon would have lopped off that big toe," Dr. Barnes informed me, "but that wouldn't have stopped the gangrene. It keeps climbing to the ankles, then the thigh. Then it usually goes to the other side and starts all over. The knife fights a delaying action—at the end of the toe, then at the ankle, at the knee, and finally at the thigh. The surgeon's knife operates the patient into disability and then, often, into death."

Dr. Barnes had an alternative. Gangrene and the stroke already told him that the patient had circulatory problems, perhaps of low-thyroid origin. Learning that Walter had lived most of his life in the state of Indiana, a part of the great United States goiter belt, he had additional evidence of possible hypothyroidism. The underarm temperature test showed a subnormal reading of 96°F, just the confirmation Dr. Barnes needed. He administered one-half grain of desiccated thyroid per day and kept a close watch on the patient. Things happened fast. Within a week, the rotten, mashed tomato appearance of Walter's right big toe began changing. A month later, the toe was completely healed.

Remarkable recoveries from diabetic complications such as this encouraged Dr. Barnes to share his discoveries with other doctors. But a giant roadblock kept the mass of the medical community from even trying his method: the lack of controlled double-blind studies to prove his findings on a completely objective level.

"Rarely can a physician in private practice conduct controlled experiments," Dr. Barnes readily admitted, "but he sometimes makes pertinent observations that deserve the attention of clinical investigators with facilities to give them further evaluation." Deserving attention and getting it were two different things.

Dr. Barnes also had fascinating experiences in reversing neuropathies, which run the gamut from annoying to devastating. If atherosclerosis damages a nerve to the eye muscle, the patient may lose his or her ability to move the eye from side to side. Deterioration of nerves in the leg could make walking difficult or impossible.

One case that Dr. Barnes described in an interview is an example of positive accomplishments that are possible with the thyroid treatment of neuropathies. A patient was referred to him by an Arizona doctor. Muscles between the man's left knee and thigh had become atrophied and weak. In excruciating pain, the patient had to take painkillers day and night. He could hobble around for short distances but only with a cane.

The man was frustrated and depressed that his pain limited his daily activities and brought him agony. After verifying that this patient was hypothyroid, Dr. Barnes explained that he was going to put him on a small daily dosage of thyroid. Skeptical but willing to try anything, the patient agreed to take the thyroid but insisted on staying in a Fort Collins, Colorado, motel near Dr. Barnes's offices in the event that thyroid did not agree with him. (He had heard some of the ancient thyroid scare stories.)

Within one week, he was able to cut down on the painkiller. His general health improvement encouraged him to go back to Arizona and continue thyroid supplementation. Within a month, he could walk painlessly without the cane and threw it away. Two years later—the last information Dr. Barnes had on the patient—his leg was completely normal.

Although some doctors still say that neuropathies in the eyes, which contribute to blindness, are caused by diabetes, this is not true. Atherosclerosis is the cause—deterioration of the tiny arteries of the eyes.

Although most doctors who have used thyroid hormone have been able to treat diabetics to prevent disabling neuropathies and blindness, perhaps the most dramatic and revealing work has been done by Michael Walczak, MD, of Studio City, California, Murray Israel, MD, of New York City, and I. R. Ross, MD, of Maryland, all members of the Vascular Research Foundation.[1]

Their findings add a ray of hope to the otherwise ominous information of the National Society for the Prevention of Blindness, which projects that some 50 percent of persons who have diabetes for at least twenty years will develop retinopathy (deterioration of the retina of the eye), while 95 percent of those who have diabetes for thirty years will probably develop this disease.

Drs. Walczak, Israel, and Ross treat impending blindness (diabetic retinopathy) with oral thyroid hormone extract and heavy intakes of vitamin B complex, vitamin C, and the natural enzyme varidase. Diuretics are also given to remove excess body fluid. Forty out of forty-five patients—twenty-five of whom were legally blind—were measurably improved after thirteen months on the above regimen. Two did not improve, and three became worse. Such startling results followed in the wake of a Harvard School of Public Health announcement that no cure exists for the progressively disabling complications of diabetes.

One of the most dramatic improvements came in a patient who had been totally blind in one eye prior to taking part in the research project. Vision in his other eye was diminishing so fast—20/200—that he almost became a vegetable and sat around in a deep depression. Elevated cholesterol and blood pressure as well as irregularities of metabolism made him seem a prime candidate for failure.

However, after five months on the Walczak-Israel-Ross modality, his blood pressure went down markedly, and his cholesterol reading plummeted from 294 to 215. Best of all, his vision improved to 20/60, and he became encouraged, recharged with optimism, more energetic, healthier, and able to work again.

One of Dr. Walczak's patients experienced an equally exciting transformation, a forty-seven-year-old woman who was weak and had pain, cold extremities, albumin in the urine, and advanced diabetic retinopathy, and was in a pregangrenous state. She entered the experiment with little hope, inasmuch as all other known treatments for retinopathy had done her no good. She was in such poor shape that Dr. Walczak wondered if she would live long enough to go blind.

On the thyroid-vitamins-enzyme-diuretic regimen, she soon reported less pain, greater warmth in her extremities, more strength and endurance, and no albumin in her urine. Rather than risk subjectivity, Dr. Walczak sent her to an impartial ophthalmologist for comparative measurement of her vision. In the words of this doctor, her progress was "almost unbelievable."

Still another of Dr. Walczak's cases, a sixty-six-year-old woman, had such deteriorating eyesight that she could see only foggy outlines of objects. A year after she joined the experiment, she could distinguish different flowers in pots 20 feet away. Then, five months later, came an incredible improvement. For the first time in years, she could read the newspaper. The independent and impartial ophthalmologist who tested her eyes found that her right eye had improved to 20/25 and the left to 20/40. Improvement continued.

Dr. Walczak believes that, effective as this form of treatment is in even seemingly impossible cases, it is even better when used preventively, in the early stages of retinopathy, when the disease has not as yet begun to hamper vision. Eleven of twelve patients with retinal deterioration showed definite and encouraging improvement on this modality in one experiment.[2] While conservative physicians may want to wait for the results of double-blind studies before adopting this regimen, every week, month, or year that passes may be critical to those with retinopathies and other complications of diabetes. There is no time for fence-sitting. Millions desperately need helpful thyroid therapy treatment such as this. It is time for those with sight and foresight to help those who are about to lose their sight and possibly their lives.

Unquestionably, much can be done to prevent arterial deterioration, as well as other diseases, including cancer, which is the one most feared by the most people. This is the subject of the next chapter.

22

Guard Yourself
Against Cancer

THAT TINY THYROID gland, weighing less than an ounce, can bring you pounds of prevention against cancer, a disease that picks its victims indiscriminately.

Interesting evidence links hypothyroidism and cancer. A survey by J. G. C. Spencer, MD, of Frenahay Hospital in Bristol, England, revealed a higher than average cancer rate in the goiter belts of fifteen nations on four continents.[1]

Subnormal thyroid function appears to invite cancer. This has been shown clinically in numerous animal experiments. Malignant tissue from rats grafted onto other rats took hold readily in animals whose thyroid glands had been removed, but rarely in those with normal thyroid function.

Findings with thousands of laboratory rats as well as with human beings by Bernard Eskin, MD, director of endocrinology in the Department of Obstetrics and Gynecology at the Medical College of Philadelphia, indicate that a deficiency of iodine, the thyroid gland's major nutrient, encourages breast cancer.[2] Dr. Eskin discovered that the highest incidence of breast cancer and deaths from it are in the goiter belts of Poland, Switzerland, Austria, and the United States. The iodine-impoverished Great Lakes region of the coast-to-coast goiter belt shows the highest death rate from breast cancer in the United States. Conversely, iodine-rich Japan and Iceland have the world's lowest rates of goiter and deaths from breast cancer. In fact, the breast cancer death rate in Japan, where iodine-rich seafood and seaweed are on the daily menu, is one-fifth that of the United States.

As stated earlier, sufficient dietary iodine does not always assure proper thyroid gland function. However, normal function of this gland— or supplementation with thyroid extract—seems to deter cancer.

Studies show that hypothyroids and hyperthyroids appear to be more cancer prone than the general population. Some years ago, there was a bitter controversy in this area. One faction named hypothyroidism a major cause. Other factions disagreed violently.

A German medical journal (*Klinical-Wochenshr.*) ran an article admitting a keen difference of opinion among experts.[3] According to the authors, one group feels that a shortage of circulating thyroid hormones makes the skin of the breasts hypersensitive to prolactin (the pituitary gland hormone that promotes milk production) and estrogen. This could contribute to cancerous growths. But they also say that thyroid hormone replacement is associated with the risk of breast cancer. Other evidence disputes this stand, and the American Thyroid Association favors hypothyroid patients' continuing thyroid therapy, if such therapy is indicated.

The authors state that excess thyroid hormones in the blood, as in hyperthyroidism, seemed to slow the growth of inoperable breast cancer. This is disputed, too, they say, and refer to other findings that relate hyperthyroidism to the development of breast cancer in premenopausal women.

A subsequent report in the journal *Cancer* concluded that "a proportion of breast cancer patients are mildly hypothyroid. . . ."[4] A year later, the *Journal of the American Medical Association* presented research by a team of eleven authorities, who conducted a case-control study to establish, once and for all, whether thyroid hormone therapy increases the risk of breast cancer.[5] The team compared 659 women with breast cancer and 1,719 control subjects and found no evidence that thyroid supplements increased the risk of breast cancer, even when they had been taken for more than fifteen years.

Thyroid replacement in hypothyroidism has been said to reverse cancer in some instances. One such case was presented in the journal *Neurology*.[6] A hypothyroid patient with a large tumor of the pituitary gland was given thyroid hormone. The tumor rapidly disappeared. Another case of a slightly different nature appeared in the *Southern Medical Journal*.[7] A woman with primary hypothyroidism was found to have a large pituitary tumor and, concurrently, the cessation of menstruation and an excessive flow of milk. Nine months after thyroid therapy was started, there was clinical and radiologic evidence that the tumor had regressed, along with the other symptoms.

These cases and the remarkable findings of John A. Myers, MD, and Fellow of the Royal Society of Health, indicate that alternatives should be carefully examined before female patients are rushed into surgery, particularly for removal of the ovaries.[8]

Dr. Myers's success in treating serious female conditions by nonsurgical methods has opened new vistas for all physicians and their patients. Although cancer is a formidable enemy, Dr. Myers believes that we should not let cancer phobia run away with rational decision making. The primitive fear of the unknown and the potent drive for survival sometimes stampede us into undesirable treatment alternatives. An atmosphere heavy with fear impels the surgeon who removes a cancerous breast to perform surgery on a normal, though susceptible, second breast.

Occasionally, patients request this as a security measure. Likewise, when a cancerous uterus is removed, sometimes a sound ovary is cut out, too, for fear that cancer will develop there. On occasion, both ovaries are taken out.

Preventive surgery of the ovaries is easier to rationalize in women beyond menopause, as Dr. Myers indicates. The ovaries produce the hormones estrogen and progesterone, as well as ova. The first two can be replaced. So why not part with the ovaries? For a very good reason. The ovaries make another important contribution to survival and wellbeing, as Dr. Myers learned while reviewing a paper on atherosclerosis by Joseph Stambul, MD, chief cardiologist, Department of Medicine, Southern Division of the Albert Einstein Medical Center.

Dr. Stambul stated that atherosclerosis in the coronary artery is six times more prevalent in men than in women, a key reason why women live longer than men. The obvious explanation—and a gross simplification—is that women produce estrogen.

However, he also said that another hormonelike substance is synthesized by the ovaries—protein-bound iodine, or diiodotyrosine—which keeps cholesterol in solution in the blood, rather than allowing it to accumulate in the lining of arteries.

Long before he learned of Dr. Stambul's thesis, Dr. Myers claims that he had used diiodotyrosine to soften the breasts of nursing women, particularly hypothyroid women. He states correctly that cysts and abscesses can develop in breasts that become caked in nursing mothers and offers an example of a patient who had a hardened and painful left breast. He administered 200 grams of diiodotyrosine and, within two days, brought the breast back to good health. In another similar case, the mother's breasts were so painful and hard that they yielded too little milk to satisfy the baby. Over a period of several hours, the mother was given 10 grams of diiodotyrosine to dissolve under her tongue. Almost immediately her breasts softened, the pain ceased, and milk began spurting from her nipples. That was the end of her nursing problems.

Still another female ailment was solved by the same method. A forty-five-year-old woman had a large abscess on her left breast and a cyst 4 mm long on her left ovary. The knowledgeable gynecologist who made the diagnosis recommended surgery for both conditions. Deeply upset, the woman appealed to Dr. Myers for treatment without surgery. Over a two-day period, he gave her some 50 grams of powdered diiodotyrosine to dissolve under her tongue, in addition to intravenous magnesium, B complex, and vitamin C. Response came quickly, and both conditions healed rapidly. Inasmuch as her breasts were still quite hard, heavy, and doughy, Dr. Myers continued the treatment. Within a matter of days, her breasts softened and regained the normal feeling of fluidity.

These are not isolated cases. Dr. Myers has had the same results in innumerable similar cases. He also tells of subduing persistent vaginal infections—trichomonas and yeast infections as well as nonspecific, treatment-resistant leukorrhea—in patients, most of whom were hypothyroid. Dr. Myers treated these patients with thyroid hormone and intravaginal iodine. Their hypothyroid conditions cleared up and so did their infections. Within minutes after the vaginal treatment with iodine, several of the women with hardened breasts felt and saw a softening. Women with cysts had them disappear in time.

Such measures help ward off conditions that, in some instances, may be forerunners of cancer. Dr. Myers has validated the Stambul findings concerning the ovaries and the importance of their secretions in numerous cases, including the following:

Several weeks after her ovaries were surgically removed, a forty-six-year-old woman found goiters swelling her throat. The woman, a Navy nurse, had had a total hysterectomy in the Navy Hospital in Bethesda, Maryland.

While recovering from her operation, she was found to have developed nodules on her thyroid gland. Alerted to the possibility of cancer, she was told to have the nodules removed. Rather than endure more surgery, she asked Dr. Myers to treat her. He did so with estrogen, iodine, vitamins, and minerals. The thyroid nodules began shrinking slowly. After two years, they disappeared. Two years later when she was examined by Navy doctors at Corpus Christi, Texas, and they reviewed her medical record from Bethesda, they refused to believe that she had ever had thyroid nodules.

Aside from Dr. Stambul's and his own observations relative to the protective, life-extending power of the ovaries, Dr. Myers cites the dog experiments of Perkin and Brown of Lahey Clinic, Boston. After the thyroid gland of a male dog has been surgically removed, his protein-bound iodine plummets to one-tenth its normal level. After the same operation, a female dog's protein-bound iodine remains the same until the ovary is removed. Then it drops to the same level as that of the male.

Over and above being protected from cardiovascular problems by ovarian secretions, women are also protected against cystic fibrosis as well as cancer of the breast and ovaries. Dr. Myers states that iodine, tyrosine, vitamins, amino acids, and trace minerals will guard a woman against numerous ailments, and that she should not give up her ovaries in panic at any point in her life, unless they have been proved to be cancerous. Then it is foolish to resist.

23

Alzheimer's Disease or Something Else?

"DR. LANGER, I guess I have Alzheimer's disease," sighed the tense, attractive, middle-aged woman across the desk from me. Aside from being slightly overweight, a condition almost hidden by her smart, tailored beige suit, Antoinette, a new patient, looked nothing like Alzheimer's disease victims I had seen.

"What makes you think so?" I asked.

"I'm so forgetful. I sometimes forget where I parked my car at the supermarket—or even that I have a car. It's so hard for me to think that I almost have to push thoughts around in my brain by strength of will."

Previously, she had recited a lengthy list of other symptoms—overwhelming fatigue, cold hands and feet, constipation, frequent depression, weight gain, and dryness of skin, among the major ones.

"I'm not a betting man," I replied. "However, if I were, I would bet that you have a condition that can be reversed within weeks—a few months at the most. You have many key symptoms of hypothyroidism."

Relief seemed to melt away her tension, and she leaned forward for more assurance. She got it from me when I said, "I sometimes can't find my car in the supermarket parking lot."

We both laughed, then I told her how to take the Barnes Basal Temperature Test and prescribed appropriate blood tests for thyroid hormone and thyroid-stimulating hormone.

Antoinette's underarm temperature turned out to be just 96.8°F—a good degree under normal for the resting state. Her blood tests showed low readings of thyroid hormones T4 and T3—and a high reading of the pituitary gland's thyroid-stimulating hormone, the latter a strong indication that her thyroid function was sluggish.

After a few weeks on one-quarter grain of Armour desiccated thyroid, she improved dramatically—far more quickly than I had anticipated, although her basal temperature was still subnormal.

"I'm beginning to remember again—and think," she bubbled. "It's almost unbelievable that a tiny bit of thyroid can help this much."

"That's just the beginning," I promised. "Your physical symptoms will soon improve, too."

They did, and she did! One more happy patient was on the verge of graduating to nonpatient status!

Antoinette's case was anything but rare. Dozens of my new patients with faulty memory and difficulty in thinking immediately assume the worst. So much has been publicized about Alzheimer's disease and senility that the first thing that patients think is that they're losing their minds. Then the power of negative thinking takes over and symptoms become even worse.

Such reactions are not always the fault of patients. Some doctors are to blame. Often when a retired person—even a former professional—tells a physician that his memory is failing and that he sometimes is in a confused state, the doctor will write off the condition to senility or Alzheimer's disease and dismiss the patient without treatment.

Even sadder is the fact that such senior citizens are sometimes institutionalized as if they have untreatable mental ailments or senile dementia when, with a careful physical examination, they will often be found to be suffering from insufficient thyroid hormones, nutritional deficiencies, or a combination—one condition influencing or even worsening the other.

Numerous studies reveal that new cases of mental or emotional disturbances are far more numerous in people older than age sixty-five than in younger individuals. However, it is a serious error to accept that advancing age means losing memory, ability to reason, and sanity. Less than 5 percent of senior citizens are institutionalized for such psychiatric disorders.

Too little thyroid hormone, the physical and mental consequences of poor nutrition, and nonchallenging or nonstimulating people or environments—particularly prevalent for sedentary retirees—make them feel they are growing old and senile.

Queen Victoria began studying Hindustani, one of the world's most difficult languages, after she was seventy-five years old. Frank Lloyd Wright created some of his greatest architectural designs after age seventy-five. Michelangelo was painting masterpieces after age eighty. Pablo Picasso turned out works of art when he was well into his nineties. Benjamin Franklin was eighty-four years old when he wrote his moving appeal to Congress for the abolition of slavery.

Mark Twain and Jules Verne did some of their best writing after age seventy. Italian playwright Luigi Pirandello never wrote a play until age fifty, and then became prolific and famous in this activity. He won the Nobel Prize for literature after he celebrated his seventy-fifth birthday.

Daniel Defoe, author of *Robinson Crusoe*, didn't think himself too old to continue his work. He wrote thirty books after the age of sixty-seven.

Significant accomplishments by superseniors are not limited to the mental area. Georges Adan, of France, made a convincing statement for believing that we improve with age. At the age of twenty-five, Georges rowed a boat across the English channel in seven hours and forty-five minutes. When he celebrated his seventieth birthday, he rowed a similar boat across the same channel in six hours and twenty-four minutes. King Gustav V of Sweden played five sets of tennis to celebrate his eighty-fifth birthday.

These accomplishments show us how well people can do when they continue to think and act young and retain their interest in themselves, others, events, career, and/or hobbies.

Memory loss, difficulty in thinking, disorientation, and confusion are sometimes caused by brain deterioration but, in most instances, they are brought on by correctable conditions. Narrowed blood vessels and arteries can do this—as can pathological nerve conditions such as tangled nerve fibers in Alzheimer's disease.

Clinical studies by Dean Ornish, MD, demonstrate that arteries can be flushed out with a diet accenting fresh vegetables and fruit. Chelation, too, can "Roto-Root" out blockages and help to restore normal blood circulation.

When a person suffers low thyroid function, blood carrying fuel and oxygen to the brain does not reach its destination with vigor and thrust, because the heart pumps languidly. Further, digestion and assimilation are slowed down by hypothyroidism, making it difficult to get maximum nutritional values from food.

Certainly Alzheimer's disease is a reality—a grim reality—sometimes related to pollutants in the environment, particularly aluminum. How the intake of aluminum, a nonnutrient mineral, affects the thyroid gland is not conclusively documented. However, there is evidence that aluminum accumulates in the brain of Alzheimer's disease victims, along with tangled nerve fibers—neurofibrils—minute nerve conductors within brain cells. In contrast, neither aluminum nor tangled neurofibrils are found in the brains of individuals who do not have Alzheimer's disease.

There are pros and cons on the subject. Some scientists ask if aluminum is a cause or an effect of Alzheimer's disease. Others say aluminum is a cause and that we shouldn't wait for complete documentation before taking it out of our bodies.

High blood levels of aluminum were discovered in many of 400 psychiatric patients suffering senile symptoms, including memory loss, reports the Brain Bio Center in Princeton, New Jersey.[1]

How does aluminum enter us in the first place? Some is absorbed through the intestines and some through the skin from toiletry products. Due to its tiny ions, aluminum can slip through the blood-brain barrier with ease. Its ions are less than half the size of those in essential minerals like calcium, magnesium, potassium, and sodium.[2]

If aluminum is truly a Trojan horse, how does it commit brain sabotage? Researchers Timothy L. MacDonald, PhD, W. Griffith Humphreys, and R. Bruce Martin, PhD, at the University of Virginia in Charlottesville, may have found the answer.[3] They believe it acts against the microtubules that support cell structure. These microtubules form what biochemists call "spindles." Cells can't divide without sound spindles. When cell replication is blocked in nerves, it is conceivable that tangled fibers are the result.

Microtubules are always in process—being assembled and taken apart—using a raw material named *tubulin*, a composite of amino acids and the mineral magnesium. The researchers discovered that magnesium and aluminum compete to be incorporated in tubulin and that aluminum is taken into tubulin ten times faster than magnesium. Aluminum is not as strong as magnesium for microtubule raw material. So cells made with aluminum, amino acid, and tubulin collapse more readily.

Aluminum invades us through food, beverages, medications, and cosmetics. It is in breads and pastries, baking powder, baking powder biscuits, cheese, cheese sauces, pickles, salad dressings, salt, and other condiments (added to keep them free-running), white flour, fruit juices in aluminum cans, cookware, and aluminum foils for wrapping and cooking foods, and municipal water supplies in the form of alum.

It is present in medicines and antacids, antidiarrhea products, antiperspirants and deodorants, some cosmetics, feminine hygiene products (including douches), some hemorrhoid preparations, lipstick, skin creams, lotions, and toothpastes.

Although not in my area of treatment, removal of aluminum through chelation is known to help some Alzheimer's patients in early or middle stages of this condition. Several of my physician friends and acquaintances have achieved positive results through chelation. Richard Casdorph, MD, of Long Beach, California, has noted improvement of

Alzheimer's disease through lowering blood concentrations of aluminum by means of the chelating agent EDTA.[4]

Foods and supplements said to block absorption of aluminum are vitamin C and calcium, magnesium, manganese, and zinc. In a six-month research project, 50 percent of Alzheimer's disease patients fed large amounts of lecithin improved in certain mental functions—remembering and thinking—and in their ability to take care of their personal needs.

Richard Wurtman, MD, of M.I.T. discovered that there is 90 percent less of the neurotransmitter acetylcholine (made from lecithin), essential for chemical contact between cells, in the brains of Alzheimer's disease patients than in individuals who do not have this disease.[5]

Much of what is considered senility in elderly patients is actually pseudosenility brought on by a multitude of conditions: physical illness, medications, glandular disorders—including low or high thyroid activity—nutritional deficiencies, and even prolonged stress.

Various diseases can invite symptoms that look like senility: anemia (insufficient red blood corpuscles to deliver enough oxygen to the brain); liver disease (improper handling of blood sugar, often due to hypothyroidism); hypoglycemia (low blood sugar that brings on many mental manifestations); and even urinary infections, resulting in body and brain toxicity.

Tranquilizers and sleeping pills used regularly cause side effects that ape symptoms of senility. A major job of the liver and kidneys is to remove toxins from the body. With age and nutritional abuse, these organs slow down their functions and toxins stay in the body longer, sometimes affecting the brain.

Deficiencies of proper nutrients created through eating a lot of junk food and processed food, which have lost most of their vitamins, minerals, and enzymes, account for many symptoms of senility, which people are too quick to attribute to Alzheimer's disease.

Fortunately, when these nutritional insults are eliminated—or at least minimized—and B-complex vitamins and vitamin C are added in generous doses, many such symptoms will disappear. However, as biochemists indicate, nutrients limited to the RDA aren't going to undo what many years, decades, or even a lifetime of deprivation have brought about.

It is no coincidence that most of the nutrients for reversing pseudosenility are those mentioned in Chapter 4, "Care and Feeding of the Thyroid," and are essential for supporting the health and full-strength function of the thyroid gland.

Four of the B vitamins are especially important to reversing symptoms of senility: B_1, niacin (B_3), pantothenic acid (B_5), and B_{12}. Many studies have shown that depriving test subjects of vitamin B brings on neurological and psychiatric symptoms that ape those of senility: memory as retentive as a sieve, jitteriness and shakes—especially common in alcoholics who have far out stripped their supply of vitamin B_1—and hair-trigger irritability and outbursts of temper.

Niacin deprivation can invite a host of pseudosenility symptoms: anxiety, confusion, depression, disorientation, and undependable memory. Abram Hoffer, MD, of Victoria, B.C., Canada, with Sir Humphry Osmond, MD, created the first effective nutritional treatment for schizophrenia with niacin and vitamin C, and advocates its use for the above-mentioned symptoms.[6]

Not only does niacin provide biochemical support for the nervous system and brain, it also is essential for a critically important reason. It keeps red blood cells from clumping into units too large to slide through the tiny capillaries of the brain. Such clumping means that oxygen carried by the red blood cells is choked off from brain cells, which consequently die. An oxygen-starved brain shows all manifestations of senility.

Our nervous systems could not survive daily living, let alone the stresses of the day, without ample pantothenic acid.

Mental and emotional symptoms of vitamin B_{12} deficiency are low mental energy, difficulty in concentrating, agitation, and hallucinations.

Antioxidants such as vitamins A, C, and E, beta-carotene, glutathione peroxidase, superoxide dismutase (SOD), and selenium are needed to keep free radicals from disabling or damaging brain cells.

And one of the little known causes of pseudosenility is a deficiency of the mineral zinc. Numerous studies show that zinc deficiency can bring on confusion and memory loss, plus diminished ability to taste and smell—necessary senses for a good appetite and taking in essential nutrients.

Magnesium, choline, and lecithin are also key nutrients for fending off or correcting symptoms of pseudosenility, often misdiagnosed as Alzheimer's disease.

Inasmuch as thyroid hormones help keep every one of your body's trillions of cells using food and oxygen efficiently, you must be sure that your thyroid gland is functioning properly or—if it isn't—that it is properly supplemented.

Another important, little-known, and, therefore, unsuspected cause of symptoms resembling those of senility is sustained stress. Glucocorticoids, steroid hormones released by the adrenal glands, may cause damage to brain cells, especially those of the hippocampus, state researchers at the Salk Institute for Biological Studies (San Diego).[7] This is the part of the brain where memories are made and kept. And stress damage can make it impossible to store new memories and recall old ones.

During periods of stress, these glucocorticoids block glucose (blood sugar) from entering many kinds of cells—including those of the brain—and conserving available fuel for physical action such as muscle movement in running or defending oneself. Cut off from glucose, the only fuel they can use, brain cells become damaged or die.

Another study that confirms the Salk findings was conducted by researchers at Washington University in St. Louis. Nineteen adults were administered either glucocorticoids or a placebo for four consecutive days.

Volunteers receiving the stress hormone showed a marked loss of memory, compared with the placebo takers. After a week off the stress hormone, the volunteers' memory returned fully.

A study by Mark Rosenthal, MD, assistant professor of medicine at the University of New Mexico, and Clare Jeanne Sanchez, MD,

FACP, assistant professor of medicine at the University of South Carolina, discloses that hypothyroidism can cause a host of symptoms similar to those of Alzheimer's disease: disorientation, irritability, loss of sound judgment, memory failure, and mental slowness.[8] Hypothyroidism is a "great masquerader," says Dr. Rosenthal.

"We know that those who act senile or demented should be screened for hypothyroidism," echoes Dr. Sanchez. "We recommend that all elderly people who come to their doctors for whatever reason should get a . . . screening for hypothyroidism. If hypothyroidism goes too far, it can cause permanent brain damage."

In any stay-young program, it is essential to have a normally working thyroid gland—or proper supplementation—because thyroid hormone is a *must* for the good health and longevity of every body and brain cell, every tissue, and every organ and gland.

24

Better Coping with Menopause

HYPOTHYROIDISM HAS MUCH in common with menopause.

Distinguishing the influences of menopause from those of hypothyroidism relative to symptoms of middle-aged women is not unlike trying to perform surgery to part Siamese twins. It is extremely difficult.

Not long ago, the American Association of Clinical Endocrinologists (AACE) made such an attempt. The AACE alerted its nearly four thousand members and the world to what seemed to be a startling fact: millions of American women are not successfully managing menopausal-like symptoms even by taking estrogen as hormone replacement therapy (HRT).[1]

These women may be suffering from undiagnosed hypothyroidism, as indicated by symptoms usually attributed to menopause: fatigue, mood swings, depression, and sleeplessness. Most women are not aware of the all-encompassing influence of the thyroid gland on every cell in every body system and should be alerted to it by their doctor. Otherwise, their basic problems will go untreated and contribute to long-term health complications.

The AACE urges all menopausal women to add thyroid hormone to the list of hormones they discuss with a physician, "because many of the symptoms of thyroid disease and menopause overlap," observes AACE president Helena Rodbard, MD, FACE. "As women approach menopause, many symptoms may be quickly attributed to this milestone in a woman's life without complete discussion of other easily treatable disorders, such as thyroid disease, that often mimic or accompany menopause."

Another facet of the subject not mentioned by the AACE in this connection is the possible danger of breast cancer and other cancers that may result from female hormone replacement.

"As endocrinologists and hormone experts, we are very concerned that the patient-physician dialogue on menopause be broadened to include discussion of thyroid hormone," states AACE past-president Stanley Feld, MD, MACE.[2] "Fewer than 25 percent of the nearly fifty million women reaching menopause are on HRT, and we know that as many as one in three of these women continue to experience symptoms that could be a direct result of an underlying thyroid disorder . . . Consider the fact that the incidence of thyroid disease increases to almost 20 percent for women over age sixty, and one can understand the seriousness of this situation."

The AACE states that, in addition to female hormones active during menopause, thyroid hormones play a basic role in complete body function. They regulate the rate of speed at which the body produces energy from nutrients, and influence the heart, brain, kidneys, liver, skin, muscle strength, reproductive functions, and appetite. Untreated, thyroid disease can diminish the quality of life, worsening osteoporosis and increasing the risk of heart disease. Many Americans have thyroid disease and do not even know it.

"As a woman is affected simultaneously by an onset of menopause, the increased risk of thyroid disease, and the natural aging process, the need for hormone management is essential," says Dr. Rodbard. "By recognizing the signs and symptoms of these processes as they appear, patients and doctors can reduce the long-term health risks that threaten women."

A public education program, "Thyroid: The Missing T in HRT," has been launched by the AACE to make women and physicians more aware that they need to include the thyroid hormone in their discussion of menopause. In this connection, the AACE is encouraging patients with menopausal symptoms—even if now on HRT—to perform a simple self-examination to see if they need to consult with their doctor about thyroid disease. This is to observe if they have an enlarged or irregular thyroid gland, indicating a thyroid condition that needs further examination by their physician.[3]

A glass of water and a hand mirror are the only required objects. Here's how to do it:

1. Focus the mirror on your neck just beneath the Adam's apple and right above the collar bone, where your thyroid gland is located.
2. Tilt your head back.
3. Swallow some water.
4. While swallowing, observe your neck for bulges or protrusions. Repeat this process a few times to make certain your observation is correct.
5. If you detect bulges or protrusions, see your doctor at once. You may have an enlarged thyroid gland or a thyroid nodule. Have your doctor check you to determine if you need treatment for thyroid disease or whether cancer may be present.

If properly treated, patients with thyroid disease can lead normal and active lives!

25

Is Fibromyalgia
Really Incurable?

FIBROMYALGIA IS A stubborn and enduring pain in muscles, ligaments and tendons—even bones—coupled with extreme fatigue. A researcher named Leonard H. Sigal, MD, characterizes the pain of fibromyalgia colorfully. When fibromyalgia sufferers are asked how they feel in the morning, they give what Dr. Sigal calls the eighteen-wheeler response: "I feel like I was hit by a Mack truck!"

The odds of being stricken with fibromyalgia are estimated at roughly twenty to one. These odds aren't fair, but 80 percent of those who develop this disorder are women from twenty to fifty years of age.

A few fibromyalgia patients have made a lasting impression on me. For instance, a young woman in her twenties, an assistant purchasing agent for an electronics firm, was totally frank, as patients should be:

"Doctor, my fatigue is so bad that I have to flog myself to go to work. At night, I just fall into bed with my clothes on. I sleep poorly, because my muscles and bones feel as if someone has driven a knife into them. When the bedsheet touches tender points on my back, buttocks, elbows, knees, neck, rib cage, and thighs, I want to scream."

I had her take the Barnes Basal Temperature Test and found her below the minimum: 97.8°F. Various symptoms indicated that she was hypothyroid. I started her on a quarter grain daily of Armour desiccated thyroid and asked her to be patient for good results.

"Why not?" she responded. "No other treatment has helped."

Two weeks later, I raised her to one-half grain. Then, within a month, she reported less pain, better sleep, a small increase in energy, and some hope that she would recover.

Three months after that, she seemed like a new person. "I can't thank you enough, doctor," she said. "I haven't felt this well in years."

Three out of four fibromyalgia patients I treated responded the same to a similar regimen, but I regarded the relationship between fibromyalgia and hypothyroidism as just a coincidence until an article in the *Annals of Rheumatic Diseases* caught my attention. Biochemist J. B. Shiroky and associates, of the division of rheumatology, Montreal General Hospital, Quebec, wrote that some 12 percent of fibromyalgia cases are triggered by low thyroid function. They suggest a test for thyroid-stimulating hormone (TSH) to see if fibromyalgia patients are actually hypothyroid.[1]

John C. Lowe, DC, Director of Research for the Fibromyalgia Research Foundation in Boulder, Colorado, considers the percentage named by Shiroky and associates too low.[2] Based on in-depth study and treatment of more than a thousand fibromyalgia patients, Dr. Lowe told Jim Scheer that in many instances fibromyalgia, is actually untreated hypothyroidism: "Inadequate tissue regulation by thyroid hormones results from two causes: (1) a deficiency of thyroid hormone, and (2) a cellular resistance to thyroid hormone."

One study Dr. Lowe conducted of thirty-eight fibromyalgia patients revealed that twenty-four (63.2 percent) were deficient in thyroid hormones and reported symptoms such as slow-wave sleep, decreased brain blood flow, impeded carbohydrate metabolism, fatigue, aches and pains, cold sensitivity, dysmenorrhea (difficult or painful menstruation), depression, and problems in learning.[3] Says Dr. Lowe, "These symptoms and hormone, neurotransmitter, and other objective findings in thyroid-deficient patients are also typical of fibromyalgia patients. So when I refer to fibromyalgia, I'm referring to a certain set of symptoms and signs of too little thyroid hormone regulation of tissues."

Dr. Lowe feels that fibromyalgia patients should be tested for a deficiency of thyroid-releasing hormone (TRH) and for triiodothyronine (T3), as well as for a TSH reading. Even if your TSH is within the so-called normal range, Dr. Lowe is convinced that you could still be suffering from one or more of sixty-four major symptoms of hypothyroidism, including fibromyalgic aches and pains and energy depletion.

In a publication in the *Clinical Bulletin of Myofascial Therapy*, Dr. Lowe and his associates write that, in a double-blind study, some patients with normal thyroid function had hypothyroid-fibromyalgia symptoms that seemed to result from partial cellular resistance to thyroid hormone. Seven patients alternately treated with T3 (dosages from 95.75 mcg to 150 mcg) and with a placebo over eight months were shown to experience "significant therapeutic effects in their T3 phases on all measures of fibromyalgia status."[4]

Their improvement was maintained even in a two-month follow-up. These dosages were significantly effective, although they produced thyroid function tests that indicated hyperthyroidism. However, the patients experienced no ill effects from this condition.

Four false beliefs held by most doctors make it possible for you to be in what is called "the normal range" and still be hypothyroid:

1. The sole cause of thyroid deficiency symptoms is hypothyroidism.
2. Only individuals with primary hypothyroidism (insufficient secretion of thyroid hormones) should be permitted to use thyroid hormone.
3. Hypothyroid patients should only be permitted to use synthetic T4 (levothyroxine formulas such as Synthroid and Levoxyl).
4. Patients' replacement dosages should be limited only to amounts that keep the TSH within normal range.[5]

Dr. Lowe maintains that these unproven guidelines followed by most physicians cause inadequate thyroid hormone regulation of many patients to remain untreated. In other words, if synthetic T4 fails to correct the symptoms of hypothyroidism, the limitations of this treatment are not blamed. The doctors conclude that the illness is something different, such as fibromyalgia or chronic fatigue syndrome.

Dr. Lowe is not surprised when stressed hypothyroids start suffering fibromyalgia-like symptoms, such as muscle aches and pains and insomnia. "Over time, hypometabolism imposes a lifestyle that can further complicate hypothyroidism," he told Mary Shomon, writer-editor of the About.com Guide to Thyroid Disease.[6] "As an illustration, the hypothyroid patient may not be able to take part in enough physical activity to maintain normal muscle mass. Metabolic status is critically dependent on muscle mass. The lower an individual's muscle mass, the lower the metabolic rate."

Stress of various kinds, such as a death in the family, loss of a job, depression, poor diet, and extreme fear, seems to trigger fibromyalgia. Most authorities admit not knowing the actual cause or causes of fibromyalgia. However, Dr. Lowe finds that many patients who develop symptoms of fibromyalgia after some traumatic experience were already hypometabolic:

> After learning what the various symptoms and signs of hypothyroidism are, many fibromyalgia patients say such things as, "You know, come to think of it, I remember having these symptoms off and on since I was in my early teens." A short period of physical inactivity after the trauma appears to decrease their muscle mass and further lower their metabolic rate. After enough time passes to permit a significant loss of muscle mass, many people develop posttraumatic fibromyalgia. . . . In many cases, the patients' metabolic insufficiency was probably worsened by the typical American diet and not taking nutritional supplements. To shorten a potentially long story, factors such as hypothyroidism (even borderline), nutritional insufficiencies, and inadequate physical activity become intertwined and interactive in impeding the person's metabo-

lism. . . . By the time I've seen some patients, the probable in-
teractions of factors that have contributed to their disabled
conditions have become impossible to comprehend. The best
I've been able to do with such patients is start working with
multiple factors that may be currently sustaining their fibromyalgia, making recommendations. Usually I've asked such
patients to try and generate a few months of faith. It may take
that long before they feel better subjectively and before our objective measures show that their fibromyalgia is improving.[7]

In order to secure treatment like that advocated by Dr. Lowe, try
to locate a holistically oriented medical doctor, a doctor of osteopa-
thy, or a naturopath in a state that licenses naturopaths.[8] These categories of physicians are usually willing to spend the time necessary to
do the clinical detective work that most other doctors have, for all
practical purposes, abandoned.

Hypothyroid patients following Dr. Lowe's treatment protocol have
reported a high degree of success. Dr. Lowe typically starts hypothyroid
patients with Armour desiccated thyroid, which he uses because it has
a higher T3 content than that in synthetic T4/T3 preparations.

"I have found that many hypothyroid patients also have cellular resistance to thyroid hormone," states Dr. Lowe. "Most of these patients
don't benefit from T4 alone, but some of them do from desiccated thyroid, presumably because of the relatively high T3 content. . . . Some
we do switch to synthetic T3 when they don't benefit from desiccated
thyroid. However, we've stopped altogether giving patients T4 alone."

With every new fibromyalgia patient, Dr. Lowe has the point
driven home to him that fibromyalgia is actually a manifestation of
hypothyroidism. "I'm so certain of this that I would put my neck on
the chopping block!" he told us. Currently, there's no research to
counter Dr. Lowe's findings, and no opposing researcher who would
risk her or his neck!

26

Stress and Free Radicals

WHOEVER SAID "THE best things in life are free" lived too long ago to know about free radicals, those molecular muggers that attack our trillions of cells and seem programmed to undermine us in body, mind, and spirit.

Physiology 101 teaches that the body's metabolism, using oxygen to turn food into energy, warmth, and body tissue, creates free radicals, also called "reactive oxidative stressors." Likewise, so do breathing and the working of the immune system. However, relative to the immune system, oxidative activity in white cells does us a good turn, killing harmful bacteria and viruses and purging us of harmful toxins.

Excess free radicals harm us, and their sources are not limited to body functions: vehicle exhaust, tobacco smoke, industrial chemicals, pesticides, chlorine and fluoride in the water supply, household cleansers, paint, fumes from gas stoves, and radiation from electrical appliances, including cell phones. These and more set off biochemical stress reactions that generate free radicals in us.

Other free radical generators are the thousands of additives in processed foods and beverages, excessive intakes of omega-6 fatty acids in vegetable oils, margarines and shortenings, partially or totally hydrogenized products, trans fats, CLA (this essential fatty acid sold for weight control, in fact, increases free radicals) too much sugar, undernutrition, certain prescription and recreational drugs, and even vigorous aerobic exercise.

Add emotional stressors to these: money worries, hating the job, unreal work deadlines, incessant commuter traffic tie-ups, nagging illnesses, marital conflict, and, among numerous others, feelings of inferiority, insecurity, anxiety, and fear.

It is virtually impossible immediately to sense the damage from these countless and continuous free radical assaults, and, consequently, we often fail to relate them to physical, psychological, or emotional ailments that may develop.

It is paradoxical that oxygen gives life and takes it away. However, without oxygen life would not exist. A peeled apple or banana turns brown and starts deteriorating, iron lawn furniture rusts, and fat in the membranes of body and brain cells becomes oxidized and deteriorates.

Initially our molecules are stable with a pair of electrons orbiting around them. Oxidation from any source causes the loss of one of these electrons. Desperate to replace it and restore its balance, the molecule commits a hostile takeover of an electron from a neighboring molecule, turning the neighbor into a free radical. Deprived of an electron, the neighbor wrests one from its neighbor, starting a chain reaction of biochemical barbarism.

You have to see results to believe what violence takes place. Biochemist Jeffrey Bland, PhD, demonstrated this many years ago while on the faculty of the University of Puget Sound.[1]

Seventy-eight volunteers in good health and on a normal diet—without the protective antioxidant vitamin E—gave blood for testing. These blood samples were exposed to air for sixteen hours and then observed through a powerful electron microscope.

An incredible change had taken place. Every cell's membrane was "budded," deformed, much like bulgy spots on a weak bicycle tire. Then, for ten days, the volunteers supplemented their same diet with 600 IU of natural vitamin E. Their blood samples were exposed to air for sixteen hours. This time only 5 percent of their cells were budded, demonstrating the power of an antioxidant to control oxidative stress.

Recent studies have confirmed the suspicions of medical researchers that hyperthyroidism, hypothyroidism, and Hashimoto's thyroiditis generate free radicals and, may, in part, be caused by excess free radicals.

This makes sense to Majid Ali, MD, professor of medicine at the Capital University of Integrative Medicine, in Washington, DC, a true research genius who pioneered the study of oxidative stress at a molecular level and observes the chronic degenerative diseases it causes. He concluded that everyone with unchecked and unrelenting stress will, in time, suffer from a breakdown of the body's temperature regulating system.[2]

Numerous enzymes that control every aspect of cellular biochemistry are temperature-sensitive. Even a slight lowering of basal body temperature, as in subclinical hypothyroidism, sharply decreases cell enzyme function and, so, boosts free radical production. Diminished enzyme action may frustrate the body's natural process of converting the abundant, but relatively inactive thyroid hormone thyroxine (T4), into the bioactive triiodothyronine (T3), almost guaranteeing subclinical or full-blown hypothyroidism.

Unfortunately, some doctors still supplement low thyroid patients only with synthetic T4 on the erroneous assumption that conversion to T3 is automatic. When they fail to respond, the doctor may conclude that they are not hypothyroid, after all, and offer no treatment, causing frustration, accelerated stress, and continued symptoms of hypothyroidism.

Like all other kinds of stress, low thyroid function trips the body's alarm system, causing the adrenal glands to pump more adrenaline, cortisol, and other stress hormones into the bloodstream. Arteries and capillaries—some so narrow that blood cells must run through in single file—constrict, reducing blood flow to the muscles and skin, further decreasing core body temperature, and spurring the body to generate more free radicals.

These free radicals often damage delicate membranes of cells, their mitochondria, energy generators, and/or DNA, and the lysosomes (minute bags of enzymes), spilling powerful chemicals that often eat away the entire cell. (This creates even more free radicals.) Such action in oxygen-carrying red blood cells may make them sticky and clumped, causing a circulatory traffic jam that intensifies chances for a stroke or heart attack. Free radical insults may even damage receptor sites on the involuntary or autonomic nervous system, further disrupting blood circulation, and lowering core body temperature, typical of low thyroid function.

Diagnosed with hypothyroidism and not responding to a synthetic hormone containing only T4, Gina, the thirty-five-year-old owner of a manufacturing company with one hundred employees, came to my offices highly stressed. Her body shook and her right hand trembled so that she couldn't fill out my medical questionnaires. My secretary had to interview her and fill in the blanks.

Nervously, she kept glancing at her wristwatch, saying she had to get right back to the office. Finally, she settled down enough to tell me the whole story. She worked seventy to eighty hours a week, hadn't had a vacation in three years, couldn't sleep, and seemed close to a physical and emotional breakdown.

"I can help you, but I've got to level with you," I told her. "You know you're in precarious health. You've got to take time off immediately! You must delegate your work to a capable person you trust."

She hesitated before responding. "My executive secretary knows the business. I can trust her, but she's never been in charge."

"If you were hospitalized, someone would have to take over."

She reflected on this briefly, then burst into tears, which helped to break her tension. Knowing she had been on synthetic T4, I immediately had her take a one grain tablet of Armour natural desiccated thyroid and a 100 mg vitamin B–complex capsule with a cup of bottled water. I also gave her enough thyroid and vitamin B-complex pills for a week—plenty of time to get the prescription filled and visit a health food store.

I explained that this thyroid supplement contains both T4 and T3 and would work even though her synthetic did not. Reluctantly, realizing she had to take an immediate vacation, she promised to put her executive secretary in charge and spend a week with a sorority sister in a nearby seaside city.

"This has to be a vacation for total rest—no work," I told her. "When you get back, I'm going to put you on a small amount of adrenal hormone, Siberian ginseng, as well as the hormone precursors DHEA and pregnenolone. I want you to use proven stress reduction techniques: easy but stress-breaking aerobic exercise, biofeedback or meditation, and pursuing a hobby. You and I want you to live to enjoy your success, so you'd better delegate more, work reasonable hours, and vacation twice a year."

Again, she burst into tears, but this time it was with relief, realizing she should have done these things years earlier. Not wanting to overwhelm her, I made a list of antioxidants to add to her daily diet later to control damaging free radicals: vitamin C, a 250 mg tablet after each meal; vitamin E, 400 IU (natural mixed tocopherols); selenium, 200 mcg; lycopene, 15 mg twice; pycnogenol extract, 300 mg; grapeseed extract, 200 mg; N-acetyl cysteine, 1 gram. I use a variety of antioxidants to cope with a variety of free radicals.

A novelist couldn't have crafted a happier ending to Gina's case. During her absence, she found that her executive secretary had done such a great job that she realized she didn't have to oversee every minute detail of the company operation. Gina rewarded her with the newly created position of executive vice president, confidently delegated more functions to her, began living a balanced life, and healed completely.

No less an authority than Denham Harman, MD, discoverer of the free radical theory of disease, told Jim Scheer at a Las Vegas antiaging conference that "unchecked free radicals appear to bring on most, if not all, of the disorders attributed to aging."

This includes assaults on fats in blood and tissue that may invite hardening of the arteries, strokes, and heart disease. Stress may also cause failures of cellular oxygen metabolism that threaten the very health of all our cells.

Stress may also be responsible for symptoms as diverse as chronic fatigue, disorders of mood and memory, skin lesions and eye dryness, excess acidity that impairs digestion and absorption, inability to detoxify systemic poisons, faulty muscle action, neurotransmitter malfunction, and thickening and reduced efficiency of lymphatic fluid that drains toxins from the body. These factors result in chronic fatigue, diminished immune system functioning, and neuromuscular disorders.

So much for enemy action. Now let's consider defense. Everybody knows that the body makes antioxidants to tame free radicals. The major ones are catalase, superoxide dismutase, and glutathione peroxidase. And almost everybody knows that these defending troops are often outnumbered by free radicals. Many of us take supplementary antioxidants such as vitamins C, E, beta carotene (a predecessor to vitamin A), selenium, lycopene (the coloring in tomatoes, watermelon, and pink grapefruit), pycnogenol, and others. We know that there's a lot of guesswork as to which to take and how much.

Now we no longer have to fly blind, because, for the first time in medical history, a patented, scientifically validated, noninvasive test—the Wellness Index—can measure the body's free radical load more accurately than any other existing test. (For more information on the Wellness Index, please see Chapter 19, "How to Prevent a Heart Attack—Your Own!")

A study in *Free Radical Biology* disclosed that high levels of isoprostane correlated with chronic fatigue, postexertion malaise, and joint pain. Never before have chronic fatigue symptoms been directly related to oxidative stress.

Abundant new research and my experience with thousands of thyroid patients convince me that hypothyroidism and hyperthyroidism are due, in part, to excessive and chronic free radical attacks on the body. Both of these disorders then generate more free radicals, undermining your health, and causing premature aging. However, as stated earlier, it is unfair to consider free radicals totally biochemical bad guys. Impeccable medical research proves they are important in fighting infectious diseases, in regulating enzymes, and in producing energy and hormones. We couldn't live without them. Yet we have to learn how to live with them. When their armies outnumber those of antioxidants, they can cause severe illness, accelerated aging, and death.

Only in recent decades have we been aware that, since the beginning of time, free radicals—along with their positive contributions—are a major cause of chronic degenerative diseases and premature aging, and what antioxidants are most beneficial for a particular clinical illness.

27

Overweight?
How to Be a Good Loser

WHOEVER FIRST CALLED the struggle to shed unwanted weight the Battle of the Bulge was guilty of a serious understatement. It seems more like the Hundred Years' War!

I am constantly besieged by patients whose best efforts at losing weight have been none too good. It is not surprising that they lose their fighting hearts. Many of them have been on every diet touted by best-selling books: high carbohydrate-low fat; high fiber; low carbohydrate-high protein; juices; fasts; and other plans conceived by the profit-motivated human mind.

Some patients lose weight, but not for long. Sooner or later—usually sooner—they slip back into old eating habits, and the fat comes back bigger and better than ever. As one of those fortunate fellows who carries no more fat than a racing greyhound, I am going to give you a plan that keeps me slim and helps my patients reduce. My system doesn't promise as quick returns as bestseller regimens, but it does work. It starts with the underlying principles of encouraging good health and proper thyroid function, which are basic to efficient weight loss.

Most overweight individuals are undernourished and suffering from subclinical malnutrition. This condition doesn't always lead to immediate catastrophic illness, but it will lead to biochemical imbalance that may cause health problems and preclude weight loss. It is important to avoid incomplete and unbalanced diets. Temporary shedding of a few pounds is not worth the loss of good health.

We are all different and therefore require different quantities of the same essential nutrients to stay healthy. No matter how complete your diet appears, you can't get from it all the essential nutrients in proper amounts. You must therefore take nutritional supplements to maintain optimal health. You must be realistic about your food supply. On its trip from the ground to your gullet, your food may lose as much as 50 percent of some essential nutrients, even before it is processed.

In order to be in good health and to lose weight, you must have normal thyroid function—or appropriate supplementation—to realize full values from your food. Even if your diet contains all essential micronutrients in proper amounts, you may not be getting full nutritional benefit from it.

Food must be broken down and absorbed through the gastrointestinal mucosa. This process is often impaired in hypothyroidism. Next, food must be processed by pancreatic enzymes and converted by the liver in order to become biochemically active.

Assimilation is often faulty in hypothyroid patients. Then the digested food must be transported by the circulatory system to the sites of use at the cellular level and successfully enter the cells to provide nutritional fuel. Lack of certain nutrients retards the process.

After all this, wastes have to be efficiently eliminated from cells, carried by the circulatory system for detoxification by the kidneys and liver, and thrown off by the bowels, urinary system, skin, and lungs—all of which function below par in hypothyroid individuals.

In hypothyroidism, a decreased rate of oxygen use and a diminished rate of heat production translate into a decrease in metabolism and an inability to lose weight, no matter how hard we try. Administration of thyroid hormone restores both oxygen consumption and metabolic functioning to the hypothyroid individual.

Now comes a key fact. All dieters are familiar with the "sticking point"—the point at which the bathroom scale stubbornly refuses to go lower. In the hypothyroid, this is attributable to a worsening of the hypothyroidism, in which the body sets its thermostat lower.

Hypothyroidism does not make you fat. Dr. Barnes always pointed out that upwards of 40 percent of his hypothyroid patients were actually underweight. However, if you are overweight and hypothyroid, you will probably need to be taking thyroid hormone to facilitate the usefulness of any diet you are on.

Your doctor has probably told you that taking thyroid hormone to lose weight is an unnecessary placebo if you don't have low thyroid blood tests. Unfortunately, this is not the case. It is possible to be hypothyroid even with an adequate thyroid hormone output because of biochemical differences in the receptor sites in our cells, and this condition will show up on the basal temperature test.

What can you do to lose weight? Follow the rules listed below.

1. Make sure your thyroid gland is functioning normally so that you can rule out hypothyroidism, a handicap to weight loss. Start with the Barnes Basal Temperature Test.
2. Eat frequent small meals from the five major food groups.
3. Increase your vegetable intake for all of its nutritional contributions, particularly live enzymes, which help the digestion and absorption process, and added dietary bulk that speeds up elimination.
4. Avoid refined carbohydrates, including sugar, white flour, and white rice.
5. Avoid foods containing preservatives and artificial additives (coloring, flavoring, stabilizing, and foaming agents).
6. Don't add salt to foods. Avoid restaurants that oversalt their food. Avoid sodium-containing additives such as MSG.
7. Avoid overcooked foods. Use leftover cooking liquids in soups and gravies.

8. Minimize your use of animal or saturated fats. Use only lean cuts of meat, trim off fat, and remove fat-laden skin from chicken.

9. Don't use heated vegetable oils. Don't fry foods in oil. Heating vegetable oils and fats makes them as harmful to the body as animal fats and robs your system of essential fatty acids.

10. Get a computerized nutritional evaluation. This will pinpoint your dietary deficiencies. Better yet, have a consultation with a physician who specializes in preventive health maintenance.

11. Improve your diet by taking nutritional supplements.

12. Add bulk to your diet with fiber.

13. Check on evening primrose oil, a supplement sold at all nutrition centers and helpful in weight reduction programs. Two capsules after each meal (or three times a day) is the recommended amount for adults.

14. Avoid diet beverages, dark teas (of the nonherbal variety), coffee, and more than 4 to 6 ounces of fruit or vegetable juices at one sitting or more than one piece of raw fruit at a single meal.

15. Never starve yourself.

16. Get professional psychological counseling if you have been overweight for more than a year. Many individuals and families working to lose weight often unconsciously sabotage their own programs for a variety of hidden reasons. A professional counselor can often unearth these problems. It is also difficult for some dieters to adjust to the success of their programs and to becoming more attractive and more socially acceptable. Such conflicts can be brought to light by counseling and, after a few brief sessions, eliminated.

17. Remember, strictly vegetarian diets are notoriously deficient in micronutrients such as vitamin B_{12} and others; this has

been mentioned in previous chapters. Such shortcomings must be corrected by dietary changes and nutritional supplementation.

18. Exercise aerobically (unless you are seriously ill or your doctor has advised against it). This is an essential part of any weight control program. The best exercise that most of us can enjoy and participate in is brisk walking for forty-five to fifty-five minutes, three or four times a week.

19. Recognize that you are responsible for the success or failure of your weight control program. You will notice that I did not include any rigid menus in this chapter for the simple reason that most of them don't work. We tend to revert to our old, established eating habits, no matter what diet we're on, because of ethnic likes and dislikes, mistrust of the new, and inertia. More important than a set of menus is an awareness of nutritional principles on which you can build your own best diet based on your food likes and dislikes. If you eat small meals from all the essential food groups and eliminate junky, refined, and convenience foods from your diet, you will almost always lose weight.

20. Don't expect perfection in following your diet. This can lead to depression if you slip. Remember, two steps forward and one step backward is better than the reverse. Strive to the best of your ability for moderation. Allow yourself to binge on rare occasions, if you consciously control when those occasions occur. If you can't do this, please reread number 16 and pay careful attention to number 21.

21. If you're following all of the previous suggestions and are still struggling to lose weight, you are probably suffering from food allergies, which often cause serious food addictions and weight gain. Food allergy and sensitivity were purposely not discussed in detail, because they fall outside the scope of this book. However, my own

clinical experience indicates that most minor food sensitivities and allergies are resolved by correcting hypothyroidism and nutritional imbalances.

22. See a physician who specializes in programs for treating food allergies—and start a food rotation diet. If there are no such specialists in your area, read a book that offers a step-by-step program for testing foods by means of an "elimination diet." Once aware of the foods to which you are sensitive, you can rotate them, eating none of the offending ones any more than once every four days.

23. Check with your doctor to make sure you don't have *Candida albicans*, a yeast infection that tends to contribute to weight gain. If you have it, follow treatment for it.

24. Inventory things that cause you stress and learn to either avoid them or cope with them through stress-reduction techniques. Relax and enjoy your program. With time and persistence, you will take off or keep off excess weight, which can contribute to a host of ailments. Some of the worst stressors that can undermine any diet are mentioned in the next two chapters.

28

Tobacco and Alcohol: Thyroid Gland Enemies

ALL SORTS OF charges have been launched against smoking and how it sabotages health by constricting arteries, limiting blood circulation, and contributing to strokes, heart attacks, asthma, emphysema, and lung cancer—and all of them are well founded. Now we know that smoking can also undermine the thyroid gland.

Researchers at University Hospital in Basel, Switzerland, studied women in the Netherlands, Sweden, and Switzerland and discovered that smoking does two harmful things to the thyroid gland: (1) decreases its ability to secrete hormones, and (2) then limits the hormones' action. In the *New England Journal of Medicine*, Beat Mueller, MD, announced that smoking may contribute to the "high incidence of subclinical hypothyroidism (diminished synthesis of thyroid hormone) and aggravate the clinical manifestations of subclinical hypothyroidism."[1]

Critiquing the Mueller study in the same issue of this magazine, Robert D. Utiger, MD, states that smoking was not found to cause hypothyroidism, only to make it more severe and to aggravate its various symptoms.[2] The evidence against smoking is compelling, in either case.

One of many harmful ingredients of cigarette smoke is cyanide, which is converted to thiocyanate in the body. We mentioned earlier in this book that thiocyanate is a suppressor of the thyroid gland. Dr. Utiger comments that thiocyanate lessens the gland's ability to absorb iodine and to synthesize its hormones from raw materials, and actually causes much iodine to escape the gland.

Another study focused on smoking and Hashimoto's thyroiditis, a disorder in which the immune system attacks the thyroid gland, causing inflammation and low thyroid function. (This usually responds to treatment with Armour natural thyroid supplement.[3]) A retrospective study of 387 women with Hashimoto's thyroiditis, averaging 50.5 years of age, included 256 nonsmokers, 110 smokers, and 21 former smokers. Hypothyroids among nonsmokers totaled 34.8 percent, among former smokers, 61.9 (suggesting that quitting smoking doesn't appear to reverse hypothyroidism), and among smokers, 76.4 percent. The percentages of smokers in the hypothyroid group, the subclinical thyroid group, and the euthyroid group (the group with normal thyroid function) were 45.2 percent, 18 percent, and 11.3 percent, respectively.

The researchers found that blood serum levels of thiocyanate, the thyroid gland suppressor, were highest in hypothyroid smokers and ex-smokers. "An increase in serum thiocyanate concentration from smoking may contribute to the development of hypothyroidism in patient's with Hashimoto's thyroiditis," write the researchers. "Our results suggest that smoking may increase the risk of hypothyroidism in patients with Hashimoto's thyroiditis."

An article by David S. Cooper, MD, FACP, in the Thyroid Foundation of America's newsletter, *The Bridge*, shows that smoking affects thyroid efficiency by introducing harmful substances into the body.[4] Further, smokers are more prone to have an enlarged thyroid gland than nonsmokers, a sign of at least subclinical hypothyroidism. It is imperative for smokers to quit at once, for life preservation, health promotion, and longevity. However, determining to quit and actually quitting are two different things.

Nicotine gum helps some people to quit smoking by degrees. However, some can quit cold turkey when made to realize that their smoke is not only jeopardizing their own health but also that of loved ones who live with them. Herbal and homeopathic remedies can also help some individuals to quit smoking.

One of the most popular antismoking herbs in Australia is coltsfoot. This was popularized by Hans Wagner, a television nutritionist.

Dried leaves of coltsfoot, available in many health food stores, are crushed to granules and added to a pipe or to roll-your-own cigarette tobacco. When smoked, coltsfoot gives off such an offensive odor and the taste is so repellent that some people develop an aversion to it. If it doesn't work at first, some individuals keep increasing the amount of coltsfoot until it does. Good luck!

My patients have had some success with a homeopathic remedy that includes lobelia inflata, nux vomica, staphisagria, and tabacum. Each of these ingredients supposedly helps curb the desire for tobacco. In addition, lobelia inflata is said to enhance breathing, particularly in asthmatics. Nux vomica supposedly helps quitters to overcome irritability. Staphisagria also works to banish irritability. Tabacum, derived from tobacco leaves before their flowers bloom, is said to reduce the powerful desire for tobacco and relieve jitteriness and trembling hands.

In her Web site online column (www.thyroid-info.com), Mary Shomon writes about herself and subscribers to her free Internet thyroid newsletter and their response to quitting smoking.[5] She and some of her readers were diagnosed as hypothyroid after quitting smoking. They also gained weight.

Like these people, most of my patients who are former smokers gained weight when they quit. However, my literature search reveals that no study supports the position that quitting causes hypothyroidism. In most cases, my patients explained this phenomenon as follows: tobacco is an appetite suppressant and tends to rev up metabolism and the adrenal system to activate sugar stored in the liver to increase energy.

As Mary Shomon writes: "My theory is that smoking/nicotine creates an artificially high metabolism that masks the fatigue/lethargy commonly seen in hypothyroidism. When the smoker quits, this masking is removed, and the full effects on the metabolism and thyroid are felt. . . . And for smokers with undiagnosed thyroid dysfunction, without proper thyroid hormone treatment, stopping seems to be a metabolic/weight gain double whammy, as they lose the appetite suppressant, metabolism-upping effects of nicotine, and experience the full effects of the hypothyroidism."[6]

Mary Shomon advocates that those who experience this should have a thyroid-stimulating hormone (TSH) test to establish or rule out hypothyroidism. I go a few steps further, recommending that they have the full panel of thyroid tests, a history of health, and questioning by their doctor to catalogue their symptoms.

Heavy smoking is not the only harmful habit that reduces the effectiveness of thyroid function. High intake of alcoholic beverages can also do this. As a highly refined carbohydrate, alcohol demands the whole family of B vitamins—particularly vitamin B_1 (thiamine)— for metabolizing. This leaves little, if any, vitamin B_1 to extract energy from foods.

In natural products such as liver and brewer's yeast, B-vitamin family members appear together, and they work together. As people age, they can't metabolize vitamin B_1 efficiently, so they must compensate by taking more.

Aging and alcoholism combine to drain vitamin B_1 and other B family members away. Depletion of vitamin B_1 is a prime cause of cardiomyopathy, inability of the heart to contract and pump blood forcefully to our farthest extremities. Could it be coincidence that, in hypothyroidism, the heart cannot pump with enough vigor?

Isobel Jennings (see Chapter 4) found that a deficiency of vitamin B_2 depresses the function of various glands and organs, including the thyroid. She also discovered that a deficiency of vitamin B_6 reduces the thyroid gland's ability to convert iodine efficiently into thyroid hormone.

Various animal and human studies show that chronic alcohol drinking and food deprivation can negatively influence three related glands—the hypothalamus, pituitary, and thyroid. A rat experiment described in the journal *Endocrine* revealed that alcohol at 10 percent of total intake along with too little food produced a decrease in TSH. At the same time, this increased thyrotropin-releasing hormone, TRH, a chemical that tells the pituitary gland to produce TSH to induce the thyroid gland to synthesize and release hormone.[7]

An article in *Clinical Experimental Research* indicates in a human study that alcoholism sometimes blunts the response of TSH to thyrotropin-releasing hormone.[8] Researchers are not certain whether this is due to alcohol-related harm that reduces the pituitary gland's ability to secrete TSH, to genetic vulnerability, or to the toxic effects of prolonged alcohol abuse.

As there is little doubt that alcohol reduces thyroid function, along with other damage it produces in the body, can something be done to counteract it?

The intake of additional vitamin B complex—as much as 100 mg of the major family members daily—has helped many of my patients. Those who drink heavily and find it difficult to quit may profit by a discovery of the late Roger J. Williams, PhD, longtime director of the Clayton Foundation Biochemical Institute, the researcher who isolated pantothenic acid, and a Hall of Fame biochemical researcher.[9] Dr. Williams experimented with L-glutamine—not glutamic acid—and found that, when given to rats, it decreases their voluntary drinking of alcohol.

How does it work? Dr. Williams theorized that L-glutamine gets into the rats' brains and protects cells in the appetite center so that they lose their desire to drink more alcohol. Enough human trials have been made to encourage its use by alcohol-addicted individuals. An interesting case study is described by Dr. Williams in *Nutrition Against Disease*. A friend was given a supply of L-glutamine to try on an alcoholic acquaintance. Dr. Williams writes that "the result was dramatic"—and due entirely to the supplement, rather than to any placebo effect. The person voluntarily stopped drinking, found work, and two years later still did not crave alcohol.

Dr. Williams got positive results from just 2 grams of L-glutamine daily. However, he sometimes needed 4 grams daily to turn an individual around. Naturally, in my practice over the years, I have used from 2 to 4 grams of L-glutamine daily for alcoholic patients. It actually worked in sixteen patients out of twenty—all hypothyroids. Not a bad record!

29

How to Thrive in a Polluted World

ONCE UPON A time, the environment was our friend. Today, pollutants assail us in the air we breathe, the food we eat, and the water we drink. Metropolitan smog has turned many a blue sky into a dirty gray. Insecticides have all but done away with once-common yellow clouds of butterflies, as well as with some of us. Additives in processed foods extend their shelf life but not our lives.

One of the worst chemicals in the environment is fluoride, since 1854 a known thyroid gland inhibitor, as we mentioned previously. A waste product from the aluminum and synthetic fertilizer industries and a former rat poison, fluoride continues to be added to the water of many cities as a preventive for cavities.

By authority of the Environmental Protection Agency (EPA), public water supplies can exceed one part per million of fluoride—up to four parts per million. Reputable medical and technical publications, however, state that it does not contribute to better teeth and that it can cause deterioration of bones and even bone cancer. These are typical excerpts from a newsletter by fluoride authority Walter Miller:[1]

> "The current decline in caries in the United States and other western industrialized nations has been observed in both fluoridated and nonfluoridated communities with the percentage reduction about the same." (*Journal of the American Dental Association*)

214

"Our committee had access to a recent dental screening of 26,000 elementary school children, and it was found that the more fluoride a child drank, the more cavities appeared in the teeth." (*Chemical and Engineering News*)

"We found a small but significant increase in the risk of hip fracture in both men and women exposed to artificial fluoridation at one part per million, suggesting that low levels of fluoride may increase the risk of hip fracture in the elderly." (*Journal of the American Medical Association*)

A study disclosed that the central nervous system is "vulnerable to fluoride and that fluoride accumulates in brain tissue and that the neurotoxic risks can be indicative of a potential for motor dysfunction, IQ deficits, and/or learning disabilities in humans."[2]

Similar reputable publications reveal that fluoride can cause nausea and vomiting, kidney failure, and a type of bone cancer.

An article in the *Journal of the International Society for Fluoride Research* states that fluoride is an antagonist to the mineral magnesium, essential to the function of more than three hundred enzyme systems:[3] "The amount of fluoride assimilated by living organisms constantly increases, and magnesium absorption diminishes as a consequence of progressively advancing industrialization. An increased intake of magnesium plays a protective role by countering and reducing toxic effects of fluoride."

The generally accepted ratio of magnesium to calcium is one to two. However, several authorities now advocate a one-to-one ratio: 1,000 mg of magnesium to 1,000 mg of calcium, for example.

Fluoride enters our bodies from many more sources than city water. These include soft drinks, fruit juices, jellies, beer, various processed foods, many TV dinners, mouthwashes, and toothpastes, as well as in other products that utilize tap water in fluoridated communities. Fluoride accumulates in our systems. Not only do we swallow it, we breathe it if we live in areas where aluminum or synthetic fertilizers are produced. So, our intake of fluoride can be frighteningly high—far above the one to four parts per million authorized by the EPA. Inasmuch as fluoride inhibits thyroid function, it probably plays an important role in the genesis of hypothyroidism.

In addition, fluoride interacts with lead water pipes and adds another thyroid suppressor to drinking water, as reported in the *British Medical Journal*.[4] "Analyzing a survey of over 280,000 Massachusetts children, investigators found that silicofluorides are associated with an increase in children's absorption of lead," states the article.

Another potent environmental toxin is perchlorate, which the EPA says inhibits the thyroid gland from absorbing iodine. You've never heard of perchlorate? Many people haven't. Still, you may be unknowingly ingesting it.

Its sources are mainly the by-products of synthetic fertilizers and solid propellants for rockets, missiles, and fireworks. Perchlorate salts are also used as a component of air bag inflators. Ever since 1950, perchlorate wastes have been stored without appropriate care and monitoring, so it has invaded surface and underground water supplies. Thanks to watchdog organizations such as Zero Waste America, which promotes the elimination of waste, toxins, and pollution, we have been alerted to its dangers.

Why didn't the EPA warn us of perchlorate's dangers and order city water suppliers to test for this hazardous chemical? The EPA informed Zero Waste America that, because perchlorate is used in military applications, secrecy was necessary.[5] Defense contractors and fertilizer makers in forty-four of the fifty states use perchlorate, so the time has come for water companies to develop appropriate tests and ways to eliminate it. The EPA's stated safe limit for adults is thirty-two parts per billion—much less for children and infants. However, far more testing is necessary to establish this figure's validity.

Still another source for possible thyroid suppression are the pesticides used on domestic and international airline flights, supposedly to discourage insects and rodents from coming aboard. The pesticides may also discourage you and me from coming aboard for any more flights than necessary.

So much emphasis is placed on dangers from radiation exposure in high-altitude flights that little was known about hazards from airplane insecticide spraying until several years ago when Karin Winegar wrote a revealing article on this subject for *Mother Jones* magazine.[6] This unfair practice is being carried on without a federal agency requirement and without warning to passengers. Dozens of studies—including some by the National Research Council and the National Institute of Environmental Health Sciences—link pesticide ingredients to many ailments, including respiratory illnesses, allergic skin reactions, nervous system damage, sexual dysfunction, cancer, and glandular disorders.

Becky Riley, spokesperson for the National Coalition for Alternatives to Pesticides, based in Portland, Oregon, reveals that pesticides, health hazardous on land, are even more so in the air, inasmuch as 50 percent of the air in airplane cabins is recycled. She is quoted in Karin Winegar's *Mother Jones* magazine article as saying, "Pesticides break down slowly in the enclosed, poorly ventilated aircraft. Passengers are sealed in a chamber that has been gassed, and sit there for hours."

Airline representatives insist that this practice is carried on for the safety and protection of passengers. Although the sight of a mouse or insect on an airplane could upset passengers, it is more likely that spraying is done for public relations purposes.

Many toxicologists quoted in the *Mother Jones* article take exception to this practice, relating it to many common medical ailments. Jack Thrasher, PhD, an immunotoxicologist in Alto, New Mexico, told Winegar, "This practice is insanity. Tralomethrin (a commonly used airline spray) contains bromide. Bromide has been shown in animal studies to cause thyroid disease," states Dr. Thrasher. Other chemicals in Tralomethrin create allergic reactions and worsen asthma. They have no business spraying pesticide. I don't care if it's .05 percent," he said.

Winegar writes that Sheila Daar, director of the Bio-Integral Re-
source Center in Berkeley, California, a developer of nonpoisonous
ways of controlling pests and weeds, insists that cleaning crews for
aircraft follow safe procedures.

First, they should check each airplane with sticky or pheromone
traps to determine if there actually is an insect problem: "Affected
planes can be treated in a number of inexpensive ways that don't involve volatile materials, or [that use] only low-toxic methods such as
caulking, cracks, traps, boric acid gels, or paste in a bait station at entry points or hiding places." Daar also notes that insects quickly develop resistance to pesticides.

Periodically the EPA meets with industry to determine how environmental chemicals impact on secretions of various glands. In one
conclave, participants focused on thyroid hormones. Unfortunately,
the only conclusions reached were that environmental chemicals do
three things to thyroid hormones: block their synthesis, change serum
transport proteins (the delivery system), or increase their catabolizing
(breaking down).

Authorities concur that the worst pollution—50 to 55 percent of
the total—is spewed from cars, trucks, buses, gas-guzzling motor
homes, and farm equipment: sulfur dioxide, carbon monoxide, benzo-
prene, tars, nitrous oxides, and ozone—the latter caused by sunlight interacting with nitrous oxide. This murderous array of chemicals reduces
thyroid function and invites lung diseases such as asthma, bronchitis,
emphysema and cancer.

Certain nutrients help, vitamin A for instance. This nutrient is
known for protecting and healing mucus membranes—mouth, throat,
and lung tissues. A fascinating study was presented to the 9th International Cancer Congress by Umberto Saffioti, a pathologist at the
Chicago Medical College.[7]

Saffioti's reasearchers simulated the way that the environment de-
livers pollutants to the lungs, attaching benzopyrene, a cancer-caus-
ing hydrocarbon in vehicle exhausts, cigarette smoke, and smoke

from oil and coal fires in homes and manufacturing plants, to minute dust particles placed in the windpipes of small animals, noted for their resistance to cancers. Carried by lung fluid, the chemicals traveled to the bronchi, tubes that channel air into the lungs. Almost all the animals developed lung cancer.

Next the research team fed a new group of the same animals vitamin A, along with the dustborne chemicals. Very few developed lung cancer. Generally, alternative physicians suggest no more than 10,000 IU of fat-soluble vitamin A daily and warn that pregnant women had better stay around 5,000 IU. It is wise to be guided by a preventive medical specialist relative to an appropriate intake of vitamin A. Best food sources of vitamin A are liver, other meat, fish, butter, eggs, cheese, and milk.

Since the Saffioti research, other scientists have found that vitamin E also protects mucus membranes from smog. Generally, 400 IU of natural vitamin E—mixed tocopherols—is the suggested amount. Best food sources of this nutrient are wheat germ, hazelnuts, codfish (and cod liver oil), cashews, oats, avocados, and pecans.

It is customary to criticize the EPA for its lack of protection for the environment and those of us in it. However, we have to do some protecting ourselves. We can use the car less, join a carpool to work, take public transportation, where available, and walk or cycle short distances. We can conserve electricity on air conditioning by keeping the blinds or shades drawn on the sunny side of the house, experiment in setting the thermostat at a higher temperature that's still comfortable, and reduce winter heating costs by wearing warmer clothing indoors.

There's a tendency to think such measures are useless, saying, "I'm just one person. What good will it do if I conserve?" That's part of the problem. Multimillions of people think that and refrain from doing anything, so multimillions add unnecessary pollution to the environment.

Sadly, pollution is no longer merely a national issue. Pollution doesn't need a passport to cross our borders. One of many examples makes this point. Daniel A. Jaffe, PhD, an environmental chemist at the University of Washington at Bothell, in addressing an annual conference of the American Geophysical Union, revealed that springtime dust storms in China and Manchuria sweep as much as 140 million tons of dust, carrying lead, mercury, and arsenic to various parts of North America, as captured by satellite images. Some of our pollutants also travel to other parts of the world.[8]

How can lead, one of the most toxic heavy metals, harm us? Let me count the ways. Lead causes nerve damage, brain dysfunction, lowered IQ, behavioral problems (attention deficit disorders and additional juvenile delinquency), and retarded skeletal growth.

The list goes on to include excessive fatigue, irritability, sleeplessness, confusion, impaired hearing—sometimes, even loss of balance. When lead accumulates in the bones, it reduces our ability to make red blood cells to carry oxygen to all the rest of our cells for metabolizing foods. It weakens our immune system and slows down thyroid function, often to the point of hypothyroidism.

Innumerable surveys disclose that we carry an unprecedented burden of lead—500 times as much as our ancestors of three generations ago. There's a lot more that can and should be said about the hazards and sources of lead. Too many individuals believe that lead disappeared many years ago when oil companies were ordered to get the lead out of their gas. Certainly this helped.

In addressing the National Academy of Sciences' Round Table on Environmental Health, Timothy E. Wirth, PhD, president of the United Nations Foundation, disclosed some of the gains:[9] "Since the elimination of lead from gasoline in the U.S, we have witnessed a 15 point drop in blood levels of lead. This gives every baby born today a gift of four to five additional IQ points."

Wirth also indicates that we need more gains. Citing the pioneering research in harmful effects of lead by Herbert L. Needleman, MD, world expert in this area, he stated that, in a study involving 200 delinquent youths and 200 nondelinquent youths in Philadelphia, Dr. Needleman found elevated lead levels only in the deliquent youths:

"He estimates that 11 to 38 percent of the nation's delinquency is attributable to high lead exposure."

There's still too much lead around. Neither Merlin magic nor oxidation has removed it all from the scene. Lead is still on highways and in the soil next to roadways, carried by wind and rain to nearby and faraway lakes, streams, wells, and reservoirs of drinking water. Lead arsenate is still sprayed on fruit trees, much of which goes underground to be absorbed by tree roots and, then, by us.

An estimated 1,800 pounds of lead arsenate may be used on an acre of land over ten years. As an insecticide, this chemical is sprayed on tobacco plants, along with other toxins, polluting the smoker and those living and working with him or her. Lead smelting plants exhale vapor inhaled by those working and/or living near them.

Lead also makes an illegal entry into us from earthenware plates whose glaze is fired at too low a temperature, from toothpaste tubes, and from sealants in metal cans containing food and beverages—good reason for eating mainly fresh foods and limiting our intake of soft drinks.

How do we rid ourseves of lead? One basic way is by chelation, a moderately costly but highly succesful chemical process by which EDTA, a synthetic amino acid, is dripped into a vein and makes the rounds of the circulatory system, seizing metals such as lead and eliminating them from the body.

Chelation was first proved during World War II on seamen who developed lead toxicity by painting ships with lead-based paint. It worked wonders. Progressive medical researchers immediately recognized it as an efficient means of carrying off harmful heavy metals. To date, millions of successful cases have validated the detoxification merits of chelation.

EDTA also etches away blockages in arteries by removing the calcium that cements arterial plaque. Up to thirty treatments—two per week—are required to remove arterial blockages.

Optimal calcium intake offers some protection from lead toxicity by competing for the same cellular absorption sites. If you ingest, absorb, and assimilate enough calcium, lead—an opportunist—can't find vacant sites.

There's yet another effective lead elimination therapy. Rhoda Papaioannou, a biochemist at the Brain Bio Center in Princeton, New Jersey, discovered it by using applied clinical nutrition. Twenty-two workers in a storage battery plant showed many symptoms of lead poisoning.[10]

Before launching the study, the Brain Bio team measured the workers' blood levels of lead. Then the workers were given 2,000 mg of vitamin C and 60 mg of zinc daily for 24 weeks. Their blood levels of lead were measured at 6, 12, and 24 weeks. At the end of the study, lead blood levels plummeted by an average of 26 percent.

Results were all the more remarkable because, throughout the study, the workers continued on the job in the same polluted environment.

"By increasing zinc and vitamin C, everyone could be better protected against inevitable lead exposure that is part of modern life," says Papaioannou. "It would be better to clean up the environment, but, in the meantime, we can at least protect our bodies."

Such a program can't be carried out indefinitely, however, because, in time, such a high daily dose of zinc could upset the zinc-copper ratio. Zinc and copper use the same absorption sites. Excessive zinc could crowd out copper, causing harm in that copper is vitally needed to make red blood corpuscles, strengthen blood vessels, nerves, tendons and bones, maintain fertility, help to promote blood clotting, and ensure proper skin coloring and healthy hair.

Usually 2 to 3 mg of copper daily should be added to a zinc-heavy regimen, says biochemist Philip A. Walraven, PhD, of the University of Colorado Health Science Center. From that point, copper intake doesn't have to rise in the same proportion to zinc.

The best food sources of zinc are herring (a saltwater fish), almonds, wheat germ, blackstrap molasses, liver, sunflower seeds, eggs, lamb, chicken, oats, rye, beef, turkey, and walnuts. Oysters, clams, and crabs top them all in zinc but live in waters close to ocean shores where most industrial pollutants are expelled.

Almost all fruit and vegetables are rich in vitamin C, and they contain fiber that's helpful in carrying off lead. Heading the list are rose hips, acerola cherries, guavas, black currants, parsley, red peppers—with twice the vitamin C of green peppers—watercress, chives, strawberries, red raspberries, oranges, grapefruit, and papaya.

Mushrooms are, by far, the food richest in copper, followed by liver, wheat germ, blackstrap molasses, Brazil nuts, cashews, oats, lentils, barley, almonds, bananas, avocado, rice, and bee pollen.

Like lead, the heavy metal mercury silently invades our body from industrial and vehicular exhausts, the burning of coal and other fossil fuels, from producing paints and plastics, manufacturing wood pulp, sprayed fungicides, even from the earth's crust when rain washes it into rivers and lakes or releases it into underground water. Most large fatty fish contain mercury contamination—swordfish, shark, marlin, and tuna. They present the greatest potential health hazard, because they eat smaller fish, adding to their load of toxins.

In his Internet health column (http:www.mercola.com), Joseph Mercola, DO, writes about the hazards of eating farmed fish, due to their crowded environment, similar to that of factory-farmed animals and hens: proneness to disease and treatment with antibiotics. "Unless you can verify that the fish has been lab-tested and found free of contaminants, don't eat it," he advises. "When you visit your supermarket, ask the fish handlers where the fish comes from. They may contact the manufacturer for you. Otherwise contact them on your own and ask if the fish has been tested for mercury and PCBs."

Charles Williamson, MD, codirector of the Toxic Studies Institute in Boca Raton, Florida, states that mercury causes a fetus to suffer decreased oxygen, amino acids, glucose, magnesium, zinc, and vitamin B_{12}.[11]

"This suppression in turn causes reduced iodine uptake and hypothyroidism, learning disabilities and impairment and reduction in IQ . . . ," he maintains. "However, mercury-contaminated fish barely scratch the surface of the overall problem. The great majority of the body-burden of mercury (87 percent) comes from dental amalgams. . . ."

The late Willem Khoe, MD, who practiced medicine in Las Vegas, Nevada, studied this issue in one hundred years of medical and dental journals and told us that most of the articles disclosed that amalgam fillings are definitely harmful to health.

Based on abundant medical literature, David W. Eggleston, DDS, of Newport Beach, California, suspected that amalgam fillings depress the immune system, among other negative actions. A clinical associate professor in the Department of Restorative Dentistry at the University of Southern California, he tested this premise in a 1983 research project.

Along with forty-seven other individuals, my collaborator Jim Scheer volunteered to have his mercury-silver fillings removed and replaced with harmless alternative fillings. Before and after removal of the amalgam fillings, each volunteer offered blood samples for comparison.

At the experiment's end, the number of Jim's T-lymphocyte cells in ratio to total lymphocyte cells rose by more than 30 percent, a dramatic gain. All volunteers showed comparable results. (These cells protect us from toxins.)

David Kennedy, DDS, a practicing dentist and longtime analyst, researcher, and historian on the subject of amalgam fillings, writes and lectures frankly on this subject: "Studies have documented that mercury causes hypothyroidism, damage of thyroid RNA, autoimmune thyroiditis (inflammation of the thyroid), and impairment of conversion of thyroid hormone T4 to the active T3 form. . . . Mercury blocks thyroid hormone production by occupying iodine-binding sites and inhibiting hormone action even when the measured thyroid levels appear to be in proper range."[12]

Of course, the best defense against mercury is avoidance. The best offense is optimal consumption of the mineral selenium that counteracts mercury. "It is clear that organisms with a diet supplemented by selenium or with high natural levels achieve added degree of protection against methyl mercury poisoning," states the Environmental Studies Board of the National Research Council.[13]

Nearly no one is free of mercury toxicity, so it's useful to know that the nonmetallic element selenium counteracts mercury and protects the kidneys from damage. Although a protective daily amount is generally considered from 200 mcg to 600 mcg, I advise my patients to take no more than 200 mcg, because selenium can be toxic at high levels.

Although not as pervasive in the environment as mercury, cadmium, another toxic metal, can be equally devastating. Highly concentrated in tobacco, cadmium enters the lungs and, over time, can cause such devastating disorders as emphysema and lung cancer. Research demonstrates that livers of terminally ill patients with emphysema and bronchitis contain three times more cadmium than those of individuals dying of other diseases.[14]

Other sources of cadmium include the smelting of copper, lead, and zinc, the burning of coal, oil, and gasoline—particularly from car exhausts—electroplating, the manufacturing of nickel-cadmium rechargeable batteries, vehicle tires, some paints, phosphate fertilizers, ice cube trays, pitchers, bowls, and ceramic ware.

As vehicles race down highways, stop, or start, they leave an almost invisible residue from their tires—rubber and cadmium. Shellfish and animal liver and kidney contain more cadmium than any other foods. Individuals on crash diets or undernourished and deficient in zinc are at some risk to develop cadmium-related disorders. The trick is to keep intake of cadmium from foods and breathing at a minimum. Cadmium and zinc have a similar chemical structure, so, if there's a deficiency of zinc, cadmium moves in.

Zinc-rich foods are herring, wheat germ, blackstrap molasses, egg yolk, lamb, chicken, brewer's yeast, oats, rye, wheat, coconut, turkey, barley, beans, avocados, peas, blue cheese, and buckwheat.

Sodium alginate, available in health food stores, binds with cadmium and may be helpful in ridding the body of it. Products vary in potency, so read the label for the recommended daily intake. Rats fed sodium alginate, then given a lethal dose of cadmium, all survived.[15]

Nearly one hundred thousand synthetic chemicals are now on the market. Authorities estimate that almost a thousand new ones are released each year. They are tested on an individual basis. However, time, costs, and the impossibility of doing blind studies—nobody is pollutant-free—leave us all vulnerable. Among these chemicals, one that has been banned for decades continues to haunt us: polychlorinated biphenyls (PCBs).

It would take a library of books to reveal the harm and antidotes (if any) for these chemicals—most of which threaten our well-being, health, and even our lives. Timothy E. Wirth, PhD, mentioned earlier, sums up the disaster of insufficiently tested chemicals:[16] "We have allowed too many compounds like DDT and PCBs to move into global use before we have understood their tragic consequences. The proper place to carry out experiments is not in our children's bodies or in the ecosystems of the world."

Does the problem of access to wholesome, nonchemicalized food seem too gigantic to be solved?

It isn't.

However, it won't be solved in Congress, the Senate, the White House, or in court. It will be settled in the stores where you buy your groceries. Twenty years ago, only a few health food stores carried organic produce, free-range meat and poultry, eggs from cage-free chickens, and hormone-free dairy products.

Today, supermarkets stock them all, because consumers like you demand and buy them. One of the national leaders among supermarkets in selling organic produce is Raley's stores in northern California and Nevada.

This chain started the trend decades ago. For shoppers who want to pay less than the prices for organic produce, Raley's also carries produce that undergoes rigorous inspection by Scientific Certification Systems (SCS) to make sure the fruits and vegetables contain no detected pesticide residues. They are marked with the Agri-Check label. Samples are regularly sent to an independent lab for testing.

There's a strong buyer undercurrent for wholesome foods. Many syndicated news and magazine stories validate this trend. The Environmental Working Group, an advocacy organization in Washington, D.C., not long ago made a list of the safest and unsafest produce sold in stores, founded on latest research from the Department of Agriculture.[17]

Vegetables and fruit with lowest levels of pesticides are asparagus, avocados, bananas, broccoli, cauliflower, sweet corn, kiwi, mangoes, onions, papaya, pineapples, and sweet peas.

Those with the highest are apples, bell peppers, celery, cherries, imported grapes, nectarines, peaches, pears, potatoes, red raspberries, spinach, and strawberries. Organic produce doesn't always have the Hollywood cosmetic beauty of chemicalized vegetables and fruit, but its nutrients are more numerous and richer in quality. A recent study indicates that organic produce can help children throw off toxic pesticides.

Cheshong Lu of Emory University, Atlanta, Georgia, and his team of researchers, conducted a fifteen-day experiment with children aged 3 to 11 in twenty-three families in a Seattle suburb.[18]

On the first three days and the last seven days, the children were fed conventionally grown foods. On the five days in between, they were given organically grown foods, prepared the same way as the children would normally eat them—fruit vegetables, juices, cereals, and pasta.

Parents collected their urine samples twice daily. During each period, the urine was tested for malathion, chlopyrifos, and several other commonly used pesticides. Lu's team bought organic foods and gave them to the parents. The researchers asked the parents to make the same meals that the children would usually eat.

Pesticides were present in the urine when the children ate conventionally grown foods but not detectable in most of the samples when they ate organically grown foods. In analyzing the results, Doug Brugge, PhD, an environmental health specialist at Tufts University

School of Medicine, Boston, told *Science News*: "Organic food is a viable intervention to control pesticide exposure. . . . "

The Union of Concerned Scientists issued the following statement:[19] "We need to de-emphasize chemical controls and start the transition to biologically based pest management techniques, which rely on prevention, soil health, resistant species, natural pest predators and, only as a last resort, pesticides."

Every one of us can speed up this cause if we deal with the problem at the right place—the cash register!

30

Live Longer,
Healthier, and Younger

AN ALL-TIME HIGH in long living was set by a fellow named Methuselah—969 years. He isn't mentioned in the *Guinness Book of World Records*, but you can find him in the Book of Genesis.

You may not expect to dethrone Methuselah, but wouldn't it be great to live several decades longer than average with great health and a sharp mind?

You can.

First, however, you should be armed with the latest solid information on this subject—psychological, physical, biochemical, and social.

Staying young starts with thinking and acting young. A positive attitude helps because, sooner or later, signs of aging appear somewhere between the top of the head and the soles of the feet. It is essential not to let an unwelcome wrinkle, a gray hair, or a joint's worth of arthritis send negativism richocheting through your mind, causing you to give in to aging.

Accentuating the negative only accelerates the aging process, as it did in the forty-five-year-old father of a school acquaintance of mine back east. His frequent comment was, "I'm getting old fast."

Returning after a decade away, I was shocked at how cruelly the years had treated him. Yet there was grim justice in the physical response to his self-image. A comparatively youthful, vigorous, middle-aged man had become bent, faltering, and stiff-legged, his hands locked like claws with arthritis. Poor self-image and negative programming were surely not the only factors in his rapid deterioration, but they were powerful determinants.

Certain psychological and social factors contribute strongly to staying young, says G. Z. Pitskhelauri, MD, a noted gerontologist, based on in-depth studies in the Republic of Georgia, reputedly the home of more hundred-year-olds (and older) than any other area in the world.[1]

Following are his major requirements for longevity, many of which can be applied in the United States: (1) close family ties—the branch should always remain a part of the family tree; if possible, several generations should live under a single roof; (2) a continuous daily work routine within the body's capabilities; (3) continued physical activity, not vegetative retirement; (4) independent pursuits within the close family structure; (5) periods of relaxation.

Dr. Pitskhelauri would take exception to Oliver Wendell Holmes's classic witticism that the best way to live long is to select your grandparents wisely. Environment is more important than heredity, at least so far as the Republic of Georgia is concerned, he maintains. Replying to the argument that many long-living Georgians also have long-living ancestors, he states that this is to be expected, because they are products of the same environment.

Dr. Pitskhelauri also says that a key to longevity is the typical Georgian diet, one that gives the back of the hand to the low cholesterol diet: fatty meats, whole milk products, native sauces, herbs, and other greens, and moderate amounts of wine.

His final words of advice are to eat in moderation; avoid hard liquor and tobacco; be active, with a lively interest in family and the community; and, of crucial importance, follow regular life patterns (including work) to try to stay free of excess stress.

Another longevity program—this one in the United States—is based on a comprehensive survey by the California State Department of Public Health.[2] Several thousand individuals were interviewed initially and then nine years later. Persons who adhered to at least six of the following rules experienced better health and more years to enjoy it than those who complied with fewer than four:

1. Sleep seven to eight hours a night.
2. Always eat breakfast.
3. Snack infrequently.
4. Keep weight to between 5 percent under and 20 percent over desirable standard weight (for males) and less than 10 percent over desirable standard (for females).
5. Exercise frequently: do some physical work such as gardening, pursue sports (swimming, golf, calisthenics), and take long walks.
6. Always keep alcoholic consumption low.
7. Do not smoke.

Such guidelines offer a helpful pattern for longevity. However, certain bits of misinformation still mislead and discourage the young on their way to advanced years, as well as those who are already there. One of them is the moss-covered cliche, "You can't teach an old dog new tricks." Another is the belief that we inevitably begin losing irreplaceable brain cells at age twenty-six and with them essential mental capacity.

More than a generation ago, studies by Irving Lorge, MD, of Columbia University, proved conclusively that old dogs not only learn new tricks but learn them well. A remarkable research project conducted by William A. Owens Jr., PhD, while he was head of the psychology department at Iowa State University, exploded the "old dogs" cliché again. He happened upon a musty treasure in the attic of a college building—scores of 179 freshmen who, in 1919, had taken the Army Alpha test, one of the first comprehensive means of measuring mental ability. Aware that he could make a tremendous contribution to psychological knowledge, Dr. Owens managed to track down 127 of these then middle-aged individuals and administered the same test, comparing performances.

What impressed him most was that, after four years of college and three decades of experience, these individuals scored higher on general information and far higher on questions requiring judgment and logic. Unquestionably, the fifty-year-olds demonstrated superior thinking ability when compared with their younger selves.

A few decades ago, the then Soviet Union issued a report to the United Nations, *The Right to Old Age*, based on tested physical and mental abilities of 21,000 elderly individuals. Its conclusion was, "The more brains and muscles are used, the less they age."

Many similar studies have been published in the past fifty years, and now scientists in laboratories are learning underlying reasons for previous findings.

One of the leaders of this alluring field of research is Marian C. Diamond, PhD, a neuroanatomist at the University of California at Berkeley. Results of her thirty years of experiments with rats have given the world enlightenment and new hope. She says that if we seek stimulation and challenge all of our lives, we can delay and even defeat mental aging. She has also shattered the misconception that we necessarily lose thousands of brain cells daily, that there is nothing we can do to replace them, and that, therefore, our mental capacity declines steadily and inevitably.[3]

To skeptics who might say, "All of this is helpful if you're a rat," Professor Diamond responds that brains are big clumps of nerve cells, and that nerve cells of rats and human beings have the same basic constituents. In the Gertrude Stein tradition, she says, "A nerve cell is a nerve cell is a nerve cell."

It is not true that the brain settles on a comfortable plateau of accomplishment in early life and declines after that. Professor Diamond learned that there can be brain growth even in rats who are in their eighties and nineties in human years. In one experiment, she moved rats who had lived boring lives in uninteresting cages with only a few companions into what she called "enriched quarters," with larger cages, a choice of toys, and sometimes twelve other rats for companionship. Toys were changed every day. She compared this group's progress with that of a control group, rats in standard dull cages with no toys and only two companions. Without stimulation or challenge, the control rats stayed in their rut, keeping to themselves, hardly moving, moping, and acting as old as they were. It was just the opposite for the rats in the enriched environment. They socialized, played with their new toys, and seemed to look forward to the next day's toys.

At the end of the experiment, when the rats were more than 120 years old in human terms, those in the enriched environment had actually increased their number of brain cells. Their cerebral cortexes were 6 percent thicker than those of the unstimulated rats. Further, their brains showed 9 percent less lipofuscin (aging pigment).

Nerve cells were designed to receive stimuli. They will react positively to stimuli at any age, Professor Diamond says. Brains that meet challenges positively don't lose cells; they gain some. Professor Diamond sees a lesson for human beings in the rat studies. We can socialize, keep our minds stimulated, and stay young, or isolate ourselves, vegetate, and age rapidly. The decision is up to us. It's a question of using or losing our brain power.

Other scientists worldwide are also uncovering secrets to keep us physically young for productive living. Most gerontologists agree that there's no point in extending life only to give ourselves an additional fifteen or twenty years to be ravaged by disease and degeneration.

Allan L. Goldstein, PhD, chairman of the biochemistry department of George Washington University Medical School and one of the foremost researchers in longevity, feels that scientists will soon discover how to use immune system energy, just as researchers decades ago learned how to release energy by splitting the atom. Effervescent with optimism, Dr. Goldstein feels that within a decade we will know how to live to age one hundred or beyond. It will be up to us to learn how to use this information.

How can immune system energy be utilized for our benefit? Before we answer, let us review what the immune system is and what it does. The immune system is an inner guard that protects us from threats to our existence, from anything that's foreign or abnormal, whether it is a transplanted organ or malaria germs, viruses, or cancer cells.

A popular theory holds that when the immune system begins to decline, that is the beginning of the end. The decline appears to start in the thymus gland, a twin-lobed, gray-pink organ located at the top of the chest. Dr. Goldstein calls the thymus (thought to be useless until the early 1960s) the immune system's master gland. Unlike other glands whose peak productivity continues for many years, the thymus slows down when we are about fourteen years old.

Protective white blood cells called T cells pass through the thymus gland to be modified and matured for action. These cells fight for our lives. Like soldiers, they have various missions—annihilating invaders, stimulating certain immune functions, shutting down others, and enhancing the ability of antibodies (cells that provide immunity against disease) to recognize enemies. As a person ages, the immune system cells lose their power to protect against infection as well as their ability to distinguish between friends and enemies. Then they sometimes mistake their own body tissues for enemies and attack. This is what happens in autoimmune disease.

When we reach the age of fifty, the immune system is operating on something like 15 percent of full efficiency. A weakened immune system loses its ability to monitor and kill abnormal cells; this is a cause for the growing threat of cancer as we grow older, according to some authorities.

As the thymus gland weakens, it is important that we supplement this organ as we do the lazy or weak thyroid gland. The main thrust of thymus research is therefore the synthesizing of a family of hormones named *thymosins*. The codiscoverer of thymosin, professor Goldstein says scientific evidence indicates that the immune system probably can be rejuvenated by thymosin. In experiments at the National Institutes of Health, these hormones proved effective in blocking, delaying, and even curing certain cancers that seem to be age-related—those of the kidney, lung, and prostate.

A controlled study of fifty-five patients afflicted with inoperable oat cell lung cancer brought rewarding results. Thymosin supplementation doubled survival time. Twenty-one subjects received extremely high doses of this hormone and were cleared of cancer. Two years later they are still free of it.

Another authority on thymosin, William Regelson, MD, Professor of Medicine and Microbiology at the Medical College of Virginia, has had some encouragement in experiments with these hormones against rheumatoid arthritis and multiple sclerosis. He says that this approach is a fundamental one, aimed at the heart of the problem, not at the edges.

Thus far, the side effects of thymosin supplementation seem negligible. The body appears to use what is required from what is injected and excretes the rest.

Not all the world's best gerontologists agree by any means that the declining immune system is the sole cause of aging, important though it is. Some maintain that the individual cells gradually lose their ability to repair DNA, the complex chemical of heredity. Still another group feels that a buildup of free radicals accelerates aging.

Protection of body cells, in which an estimated thousand chemical processes go on, is accomplished by antioxidants, including vitamins A, C, and E, lycopene, pycnogenol, various carotenes, and, among many others, selenium, a trace mineral that cooperates with vitamin E, and iodine.

The late Benjamin Frank, MD, believed that supplementary nucleic acids—DNA and RNA—protect cell integrity, too, and even reverse aging. The best sources of nucleic acids, which he advised taking with plenty of fluids, are brewer's yeast, sardines, and leafy green vegetables. Nucleic acids supposedly minimize production of free radicals within cells.

Various authorities feel that high-quality nutrition, regular exercise, and care of the heart and arteries contribute to longer life.

Linus Pauling, PhD, favored taking in 8 to 10 grams of vitamin C daily, a practice that he believed may extend lifespan by twenty-four years. His own daily intake of vitamin C was 18 grams.

The late Roy L. Walford, MD, of the University of California at Los Angeles, advocated a severe restriction of food as one of the best ways to prolong life, particularly starting in the early years. His experiments with mice demonstrate the validity of his thesis.[4] While the Walford system appears to work, it is doubtful whether most individuals could endure his Spartan limitations. Furthermore, the pleasure of eating (not overeating) is part of our enjoyment of life.

Aside from deficiencies in critically needed vitamins, minerals, nucleic acids, and sometimes proteins, the greatest problem in nutrition for longer life is overeating and its natural consequence, obesity. As fat accumulates in all the old familiar places, chances of becoming a victim of brain disease, cancer, diabetes, gallbladder trouble, heart disease, and liver ailments soar, says Grant Gwinup, MD, Professor of Medicine at the University of California, Irvine.

"Stay active physically if you want to live long," insist advocates of daily exercise. Lawrence Morehouse, PhD, professor of exercise physiology at UCLA, states in his book *Total Fitness in 30 Minutes a Week* that 80 percent of the adult American population doesn't exercise properly or sufficiently to stop physical decay.

Although many authorities find that we benefit most from a lifetime of physical exercise, Herbert deVries, PhD, FACSM, exercise physiologist at the University of Southern California Gerontology Center, insists that older people can also profit from exercise even if they start late in life. Men between the ages of fifty-two and eighty-eight at Leisure World, a retirement colony at Laguna Hills, California, were put through carefully monitored exercise routines by Professor deVries and showed surprising improvement: 35 percent greater breathing capacity and 30 percent increased ability of the blood to transport oxygen to tissues. They also realized greater ability to relax and to release pent-up feelings of frustration, aggression, and hostility.

All too often, individuals who are indifferent to the needs of their bodies for exercise, rest, and proper diet receive painful reminders in the form of degenerative diseases, including arthritis, one of the most exquisite tortures ever to twist and gnarl the human frame and appendages.

As early as the late nineteenth century, researchers found thyroid supplements effective in managing arthritis in hypothyroids. They came to this knowledge by accident. In subnormal thyroid function, when the thyroid gland became enlarged and choked off the windpipe and breathing and doctors surgically removed the entire gland, they discovered that arthritis usually became worse. This valuable information was buried under the landslide of new scientific information. A Harvard University study showed that two-thirds of 312 patients with arthritis were hypothyroid. Loring T. Swaim, MD, who was in charge of the project, suggested that arthritis develops in persons with low metabolism.[5]

Dr. Broda Barnes, following Dr. Swaim's lead, made a similar discovery in his study of 300 arthritics, and published his findings in a prestigious medical journal.[6]

"There is a characteristic pattern marking the patient with crippling arthritis," he once told me. "First, it is poor circulation, then repeated infections throughout the years, and other symptoms that come from low thyroid function. In the late stage of this disease, thyroid therapy alone may not be entirely effective against arthritis, even though other characteristic symptoms of hypothyroidism may respond satisfactorily."

Stubborn cases have responded to Dr. Barnes's daily administration of as little as 5 mg of prednisone, one of the least harmful of the corticosteroids. Aware of the dangers of corticosteroids, I approached this treatment carefully. However, I have had excellent results with it, too.

One convincing fact arises from various research projects: the best time to treat arthritis by thyroid therapy is before you have it or in its earliest stages.

Hypothyroidism is not the cause of an illness. In diagnosis, however, it should be considered as a possible basic cause until ruled out by accurate testing, a check of symptoms, and a complete medical history.

Efficiency of your thyroid gland is not something to take for granted. Everyone's status can change, as we pointed out when discussing the thyroid's many subtle suppressants mentioned throughout this book, particularly in Chapter 4, "Care and Feeding of the Thyroid."

With enough thyroid hormone circulating in your five quarts of blood, you can fend off life-shortening infections, allergies, and a negative outlook. You can stall or even stop debilitating degenerative diseases such as cardiovascular ailments.

Your heart will beat vigorously and regularly and pump a rich volume of blood through resilient, clean, and smooth arteries to nearby and distant destinations, efficiently delivering food and oxygen to every cell and carrying off wastes.

All the information in this chapter and in previous ones will prove valuable in assuring that you live longer, healthier, and younger. It would be good to remember, however, that even a normal thyroid gland slows down with the passing years, although at a much lesser rate than the thymus. Then, perhaps, it will need a little help from its friend: you!

Best of luck!

31

Some Things
You Ought to Know . . .

Antidepressants Can
Depress the Thyroid

Beware of antidepressants if you are hypothyroid and are on a synthetic thyroid hormone! A study in the *New England Journal of Medicine* shows that if you take synthetic levothyroxine sodium such as Euthyrox, Levothyroid, Levoxyl, or the most familiar brand, Synthroid, the antidepressant Zoloft, which contains sertraline, can reduce the effectiveness of your thyroid formula.[1] The manufacturer of Zoloft claims that the same results have been observed in patients using other treatments for illness, such as carbazepine, lithium, and certain serotonin-reuptake and tricyclic antidepressants. If you take antidepressants, let your doctor know about the results of the *New England Journal of Medicine* study so he will check you with periodic tests to make certain your thyroid function isn't too low.[2]

Separate Calcium and
Synthetic Thyroid Intake

To prevent or to cope with bone-riddling osteoporosis, many hypothyroid women take a calcium supplement. They often take it at the wrong time, however—along with their synthetic thyroid hormone, levothyroxine.

Results of a small sampling (three patients) motivated Christine Schneyer, MD, of the Sinai Hospital of Baltimore, the Johns Hopkins School of Medicine, to share her findings in a letter to the *Journal of the American Medical Association*.[3] The calcium supplement reduced thyroid function, as shown in an increase of thyroid-stimulating hormone (TSH) levels and symptoms of fatigue and weight gain. One patient stopped taking calcium, but continued with her thyroid hormone, and within three weeks, her TSH level declined markedly. Rather than discontinue needed calcium, the other two patients changed their supplementation pattern. They took their thyroid hormone in the morning and their calcium after lunch and dinner. This restored the effectiveness of their thyroid function. (Numerous studies demonstrate that calcium is best absorbed before bedtime.)

Dr. Schneyer also comments that simultaneous ingestion of synthetic thyroid hormone with aluminum-containing antacids, cholestyramine (a cholesterol-lowering chemical), and iron also may diminish the efficacy of the hormone. Separating the intake of calcium supplements and medicines from synthetic thyroid hormone by at least four hours should help maintain the desired level of thyroid function. Dr. Schneyer felt it necessary to share experiences of her three patients because suppression of thyroid gland efficiency by calcium and other supplements and drugs is likely to be a "widespread phenomenon."

Be Aware of the Relationship Between Synthetic Hormones and Allergies

A little-considered aspect of taking synthetic thyroid hormone is the fact that it can cause allergies in some patients, as I have observed in thirty years of practice. These allergies, often thought to be caused by foods or environmental pollutants, can be triggered by the various coloring agents included in some synthetic thyroid hormones, such as red and yellow dyes, or even by lactose (milk sugar). This is yet another argument in favor of taking a natural supplement such as Armour desiccated thyroid (see Chapter 21, for others).

Hypothyroidism May Cause Sleep Apnea

A frightening ailment, sleep apnea (the stopping of breathing during sleep, sometimes for long periods) has many causes. Rita Wittman, PhD, a sleep specialist at the University of British Columbia, reports that hypothyroidism has been found to bring on sleep apnea, in a small number of patients.[4] Dr. Wittman and associates conducted the largest retrospective study on this subject and discovered that 4.2 percent of 833 obstructive sleep apnea patients tested were found to be hypothyroid. The more extreme the condition, the more likely the person was to be hypothyroid, said Dr. Wittman.

Be Sure You're Tested for Hashimoto's Thyroiditis

Sometimes a patient will have so many symptoms that it is difficult to make an accurate diagnosis. This is especially true in the case of Hashimoto's thyroiditis.

In Hashimoto's thyroiditis, the thyroid gland is a bit enlarged, with little or no pain. However, the autoimmune system is involved, because the body unleashes antibodies against its own thyroid gland, as if it is a threatening enemy.

Hashimoto's thyroiditis runs in families, and most individuals afflicted are between the ages of thirteen and forty-three. Symptoms range from mental to physical: a faulty memory; difficulty in thinking; depression; nervousness; allergies; irregular heartbeat; palpitations; muscle and joint pains (as in fibromyalgia); disturbed sleep; wakefulness in bed while the mind races and the heart beats fast; diminished interest in sex; menstrual problems such as too little flow, too much flow, or shortened periods; frequent headaches; digestive disorders and intestinal ailments, ranging from constipation to diarrhea; and the feeling that there's a lump in the throat (a slightly swollen thyroid gland).

Many of these symptoms cause me to routinely order tests of the patient's antibodies. Sadly, most physicians don't insist on these tests, so they fail to make the proper diagnosis. If you have many such symptoms, please insist upon testing. Thyroid antibody tests should be run on anyone with chronic health problems. T4 and TSH may be normal, so they don't reveal autoimmune thyroiditis. Even a low elevation of thyroid antibodies will prompt me to start patients on a low dose of thyroid hormone, despite the fact that their blood thyroid hormone levels give a reading of normal.

In an article in the magazine *Alternative Medicine*, a leading health publication, I mentioned the case of Theodora, aged forty-three, who had a medical book full of symptoms.[5] Theodora had numerous upper respiratory infections, many sore throats, one cold that merged into another, nasal blockage, heart palpitations, irregular periods, intestinal bloating, indigestion, and alternating constipation and diarrhea, pain in joints and muscles throughout her body, headaches, and sleeplessness. Although her thyroid hormone levels were in the normal range, her level of thyroid antibodies was sky high.

As with most patients, I started her on a quarter grain of Armour natural desiccated thyroid daily and, over the next year, gradually increased it to three grains. One of her lab tests indicated she was deficient in three amino acids, as well as other nutrients: vitamin B_5 (pantothenic acid), inositol, and the mineral zinc. Instead of prescribing these individual amino acids, I had her increase her protein intake—more dairy products, lean meat, and poultry—and take a high-potency multiple vitamin and a multiple mineral formula.

I also found that Theodora had an elevated *Candida albicans* yeast infection in her intestines, so I started her on a high-complex-carbohydrate diet and had her avoid refined sugars, sweets, and fruits.

Theodora began rotating her foods so that her system did not always have to process the same foods. Through allergy testing, I determined that she was sensitive to a lengthy list of foods: kidney beans, rye grain, cheddar cheese, egg yolk, wheat, almonds, figs, and kale. She avoided these foods.

Additionally, I gave her three supplements to detoxify her intestines: grapefruit seed extract (500 mg, three times daily); acidophilus capsules (two capsules, three times daily to recolonize her intestines with friendly bacteria); and a high-potency, odor-free, garlic tablet twice daily.

Six months later, Theodora's symptoms were reduced in intensity, and, after a year, she was almost symptom free. Her energy level was much higher. For the first time in her memory, her upper respiratory infections were gone with no signs of a cold or the flu.

Her pains were so diminished that she could exercise again. Her digestion was almost normal.

Hashimoto's thyroiditis is no easy ailment to control and eliminate. It takes patience from both the patient and the doctor, because progress is slow. However, when treated correctly it improves steadily, and that can be encouraging.

32

For Doctors Only

THERE'S AN OFTEN unsuspected cause for many chronic health problems. I am referring to hypothyroidism, which affects every major organ and controls the metabolism of every cell in the body. Its symptoms are numerous and protean.

Suffice it to say that there is no clear-cut hypothyroid syndrome. The symptoms of hypothyroidism can mimic many of the physiologic disturbances we see on a day-to-day basis. To ignore the thyroid connection, however, is merely to treat our patients symptomatically and not to treat the underlying causative factors of their illnesses.

Simple examples of this are patients with recurrent infections who are chronically treated with antibiotics. These patients are frequently hypothyroid. As noted later in this chapter, this is in part due to the thyroid hormone's control of certain immune functions. I can cite many other examples, but these are included in the section on thyroid physiology.

An accurate way to diagnose hypothyroidism is by means of the Barnes Basal Temperature Test. More than a hundred years of research has established a definite relationship between subnormal temperature, no matter how slight, and hypothyroidism. Broda O. Barnes, MD, PhD, refined the test. A clinical researcher in hypothyroidism for half a century, Dr. Barnes published more than a hundred papers on his investigations in the most reputable medical journals. He has had a strong influence on my career as a physician.

Initially, I approached his work with more than a tincture of skepticism, despite the fact that full details of how he evolved the test and proved its reliability had been published in the respected *Journal of the American Medical Association.*[1]

Over several years, Dr. Barnes had correlated the basal temperature of more than two thousand individuals with metabolic rate (BMR) tests, which he had performed himself to minimize the possibility of skewing results, and with the thyroid blood chemistry results. Through the years, he found a much higher correlation of low BMR results with his patients' basal metabolic temperature than with results of any other test for hypothyroidism. In addition, many of these clinically hypothyroid patients actually had euthyroid blood tests.

Even though the basal temperature test had appeared in the *Physician's Desk Reference* for years, it initially failed to impress me. However, in the interest of fairness, I kept an open mind about the test, which is carried out as follows: Shake down a thermometer before going to bed at night and leave it on your bedside table. Immediately upon awakening in the morning, insert the thermometer snugly under your arm for ten minutes as you lie quietly in bed. Basal temperature range reading is between 97.8°F to 98.2°F. A lower temperature indicates possible hypothyroidism. The basal temperature test should be performed on two consecutive days. Women obtain the most accurate readings if not menstruating or on the second and third day of their menstrual period.

Some years ago, shortly after a long-distance telephone interview with Dr. Barnes on the medical talk show I then hosted on a San Francisco radio station, I tried the basal temperature test on myself. To my amazement, my basal temperature was low. Therefore, each day I took a small amount of natural desiccated thyroid. (Dr. Barnes and his more than one hundred followers used the natural, desiccated thyroid preparation, as I do, based on the premise that what's natural is more complete and, so, should provide better clinical results.) In a short time, my energy level increased. My ability to concentrate improved dramatically, and many minor, nagging symptoms disappeared.

Next, I began using the basal temperature test on a number of problem patients who had failed to respond to the usual medications.

When indicated, I gave them thyroid supplementation. Their quick, positive responses dissipated the last vestiges of my skepticism.

I will frequently start a new patient on thyroid therapy even if the thyroid lab work is normal, and I believe there is clinical justification to use it. Thyroid medication given to carefully screened patients is, in my experience, almost always helpful. I start all my patients on the equivalent of one-fourth to one-half grain of the Armour desiccated thyroid preparation, and increase their dosage in one-fourth grain increments every seven to fourteen days until an optimal thyroid hormone level consistent with the desired clinical results are obtained.

The dosage I use most commonly in adults is one to two grains. I have never put a patient on more than four grains of thyroid hormone per day, as in most of these patients we achieved the desired therapeutic result with the smaller dosage.

During the time my patients are titrated with a thyroid preparation, I have them check their basal temperatures regularly. I also retest their thyroid hormone levels regularly. I refrain from increasing their dosage if their basal temperature goes above 98.2°F, if their resting heartbeat is above 85 per minute, if on history they relate episodes of either constant jitteriness or palpitations, or if their lab results indicate they're taking too much thyroid.

Fortunately, these symptoms are rarely encountered. Once my patients are receiving an optimal dose of the thyroid hormone and they are symptomatically improved, I see them a minimum of once every one to three months for a year to make sure they are still doing well clinically. In most instances the use of thyroid medication alone is sufficient to correct many of the symptoms I will discuss. The hormonal effects are greatly amplified by the judicious use of applied clinical nutrition.

The main complaint I encounter from physicians is that the basal temperature test is unscientific; they feel that hypothyroidism can be diagnosed only by the standard laboratory blood work. That is exactly what I once thought. Now the basal temperature test is invariably the starting point of my four-pronged diagnostic approach that includes basal temperature, clinical symptoms, medical history, and blood chemistry.

Today, the vast majority of physicians rely heavily on results of blood tests for diagnosing thyroid function, perhaps too heavily. I make this statement because many of my patients—and those of Dr. Barnes—have been declared euthyroid by blood tests and proved to be conclusively hypothyroid according to the basal temperature test, symptoms, and medical history.

A Mayo Clinic study by Joseph C. Scott Jr., MD, and Elizabeth Mussey, MD, determined that the diagnosis of thyroid function should be done carefully and judiciously to avoid errors.[2] A patient considered to be mildly hypothyroid by one doctor may be regarded as euthyroid by a second physician, if conclusions are based on just one interview or test.

"No single test procedure will define the status of the thyroid gland," they write. "Further, any combination of methods may lead to erroneous interpretation or to inconsistent results. The clinician must have the faculty of correlating the clinical appearance of the patient with laboratory findings."

The subtle development of hypothyroidism, too, makes diagnosis difficult; this is graphically reported in an article by Mark Gold, MD, H. Rowland Pearsall, MD, and A. Carter Pottash, MD, in *Diagnosis*.[3] Dr. Gold and his associates studied 250 consecutive inpatients admitted to a psychiatric hospital for evaluation and discovered that an often undetected cause of depression is hypothyroidism, whose symptoms overlap those of depression. They stated that thyroid hypofunction first appears in subclinical form (grade three) manifested by decreased energy and depressed mood. Next, the condition deteriorates to mild hypothyroidism (grade two) whose symptoms are fatigue, dry skin, and constipation. Blood levels of thyroid hormone are usually still normal, however. Then comes overt hypothyroidism (grade one), which presents the classical signs: a measurable decrease in circulating thyroid hormone, extreme weakness, dry skin, coarsening of hair, constipation, lethargy, memory impairment, a sensation of cold, slowed speech, and weight gain.

"It is not correct to say that hypothyroidism is present or absent; rather, there are grades of thyroid function," write the doctors. They conclude that one of every ten patients with initial complaints of depressed mood or decreased energy may have subclinical hypothyroidism.

"In our experience, thyroid hormone replacement is more effective therapy for such patients than antidepressant drugs," they state.

These physicians stress the need for careful evaluation of depressed patients who have not responded to conventional treatment to determine if they are suffering from either hyperthyroidism or hypothyroidism.

Hypothyroidism is often such an extremely subtle disease that physicians misinterpret its symptoms, states Gerald S. Levey, MD, an endocrinologist and the vice chancellor of medical sciences and dean of the David Geffen School of Medicine at UCLA, in a journal article, "Hypothyroidism: A Treacherous Masquerader."[4]

The correct diagnosis is frequently missed, because a broad range of symptoms is generally not associated with hypothyroidism, he says: musculoskeletal disorders such as severe muscle cramps, particularly at night; long-standing low back pain; hematologic disturbances (one-third to one-half of hypothyroids show some loss of blood cell mass, resulting in anemia); coagulability ailments (easy bruising, minor bleeding, and menorrhagia); rheumatologic conditions (stiffness, arthralgias, and paresthesias in hands and feet with accent on stiffness, rather than pain); myalgic complaints and synovial effusions, mainly in the knees; hyperuricemia; and a decrease in heart muscle contractility.

These conditions can be improved or reversed with thyroid hormone replacement, he says. Regarding routine screening for thyroid function, Dr. Levey states that this would not be cost effective, inasmuch as numerous factors, among them drugs and systemic states, affect such tests.

In my opinion, it is prudent for physicians with chronically ill patients who present with persistently low basal temperatures to consider using thyroid hormone replacement therapy before using toxic drugs and irreversible surgical procedures.

The importance of thyroid function to good health should not be underestimated. The thyroid gland is the largest endocrine gland in the human body. It weighs less than an ounce, secretes less than a teaspoon of hormone a year, and controls the metabolic activity of all of our cells. As Dr. Barnes said, "Cellular health depends on three factors, a steady supply of nutrients, oxygen, and thyroid hormones." The thyroid hormones stimulate oxidative metabolism, thereby increasing the oxygen consumption of every cell.

Thyroid hormone also stimulates protein synthesis; that is, the buildup of protein from amino acids. Protein is necessary for replacing worn-out cells and for the manufacture of enzymes, which moderate the speed at which biochemical reactions take place within the cells. Thyroid hormone potentiates the effect of other body hormones such as adrenaline, is necessary for the secretion of the sex-activating hormones such as the gonadotrophins of the pituitary gland, and is, in large part, responsible for controlling the rate of absorption of nutrients in the gastrointestinal tract.

In hypothyroidism, blood cholesterol and triglycerides are higher than average, a condition often predictive of cardiovascular disorders. Thyroid supplementation causes them to decrease.

Thyroid hormone is partly responsible for production of a compound known as *retinine*, essential for visual acuity at night. It is also necessary for the synthesis or activation of specific enzymatic proteins within cells and for the translation and transcription of nucleic acids. The major sites of thyroid hormone activity are the cell membranes, mitochondria, ribosomes, and nuclei.

Thyroid hormone stimulates both the sodium pump and the glycolytic pathways, leading to oxidative phosphorylation in tissues such as the liver, kidneys, and muscles.

Hypothyroids characteristically have thick and puffy skin, due to an accumulation of a mucinlike substance called *hyaluronic acid*, which binds water. The most frequent complaint of such patients is that they accumulate fluid. Powerful diuretics rid the body of this substance, but it returns as soon as the water pills are discontinued. Low-thyroid individuals are usually the patients who can't lose weight unless they subject their bodies to the rigors of spas, exercise, and a low-calorie diet.

The swollen features of hypothyroids are characteristically non-pitting fluid accumulations around the eyes, hands, ankles, and feet. The skin is usually pale and cool, as a result of generalized blood vessel constriction. Low-thyroid patients often complain of an inability to sweat even in great heat, and of being cold all the time. Their skin is often dry and coarse, because of decreased secretion of the sebaceous glands. As a result of diminished blood supply and decreased skin metabolism, their wounds heal slowly. This is particularly true in diabetics, many of whom tend to be hypothyroid.

Low-thyroid patients will frequently have severe hair loss. In the differential diagnosis of alopecia, hypothyroidism should always be a prime suspect. Nails grow slowly, tend to be weak and brittle, and are usually striated both longitudinally and transversely.

The hypothyroid patient's heart is characterized by a low stroke volume and decreased cardiac output. To compensate for this, the body increases blood vessel resistance in the skin, resulting in the coolness and pallor already described. There may also be a compensatory increase in blood pressure and this, coupled with an increased cholesterol and triglyceride level, often predisposes the patients to a greater incidence of coronary artery disease.

Hypothyroidism may also cause EKG and blood chemistry changes mimicking heart attacks and other cardiovascular disorders. The most common electrocardiographic changes are flattening or inversion of the T-wave, particularly in lead 2, along with generalized low P-wave, QRS, and T-wave amplitude. Nonspecific T-wave flattening and sinus bradycardia are frequently seen.

Cerebral blood flow and oxygen consumption may be decreased in hypothyroidism. Renal and glomerular blood flow is slightly decreased.

The digestive changes in the low-thyroid patient are quite common and reflect the general sluggishness of every tissue, cell, and organ. The hypothyroid's common problems are loss of appetite with either no weight loss or an actual weight increase and decreased peristaltic activity of all gastrointestinal cells, often resulting in chronic constipation.

Gaseous distention is another frequent complaint. Should this be accompanied by colicky pain, indigestion, and vomiting, it may be mistaken for a mechanical ileus or other related GI problems, and result in unnecessary surgery.

In certain cases, hypothyroidism may also contribute to an inability of the stomach to secrete enough acid for proper digestion, causing a general inability to reabsorb and utilize the essential nutrients calcium and vitamin B_{12}. It has been estimated that true pernicious anemia occurs in 12 percent of the hypothyroid population.

Serum chemistry determinations of SGOT, LDH, and CPK are frequently increased in hypothyroidism. These blood chemistries will generally return to normal in two to four weeks after thyroid hormone therapy is begun. They are thought to represent changes in enzyme metabolism and not hepatic or cardiovascular damage. Serum amylase levels may likewise be increased. This is often accompanied by a decrease in gallbladder motility. All too frequently gallbladder disease is diagnosed in these cases, and may again result in unnecessary surgery.

The digestive change in hypothyroidism may, in many cases, leave an investigating clinician with a false sense that GI absorption is normal or even increased, due to the fact that decreased absorption is often offset by a decrease in the patient's intestinal motility.

Neurologically, the hypothyroid individual often suffers decreased circulation to the brain, which may contribute to a generalized slowing of all intellectual functions, including speech. These persons frequently lack initiative and may even be described as slow-witted. Memory frequently appears impaired, with a decrease in the powers of retention and desire to think, and, frequently, an increased level of irritability. Reasoning power, however, is generally good. Questions may be answered slowly but with enthusiasm. Sleepiness is another common symptom.

Behavior in the hypothyroid patient may run the gamut from hyperactivity to lethargy, depending on how he or she responds to profound mental fatigue. Hypothyroidism should always be considered in the differential diagnosis of children who are hyperactive. Low-thyroid patients are often classified psychiatrically as paranoid personalities or depressive types. Thyroid hormone therapy has been studied intensively in depressed patients.

Hypothyroid individuals show a characteristic electroencephalogram: abnormally flat, low voltage or lacking alpha waves. They may therefore be diagnosed as suffering from a primary brain dysfunction or neurological disorder. Such EEG changes will generally revert to normal once the patients are treated with thyroid hormone. In severe cases of hypothyroidism, patients may be predisposed to epileptic seizure. Hypothyroidism should always be included in any differential diagnosis of epilepsy.

Many low-thyroid patients complain of night blindness. This condition is generally caused by a deficiency of the vitamin A–metabolized retinine A, which requires thyroid hormone for its generation, and is generally reversible following the administration of vitamin A and thyroid hormone.

Slurred speech and hoarseness are likewise found occasionally in hypothyroidism, due to a buildup of mucopolysaccharides in the tongue and the larynx.

Vertigo, sensory neural hearing loss, and Ménière's disease may also accompany hypothyroidism. Dry ears often occur because of decreased activity of the cerumen glands. Sore throats, dysphagia, nasal congestion, and headaches are likewise frequent.

Women are particularly vulnerable to undetected hypothyroidism. Complaints of diminished libido and menstrual irregularities such as menorrhagia and metrorrhagia are common, as are menstrual cramping and amenorrhea. As a result, these women may be subjected to unnecessary D & Cs as well as hysterectomies.

Hypothyroidism in the prepubertal girl may be associated with delayed growth or delay of menarche, and, if prolonged, may give rise to premature vaginal bleeding and premature breast development.

Diagnosis of hypothyroidism during pregnancy is essential, inasmuch as animal studies and clinical investigations strongly indicate that thyroid hormone is essential to normal fetal brain development. It is likewise essential to rule out hypothyroidism in patients with either chronic undiagnosed infertility or multiple miscarriages, as first-trimester fetal loss in hypothyroidism is common, approaching 50 percent or more in certain studies.

Thyroid hormone deficiency in the prepubertal male may result in delayed gonadal development, delayed sexual maturation, and, in the adult, a decrease in sperm count and sperm motility. Men with decreased sperm motility who have hypothyroidism diagnosed as the underlying causative factor should never be treated with human chorionic gonadotropin (HCG) or testosterone unless hypothyroidism has been effectively ruled out and the symptoms persist despite a year or more of adequate hormone replacement. Premature use of androgen therapy in the preadolescent may mask or further delay the onset of normal puberty. The most common complaint of the hypothyroid adult male involving the reproductive system is a general diminution of sex drive and libido. Suspect hypothyroidism in anyone who complains of a diminished libido.

Carbohydrate metabolism in hypothyroidism is characterized by a decreased release of glycerol from adipose tissue, diminished glucose absorption, and a decreased availability of amino acids and glycerol for gluconeogenesis. There is also frequently a characteristic flat glucose tolerance curve in these people because of their inability to absorb glucose from the GI tract.

In addition, a high serum amylase level is found in severely hypothyroid patients and is considered to reflect chronic pancreatitis. The mechanism is thought to be related to hypothermia, which is known to be a cause of pancreatitis. Thus, diabetes mellitus, which has long been attributed to an insulin imbalance, should, by definition, encompass a concept of generalized pancreatic insufficiency, which may be due in no small part to chronic hypothyroidism and superimposed nutritional imbalances, leading to a breakdown of pancreas production of bicarbonate, secretion of proteolytic enzymes, and insulin production.

The possible mechanism of diabetes and the chronic metabolic disturbances of pancreatic insufficiency caused by an unsuspected hypothyroid condition have been elucidated by William H. Philpott, MD, in his book *Victory over Diabetes*, in the following terms: Hypothyroidism (1) → gives rise to pancreatitis → gives rise to pancreatic insufficiency, which results in insufficiency of proteolytic enzymes, → gives rise to amino acid deficiencies → contributing to greater deficiency of proteolytic enzymes which are manufactured from amino acids; (2) decreases the quality and quantity of insulin, which is, in fact, built from amino acids; (3) decreases lipase activity → gives rise to increased fatty acids in the blood → increased arteriosclerosis and heart disease; (4) increases absorption through the gut of poorly digested protein particles → yields kinin or inflammatory reactions in body tissues and organs, giving possible rise to atherosclerosis and/or severe mental changes, if the reactions take place in the brain, and also an increased absorption of circulating blood lipids into the arterial intima, possibly resulting in arteriosclerotic plaque; (5) decreases the production of pancreatic bicarbonate, which is necessary for the alkaline medium of the small intestine → giving rise to metabolic acidosis after meals, since the pancreatic bicarbonate or HCO_3 has not neutralized the stomach acid as it empties into the duodenum → giving rise to further effective reduction of any pancreatic proteolytic enzymes, as they require an alkaline medium in the small intestine to function best.

More than 80 percent of insulin-dependent diabetics had abnormal output of proteolytic enzymes, and most diabetics of more than five years' duration had an abnormal bicarbonate secretory response.

Drug metabolism is frequently changed in hypothyroidism. Such drugs as Digoxin are increased in the plasma, due to an increase in the half-life caused by a decreased glomerular filtration, as well as a decrease in peripheral metabolism. Drug therapy in hypothyroid patients should be undertaken with particular judiciousness. In fact, caution should be exercised with any patient, because so much hidden hypothyroidism exists.

Decreased thyroid function retards growth and delays maturation of the skeletal system, and this can be largely prevented or corrected by administration of the desiccated thyroid preparation.

Hypothyroid patients may complain of vague muscular and articular pains as well as coldness and stiffness of the extremities that resemble fibrositis and rheumatoid arthritis. Clinically, they may present with a laxity of the ligament capsules and tendons, causing joint instability, aching on motion, joint stiffness, and pain. Symptoms are often worse in the morning or after immobilization and are exacerbated by cold and dampness. Infrequently, the hypothyroid patient presenting with musculoskeletal problems is found to have the characteristic articular deterioration of the person who has rheumatoid arthritis.

One study of hypothyroid patients in regard to the musculoskeletal system shows that nine of eleven test subjects had generalized osteoporosis. Another study revealed that 10 percent of persons with low thyroid function had an increased incidence of carpal tunnel syndrome. There tends to be an increased uric acid level in hypothyroid patients with musculoskeletal problems and generally an increase in their sedimentation rate, so these lab studies, although abnormal, may be misleading.

Muscle condition in hypothyroids may differ appreciably, from normal strength and firm to weak and flabby. Transient pain, stiffness, and cramps—frequent complaints—are often due to mineral imbalances caused by this ailment.

A high percentage of hypothyroid patients suffer from iron-deficiency anemia. The hypoplastic anemia of the low-thyroid patient is brought about by decreased production of circulating blood cells as an adaptive response to decreased tissue oxygen needs. In other words, diminished tissue oxygen consumption gives rise to a decrease in tissue hypoxia, which is a normal trigger for erythropoetin, which, under normal circumstances, increases the number of circulating red blood cells. There is, therefore, a decrease in iron turnover.

This type of anemia strongly resembles an adaptive anemia and the protein-calorie malnutrition that is frequently superimposed on it, and may further cloud the clinical picture. In general, though, the hypoplastic anemia of hypothyroidism is mild, with hemoglobin levels about 9 grams per 100 mls. A hemoglobin below 9 should cause suspicion that the anemia of the hypothyroid patient is perhaps superimposed on another type of anemia.

Environmental factors play a large role in thyroid functioning. Sulfonamide drugs have a potent antithyroid effect, as do all antidiabetic drugs. These inhibit the formation of thyroid hormone by inhibiting iodine uptake. Adrenal corticosteroids, too, have a depressing effect on thyroid function. Again, corticosteroids, prednisone, and the like should be used judiciously in the patient with known hypothyroidism or with a suspected hypothyroid condition.

Defining hypothyroidism as purely an endocrine dysfunction is myopic in that the primary problem may not be in the glandular secretions themselves, but rather due to impaired cell surface binding, so that the physiology of these cells is abnormal even with a normal range of thyroid hormone.

In addition, different tissue types often have different responses to the same level of thyroid hormone so that, due to biochemical individuality, a thyroid hormone level within normal limits may be adequate for the smooth physiological function of a person's skeletal muscle but inadequate for optimal cardiac physiology. Also, the symptoms of subclinical hypothyroidism such as chronic fatigue, depression, mild anemias, inability to lose weight, and the like, may be easily mistaken for a host of other disorders and written off as neurotic or psychosomatic complaints.

Thyroid hormone is secreted into the bloodstream predominantly bound to three proteins: thyroid-binding protein, thyroid-binding-prealbumin, and albumin. Only a minuscule percentage of the thyroid hormone is active at the peripheral tissues in a free form. It is therefore possible, because of biochemical individuality, for the body to have an adequate total output of thyroid hormone but to be hypothyroid, because more than the optimal amount of hormone for a particular individual is bound by protein and therefore inactive. It is also possible, because of the liver's role in the T4 to T3 conversion, to have an over- or underconversion of T4 as a result of liver function. Patients with conditions such as hepatitis or the nephrotic syndrome will often have an accompanying thyroid dysfunction. In short, there is a difference in the output of thyroid by the gland and the level of activity of that hormone.

It is probably true that the parameters of normal that we now use in the diagnosis of thyroid illness are not wide enough to pick up the vast amount of hypothyroid pathology that exists. Some researchers suggest that the lower unit of the total T4 range be around 65 to 70 mcg per liter rather than the present 50, because of what was found to be a five times greater prevalence of hypothyroidism at the level of 65 mcg. This same determination has been made with all other commonly measured parameters of thyroid hormone with the same results.

It is apparent, therefore, that the blood test criteria for thyroid disease should never be the be-all or end-all in the diagnosis of hypothyroidism but rather just one parameter.

Elsewhere in this book, it was explained that the body's basal temperature is one of the most sensitive indicators of thyroid hypofunction. It is therefore clinically more accurate than blood tests in those patients whose symptoms are highly indicative of low thyroid but whose blood work says otherwise.

In accordance with research by biochemist Dr. Jeffrey Bland's group, there are certain other blood test criteria to corroborate the hypothyroid diagnosis with the Barnes Basal Temperature Test: (1) cholesterol in excess of 252; (2) a triglyceride level greater than 200; (3) a total CPK level above 30; (4) a BUN-to-creatinine ratio less than 12; (5) an LDH level greater than 40; (6) a cholesterol-to-HDL level greater than 5; and (7) an increased B-2 fraction in lipoprotein electrophoresis.

Pharmacologic doses of estrogen depress the secretion of thyroid hormone by suppressing TSH. This is very important in the population of women on oral contraceptive pills. Dr. Barnes's research indicated that many women who are taking birth control pills develop cardiovascular difficulties because of their underactive thyroid conditions and not as a result of the side effects of the birth control medication itself.

The biologic reducing agents cystine and glutathione can markedly inhibit the thyroid gland's function. Cystine and glutathione are two of the major components of the glucose tolerance factor molecule, which is necessary for carbohydrate metabolism.

The B vitamin PABA, if taken in large doses, has an inhibitory effect on the thyroid gland.

The cyanide molecule is a potent inhibitor of the thyroid. Cigarette smoking can increase the body's concentration of certain cyanide-containing molecules. So cigarette smoking, in addition to all the other things we know about, can, in some cases, cause a fairly powerful inhibition of the thyroid gland.

Whatever pollutants diminish thyroid gland function, the TSH test, as originally structured, can no longer be a solo act in diagnosing or evaluating the status of the thyroid gland. Sadly, the range of normal TSH values—0.4–6.0 IU/ml—in most labs is very often misleading.

My conviction, backed by many decades of clinical experience, indicates that chronically ill patients who present with symptoms of hypothyroidism have a TSH above 2.0 and have no contraindications to thyroid replacement. Therefore, I start them on 15 mg/day (one-quarter grain) of desiccated thyroid, increasing the dose in 15 mg increments biweekly.

Be sure to repeat the TSH levels test with every 30 mg increase in dosage. If the TSH is 0.8–1.0 and the patient is clinically improved, I keep her or him on thyroid therapy and work to optimize other health aspects—nutritional status, bowel function, immune status, physical/cardiovascular status, and endocrine gland status.

Additionally, I often recommend that my patients buy a glucometer to check their blood sugar levels when they become symptomatic and periodically to check for hypoglycemia, prediabetes, or diabetes.

Have your patients get a fasting glucose level upon arising, then after a substantial breakfast, repeat glucose checks at thirty minutes, one hour, and each hour up to six hours after eating. During this period, patients eat no other food unless they feel they can't make it. Then they should eat.

Perhaps many of your patients, like mine, are prediabetic and/or hypoglycemic and should be treated accordingly. Throughout this book, I have stressed that I almost always start my patients with natural Armour desiccated thyroid. This contains physiological amounts of T4/T3, as well as T1 and T2. I feel that the latter two play an important role in overall thyroid functioning.

However, there are patients who, for many reasons, do better clinically on a combination of desiccated thyroid and synthetic T3 and/or T4. This is the art of medicine, which must be finessed based on your clinical experience as a physician and how the patient responds to thyroid therapy. I'm not locked into strictly natural thyroid but prefer to provide whatever combination of thyroid remedies is necessary to achieve a desired clinical response.

On a related subject, it is important to call your attention to a little-considered possible cause of hypothyroidism and hyperthyroidism: free radicals generated by oxidative stress in the body. Such conditions may themselves become free radical generators, a potential risk to the viability of every cell in the body.

Overproduction of free radicals has been tied to the most devastating degenerative diseases, among them myocardial infarction, arteriosclerosis, peripheral artery disease, diabetes, metabolic syndrome, autism, arthritis, chronic obstructive pulmonary disease, Alzheimer's disease, cancer, and chronic skin disease. The list is endless.

Fortunately, a new and noninvasive test is being introduced that diagnoses and monitors, via a simple dipstick, the presence of abnormal amounts of toxic free radicals. Known as the Wellness Index, the test measures the level of a biomarker called *isoprostane*, which is generated by the oxidation of fatty acids anywhere in the body. More information about isoprostane and the Wellness Index can be found online at www.thyroidmd.com.

These fatty acids are particularly concentrated in cellular membranes, where oxidation can compromise the viability of a cell and may, if serious enough, cause either mutations in cellular DNA or even cellular death. Knowing the patient's Wellness Index is, therefore, more important for total health and well-being than any other biomarker in the body. Isoprostane research is taking place all over the world, and, at this writing, there are nearly two thousand published papers in scientific and medical journals attesting to its importance as "the gold standard" measurement for oxidative stress.

For the first time in medical history, a noninvasive, inexpensive test provides a precise measurement of free radicals in the patient's system. The information gleaned from knowing a patient's Wellness Index will catapult medicine into the next century.

As a clinician, you will be able to know precisely the total free radical load of your patients and be able to determine the efficacy of nutritional/antioxidant therapies to neutralize free radicals.

Prior to this, even the most motivated practitioner could only guess the extent of damage occurring on the cellular level. You can secure more detailed information at www.thyroidmd.com. I recommend that you, as a clinician, use the Wellness Index in conjunction with all of your other valuable diagnostic tests to insure the optimal health and well-being of your patients.

There is a small subset of patients with diagnosed hypothyroidism and/or Hashimotos's thyroiditis, who are exquisitely sensitive to any amount—even the smallest—of thyroid replacement therapy from natural or synthetic. Many of these diagnosed patients suffer needlessly—sometimes for years—because they cannot tolerate thyroid medication in any form.

They are often told they're stressed out or called hysterical complainers and are inappropriately recommended for psychotherapy—or worse, placed on psychotropic antidepressant medication to bury the symptoms of what is primarily a thyroid dysfunction.

Virtually 100 percent of these patients can experience a remarkable recovery when placed on a water-based solution of thyroid hormone. The exact treatment protocol differs from patient to patient. However, when patients are placed on a tiny dose of liquid thyroid that can be increased gradually over time, most of them can achieve and tolerate the more traditional pill form of therapeutic thyroid hormone level that insures optimal health.

As a thyroidologist for many decades, I am pleased to have had the opportunity to share my clinical findings with you!

33

Conclusion

Solved: The Riddle of Illness has established that hypothyroidism and Hashimoto's thyroiditis are the two most common undiagnosed causes of chronic medical problems in the United States today. Sadly, undertreatment of diagnosed hypothyroidism and Hashimoto's thyroiditis is also widespread. These patients have been placed on thyroid medication, and when their levels of thyroid hormones and the TSH are somewhere in the normal range, they are told they're on adequate doses of thyroid hormones.

This is often far from the truth, and these unfortunate people often suffer unnecessarily for years with many of the same symptoms (although less extreme) and are often dismissed with such remarks as, "It's all in your head," "Go home and live with it," "You're depressed," "You're under stress," "It's just middle age," "This happens to the elderly," or "Everyone has the same complaints." Even worse, some are started on antidepressants or tranquilizers—a practice not unlike removing a flashing red light from your car's dashboard and feeling that the mechanical problem indicated has been solved.

There are a few important scenarios to consider if you're already being treated for hypothyroidism or Hashimoto's thyroiditis but still have many of the same symptoms you had before.

1. You're not getting enough thyroid hormone. Most doctors monitor your medical progress by taking a blood level of TSH (thyroid-stimulating hormone), the normal range of which in many labs is 0.4–5.5.

Too often, a post-treatment TSH level anywhere within normal limits is considered acceptable. TSH is produced by the pituitary gland and controls the output of thyroid hormones. The higher the blood level of thyroid hormone—from your own thyroid gland and from what the doctor has given you—the lower the TSH level. Many patients don't begin to feel well until their TSH levels are at the low end of the normal range and they are on higher doses of thyroid medication.

So, if your symptoms persist, and your TSH is in the high-normal range, it's not "all in your head." You may still be undertreated and should work with your physician to increase the level of your thyroid supplementation.

2. Your TSH is in the low-normal range, but you're still suffering with symptoms. Many patients in this category are being treated with synthetic T4 only, and are not getting the therapeutic benefit of T3 found in the natural hormone. In such cases, I slowly change patients' medication to natural thyroid. Remember this conversion: 0.1 mg of T4 equals one grain (60 mg) of natural thyroid.

3. If you're on an adequate dose of natural thyroid and still have symptoms, make sure you're taking the brand name thyroid—Armour (my favorite), Westhroid, or NaturThroid—as generic thyroid.

4. If your thyroid condition is sufficiently treated and you're still having symptoms, you're probably suffering from another problem.

Remember, it's always best to have your thyroid medication adjusted in conjunction with a complete holistic medical evaluation, including nutritional status, food and environmental allergy evaluation, bowel function, environmental toxicity, and adrenal gland status, as well as a complete history and physical evaluation.

5. If nothing seems to work, get a fresh point of view by seeking a second opinion to rule out a wide range of other body/mind imbalances that can keep you from experiencing complete wellness.

The best of health to you!

Afterword

THERE ARE ALWAYS some people whose symptoms seem to indicate hypothyroidism but whose physical exam, clinical lab results, and Barnes Basal Temperature Test are all within normal limits.

You may be one of them. Should you then consult your nearest psychiatrist? The answer is, "Possibly." We all have unfinished business psychologically. In certain instances, these problems may be converted into physical complaints. A purely psychological diagnosis is always one of exclusion. I will never tell a patient, "It's all in your mind," before attempting to rule out as many of the unsuspected causes of illness as I can, because—let's face it—a psychiatric diagnosis follows you around forever. Unfortunately, there are no recovered schizophrenics in the eyes of many employers. Once you've had a "nervous breakdown," you're always suspect by the narrow minds that pass uneducated judgment about everything.

The following are the main unsuspected causes of illness that I have encountered professionally. These should be checked into if the thyroid solution discussed in the book does not solve your own particular clinical problems.

A major unsuspected cause of clinical problems is food and environmental allergies. These allergies, beyond any doubt, mimic most of the disorders discussed elsewhere in this book. If treatment of patients' hypothyroidism, coupled with an optimal nutritional program, is not getting the proper clinical results, I always test them for food and environmental allergies and sensitivities or refer them to a physician who specializes exclusively in this area.

Candida albicans is an insidious yeast infection, which is growing in epidemic proportions. It affects mainly women in their childbearing years but can strike anyone—even infants. It assumes a wide variety of symptoms and can cause untold distress. Common major symptoms of chronic yeast infection include fatigue, poor memory, "spacy" feelings, depression, joint swelling or pain, constipation, diarrhea, bloating, impotence, endometriosis, and premenstrual tension.

Candida victims can fight back by using a combination of diet, food supplements, and drugs. You may obtain more information about yeast infections and how to deal with them by reading *The Yeast Connection* by William G. Crook, published by Professional Books, P.O. Box 3494, Jackson, TN 38301.

Adrenal exhaustion is a condition that may preclude substantive improvement of your symptoms. Your own nutritionally oriented physician may be able to help strengthen your adrenals by placing you on a small amount of hydrocortisone (5 mg four times a day, after meals and at bedtime). This regimen has been clinically tested for many decades by William McKendree Jeffries, MD, and I urge you to have your doctor read Professor Jeffries' book, *Safe Uses of Cortisone,* published by Charles C Thomas, which documents why and how to use cortisone to help restore you to peak health.

Last but certainly not least is malnutrition—imbalances in one or more of the dozens of essential nutrients without which your body cannot stay healthy. There are literally hundreds of available tests to ascertain your nutrition status that are virtually never used. If your health complaints persist, see a specialist in nutritional medicine who can help you unravel this complex but vital path to health and wellness. More information can be found on my Web site at www.thyroidmd.com.

Notes

Chapter 1

1. Rubin, Herman H., *Glands, Sex, and Personality* (New York: Wilfred Funk, Inc., 1952), 36.
2. Berman, Louis, *The Glands Regulating Personality* (New York: The Macmillan Company, 1921), 55.
3. Scott, J. C., Jr., and Elizabeth Mussey, "Menstrual Patterns in Myxedema," *American Journal of Obstetrics and Gynecology* 90 (1965): 161.
4. Stone, B., *American Medical News*, May 23, 1980.
5. Pinckney, E. R., "The Accuracy and Significance of Medical Testing," *Archives of Internal Medicine* 143, no. 3 (March 1983): 512.
6. Jackson, A. S., "Hypothyroidism," *Journal of the American Medical Association* (1957): 121–65.
7. Williams, Roger J., *Free and Unequal* (Austin, TX: University of Texas Press, 1953), 19.
8. Wren, J. C., "Thyroid Function and Coronary Atherosclerosis," *Journal of the American Geriatric Society* 16 (1968): 696–704.
9. Levey, Gerald S., "Hypothyroidism: A Treacherous Masquerader," *Acute Care Medicine* (May 1984), 34–36.

Chapter 2

1. News Story, University of Mississippi Medical Center, Jackson, MS, May 1983.
2. Williams, Roger J., *Free and Unequal* (Austin, TX: University of Texas Press, 1953), 19.
3. Masor, Nathan, *The New Psychiatry* (New York: Philosophical Library, 1959), 99–100.
4. Ibid., 102, 103.
5. Ibid., 105.
6. "Age and the Thyroid Gland," *Prevention* (August 1971): 166.

Chapter 3

1. Raloff, Janet, "Geologically Induced Goiters," *Science News* (May 3, 1986).
2. Ibid.
3. *The Encyclopedia of Common Diseases* (Emmaus, PA: Rodale Press, 1976): 754–55.
4. Raloff, Janet, "Goiter? Do You Eat Millet?" *Science News* (May 3, 1986).

Chapter 4

1. Block, Gladys, "Fruit, Vegetables and Cancer Prevention: A Review of Epidemiological Evidence," *Nutrition and Cancer* 18 (1992): 1–29.
2. Malter, M., "Natural Killer Cells, Vitamins and Other Blood Components of Vegetarian and Omniverous Men," *Nutrition and Cancer* 12, no. 3 (1989): 271–78.
3. Snowdon, David, "Study of Seventh Day Adventist Diet," *American Journal of Public Health* 75 (May 1985): 507.
4. Jennings, Isobel, *Vitamins in Endocrine Metabolism* (Springfield, IL: Charles C Thomas, 1970), 41.
5. Ibid.
6. Ibid., 45.
7. Ibid., 65.
8. Ibid.
9. Ibid.
10. Ibid., 75.
11. Ibid., 80.
12. Ibid., 69.
13. Ibid.
14. Raloff, Janet, "From Muscle Strength to Immunity, Scientists Find New Vitamin D Benefits," *Science News* (October 9, 2004): 232–33.
15. Chang, Kenneth, "Unsolved Mystery: Sunshine Hits Dimmer Switch on Earth," *New York Times*, May 12, 2004.
16. Perkins, Sid, "Dim View: Darkening Skies a Regional Phenomenon," *Science News* 168 (September 24, 2005): 196.

Chapter 5

1. Bunevicius, Robertas, et al., "Effects of Thyroxine Compared with Thyroxine Plus Triiodythyronine in Patients with Hypothyroidism," *New England Journal of Medicine* 340 (February 11, 1999).

2. Ridha, Arem, *The Thyroid Solution* (New York: Ballantine Books, 1999), 244.
3. Schachter, Michael, "The Diagnosis and Treatment of Hypothyroidism," Health World Online, www.healthy.net.
4. Shomon, Mary, "Research Finds Most Patients Feel Better with Addition of T3, Not Levothyroxine (Synthroid) Alone," About.com Guide to Thyroid Disease, February 12, 1999, www.thyroid.about.com.

Chapter 6
1. *The Complete Book of Vitamins* (Emmaus, PA: Rodale Press, 1976), 507.
2. Ibid., 507, 508.
3. *The Encyclopedia of Common Diseases* (Emmaus, PA: Rodale Press, 1976), 44.
4. Marshall, Noel K., "A Chilling Effect," *Psychology Today* (February 1982): 92.
5. Ibid.
6. Sokoloff, Boris, *Middle Age Is What You Make It* (Garden City, NY: Garden City Publishing Company, 1942), 124.
7. Atkins, E., "Fever—New Perspectives on an Old Phenomenon," *New England Journal of Medicine* 308, no. 16 (April 21, 1983): 958.
8. Ibid.
9. Ibid., 958, 959.
10. Ibid., 959.
11. Barnes, Broda O., and Lawrence Galton, *Hypothyroidism: The Unsuspected Illness* (New York: Thomas Y. Crowell Company, 1976), 102.

Chapter 7
1. Curtis, A. H., and John W. Huffman, *A Textbook of Gynecology* (London: W. B. Saunders Company, 1950), 148.
2. Taylor, E. S., *Essentials of Gynecology* (Philadelphia: Lea & Febiger, 1969), 462.
3. *The Thyroid Gland* (Chicago: Armour Laboratories, 1945), 71.
4. Ylostalou, P., et al., "Amenorrhea with Low Normal Thyroid Function and Thyroxine Treatment," *International Journal of Gynecological Obstetrics* 18, no. 3 (1980): 176–80.
5. Matveeva, L. S., "Effect of Thyroliberin on the Prolactin Level in the Blood Serum of Primary Hypothyroid Patients," *Problems of Endocrinology* 26, no. 5 (1980): 15–22.

6. Vonderhaar, B. K., and A. E. Greco, "Lobulo-Alveolar Development of Mouse Mammary Glands Is Regulated by Thyroid Hormones," *Endocrinology* 104, no. 2 (February 1979): 409–18.
7. Barnes, Broda O., and Lawrence Galton, *Hypothyroidism: The Unsuspected Illness* (New York: Thomas Y. Crowell, 1976), 135.
8. Novak, Emil, *Gynecology and Female Endocrinology* (Boston: Little Brown and Company, 1941), 465.
9. Barnes, Broda O., "Making the Pill Safer with Thyroid," Federation Proceedings 29 (March 1970): 2.

Chapter 8

1. Webster-Barnes Foundation Conference on Thyroid, Dallas, June 6, 7, 8, 1980.
2. Ibid.
3. Ibid.
4. Ibid.
5. Ibid.
6. Aakvaag, A., et al., "Hormonal Changes in Serum in Young Men During Prolonged Physical Stress," *European Journal of Applied Physiology* 39, no. 4 (October 20, 1978): 283–91.
7. Werner, Sidney C., and Sidney H. Ingar, eds., *The Thyroid* (New York: Harper & Row, 1965), 765.
8. Singer, Peter A., "Effects of Hypothyroidism and Hyperthyroidism on Sexual Function," *Medical Aspects of Human Sexuality* 15, no. 8 (August 1981): 56R.

Chapter 9

1. Izakson, Orna, "Pesticides Causing Infertility in the Heartland," *E/The Environmental Magazine*, April 2004.
2. Wong, W. Y., et al., "Effects of Folic Acid and Zinc Sulfate on Male Subfertility," *Fertility and Sterility,* 77, no. 3 (March 2002): 491–98.
3. Dawson, Earl B., et al., "Effect of Ascorbic Acid on Male Fertility," *Annals of the New York Academy of Science*, 498 (1987): 312–23.
4. "Alternative Therapies for Infertility in Men," Infertility Holistic Online, ICBS, Inc., August 2000.
5. Ibid.

6. Sharpe, Richard M., and Stephen Franks, "Environmental, Lifestyle and Infertility: An Intergenerational Issue," published online October 2002.

7. Edwards, M., ed., *A Stairstep Approach to Fertility* (Freedom, CA: Freedom Crossing Press, 1989), 103.

8. Zaadstra, B. M., et al., "Fat and Female Fecundity: Prospective Study of Effect of Body Fat Distribution on Conception Rates," *British Medical Journal* 306, no. 6876 (1993): 484–87.

9. Braun, Kirsten (Revision) "A Natural Approach to Infertility," Women's Health Queensland Wide, February 2002, www.womhealth.org.au/factsheets/naturalandalt_infertility.htm.

10. Domar, A. D., Seibel, M. M., and Benson, H., "The Mind/Body Program for Infertility: A New Behavioral Treatment Approach for Women with Infertility, Fertility, and Sterility" (1990) Feb; 53(2): 246–9

11. Rostami, K., "Celiac Disease and Reproductive Disorders: A Neglected Association," *European Journal of Obstetrics*, Gynecology and Reproductive Biology 96, no. 2 (2001): 146–49.

12. Pauling, Linus, *How to Live Longer and Feel Better* (New York: W. H. Freeman and Co., 1986), 358.

13. Cuskelly, G. J., et al., "Effect of Increasing Dietary Folate on Red Cell Folate: Implications for Prevention of Neural Tube Defects," *The Lancet* 347 (March 9, 1996).

14. Haddow, James E., et al., "Maternal Thyroid Deficiency During Pregnancy and Subsequent Neuropsychological Development in the Child," *New England Journal of Medicine* 341, no. 8 (August 1999).

Chapter 11

1. Williams, Roger J., *The Wonderful World Within You* (New York: Bantam Books, 1977), 64.

2. Blumenthal, M., et al., eds., *The Complete Commission E Monographs: Therapeutic Guide to Herbal Medicines* (Boston: Integrative Medicine Communications, 1998), 98–99.

3. Ibid.

4. Duke, James A., *The Green Pharmacy* (Emmaus, PA: Rodale Press, 1997), 228.

5. Fallon, Sally, et al., *Nourishing Traditions* (San Diego: ProMotion Publishing, 1995), 32.

6. Personal Communication.
7. Reid, Jeri R., and Stephen F. Wheeler, "Hyperthyroidism: Diagnosis and Treatment," *American Family Physician* (August 15, 2005): 629.

Chapter 12

1. Passwater, Richard, "New Discoveries Expand Our Knowledge About Selenium's Importance," *Whole Foods Magazine*, May 1999.
2. Foster, Harold D., "Selenium and Cancer: A Geographic Perspective," *Journal of Orthomolecular Medicine* (First Quarter, 1998), 8.
3. Quillin, Patrick, *Healing Nutrients* (Chicago: Contemporary Books, 1987), 9, 129.

Chapter 13

1. "Iodine's Role in Learning," *Science News* 149, no. 26 (June 29, 1996): 410.
2. Haas, Elson M., "Minerals: Iodine," from *Staying Healthy with Nutrition,* reported in Health World Online, www.healthy.net.
3. Langer, Stephen, and James F. Scheer, *Raise Your IQ!* (New York: Kensington Books, 1999), 165.
4. Price, Weston A., *Nutrition and Physical Degeneration,* 6th ed. (Los Angeles: Keats Publishing, Inc., 1997), 401.
5. Haddow, James E., et al., "Babies Born to Mothers with Untreated Hypothyroidism Have Lower I.Q.s," *New England Journal of Medicine* (August 19, 1999).

Chapter 14

1. Barnes, Broda O., and Lawrence Galton, *Hypothyroidism: The Unsuspected Illness* (New York: Thomas Y. Crowell Company, 1976), 110.
2. News Feature, Royal Hallamshire Hospital, Sheffield, England, April 1988.

Chapter 15

1. Hoskins, Roy G., *The Biology of Schizophrenia* (New York: W. W. Norton & Company, Inc., 1946), 110.
2. Barnes, Broda O., and Lawrence Galton, *Hypothyroidism: The Unsuspected Illness* (New York: Thomas Y. Crowell Company, 1976), 79.
3. Masor, Nathan, *The New Psychiatry* (New York: Philosophical Library, Inc., 1959), 45.

4. Pinckney, Edward R., and Cathey Pinckney, *The Fallacy of Freud and Psychoanalysis* (Englewood Cliffs, NJ: Prentice-Hall, Inc., 1965), 101–2.

5. Whybrow, P. C., et al., "Mental Changes Accompanying Thyroid Gland Dysfunction," *Archives of General Psychiatry* 20 (1969): 48.

6. Barnes and Galton, *Hypothyroidism,* 82.

7. Masor, *Psychiatry,* 21.

8. Elwood, Cathryn, *Feel Like a Million* (New York: Devin-Adair Co., 1956), 235.

9. Holmes, J. M., *British Medical Journal,* no. 5006: 1394–98.

10. Masor, *Psychiatry,* 20.

Chapter 16

1. Gold, Mark, "Significant Number of Depressives May Have Hypothyroidism," *Family Practice News* (November 1982): 1.

2. Coppen, A., P. C. Whybrow, et al., "The Comparative Antidepressant Value of L-Tryptophan and Imipramine with and Without Attempted Potentiation by Liothyronine," *Archives of General Psychiatry* 26 (1972): 234–41.

3. Jensen, K., et al., "Depression," *Lancet* (November 8, 1975): 920.

4. Rabin, P. L., and D. C. Evans, "Exophthalmos and Elevated Thyroxine Levels in Association with Lithium Therapy," *Journal of Clinical Psychiatry* 42, no. 10 (October 1981): 398–400.

Chapter 17

1. Fredericks, Carlton, and Herman Goodman, *Low Blood Sugar and You* (New York: Constellation International), 18–23.

Chapter 18

1. *Encyclopedia of Common Diseases* (Emmaus, PA: Rodale Press, 1976), 461.

2. "Conference on Diabetes and Obesity," *The Sciences* 7, no. 1 (June 1967): 13, 14.

3. "Diabetes," United Press International release, November 21, 1981.

4. Addanski, Somasundaram, "Roles of Nutrition, Obesity, and Estrogen in Diabetes Mellitus: Human Leads to an Experimental Approach to Prevention," *Preventive Medicine* 10 (1981): 577–89.

5. Philpott, William H., and Dwight K. Kalita, *Victory over Diabetes* (New Canaan, CT: Keats Publishing, Inc., 1983), 56–65.

6. Eaton, C. D., "Co-Existence of Hypothyroidism with Diabetes Mellitus," *The Journal of the Michigan Medical Society* 53 (1954): 1101.

Chapter 19

1. *Time,* March 26, 1984, 58–59.
2. *Modern Medicine,* March 1, 1984, 268.
3. Malysheva, L. V., "Tissue Respiration Rate in Certain Organs in Experimental Hypercholesteremia in Atherosclerosis," Federation Proceedings Translation Supplement 23 (1964): T562.
4. Friedland, I. B., "Investigations on the Influence of Thyroid Preparations on Experimental Hypercholesterolemia and Atherosclerosis," *Zeitung Ges. Exp. Med.* 87 (1933): 683.
5. Barnes, Broda O., and Charlotte W. Barnes, *Heart Attack Rareness in Thyroid-Treated Patients* (Springfield, IL: Charles C Thomas, 1972), 75.
6. Ibid., 76.
7. Pinckney, Edward R., and Cathey Pinckney, *The Cholesterol Controversy* (Los Angeles: Sherbourne Press, 1973), 7–8.
8. *Los Angeles Times,* sec. 1, October 2, 1975, 2.
9. Passwater, Richard, *Supernutrition for Healthy Hearts* (New York: Dial Press, 1976), 57.
10. Gersovitz, M. K., et al., *American Journal of Clinical Nutrition* 35, no. 1 (1982): 6–14.
11. Pinckney, E., and C., *Cholesterol,* 36.
12. *Journal of the American Medical Association* 188 (June 8, 1964): 845.
13. Pinckney, E., and C., *Cholesterol,* 33.
14. Ibid.
15. "Side Effects of Hypothyroidism," undated, Alternative Medicine Angel, http://illness.altmedangel.com/hypothy.htm.
16. Hussein, W. I., "Normalization of Hyperhomocysteinemia with L-Thyroxine in Hypothyroidism," *Annals of Internal Medicine* 131, no. 5 (1999): 348–51.
17. "Hypothyroidism and Homocysteine," undated, The Thyroid Foundation of America.
18. "How Serious is Hypothyroidism?" University of Maryland Medical Center Report, 2004.

Chapter 20

1. Barnes, Broda O., and Charlotte W. Barnes, *Heart Attack Rareness in Thyroid-Treated Patients* (Springfield, IL: Charles C Thomas, 1972), 25–27.
2. Chappell, Frank, "Obesity Rather Than Diet Blamed in High Cholesterol," American Medical Association news story, October 25, 1976.
3. Hurxthal L. M., "Blood Cholesterol and Thyroid Disease," *Archives of Internal Medicine* 53 (1934): 825.
4. Bodansky, Meyer, and Oscar Bodansky, *The Biochemistry of Disease* (New York: The Macmillan Company, 1940), 341.
5. Wilson, J. D., et al., "Influence of Dietary Cholesterol in Cholesterol Metabolism," *Annals of New York Academy of Science* 149 (1968): 808–21.
6. Johnson, Timothy G., and Stephen Goldfinger, *The Harvard Medical School Health Letter Book* (New York: Warner Books, 1981), 229–30.
7. Kountz, William B., *Thyroid Function and Its Possible Role in Vascular Degeneration* (Springfield, IL: Charles C Thomas, 1951).
8. Rath, Matthias, "How Vitamin C Prevents Heart Attack and Stroke," a publication of the Linus Pauling Heart Foundation, 1992.
9. Bricklin, Mark, *The Practical Encyclopedia of Natural Healing* (Emmaus, PA: Rodale Press, 1976), 196.
10. *The Complete Book of Vitamins* (Emmaus, PA: Rodale Press, 1977), 314–15.
11. Ibid., 315–16.
12. Ibid., 198.
13. Bricklin, *Practical Encyclopedia*, 310–11.

Chapter 21

1. *The Encyclopedia of Common Diseases* (Emmaus, PA: Rodale Press, 1976), 667–70.
2. Ibid.

Chapter 22

1. Spencer, J. G. C., "The Influence of the Thyroid in Malignant Disease," *British Journal of Cancer* 8 (1954): 393.
2. *The Encyclopedia of Common Diseases* (Emmaus, PA: Rodale Press, 1976), 294–95.

3. Vorheer, H., "Thyroid Disease in Relation to Breast Cancer," *Klinische Wochenschrift* 23, no. 56 (December 1978): 1139–45.
4. Rose, D. P., and T. E. Davis, "Plasma Triiodothyronine Concentration in Breast Cancer," *Cancer* 43, no. 4 (April 1979): 1434–38.
5. Shapiro, S., et al., "Use of Thyroid Supplements in Relation to the Risk of Breast Cancer," *Journal of the American Medical Association* 244, no. 15 (October 10, 1980): 1685–87.
6. Pita, J. C., Jr., et al., "Diminution of Large Pituitary Tumor After Replacement Therapy for Primary Hypothyroidism," *Neurology* 29, no. 8 (August 29, 1979): 1169–72.
7. Guerrero, L. A., and R. Carnovale, "Regression of Pituitary Tumor After Thyroid Replacement in Primary Hypothyroidism," *Southern Medical Journal* 76, no. 4 (April 1983): 529–31.
8. Myers, John A., with Carl H. Schutte, *Metabolic Aspects of Health: Nutritional Elements in Health and Disease* (Kentfield, CA: Discovery Press, 1979).

Chapter 23

1. Alfrey, Allen C., et al., "The Dialysis Encephalopathy Syndrome: Possible Aluminum Intoxication," *New England Journal of Medicine* (January 22, 1976), 185–86.
2. Johnson, Robert J., "Aluminum: A Threat to Mental Health," *Bestways* (December 1986): 28.
3. "A Reason for Alzheimer's Disease?" *Science News* (September 15, 1984): 167.
4. Personal Communication with Richard Casdorph, MD.
5. Zeaven, Edna, "Foods That Influence Human Behavior," *Bestways* (September 1985), 11.
6. Hoffer, Abram, *Orthomolecular Medicine for Physicians* (New Canaan, CT: Keats Publishing, Inc., 1989), 204–6.
7. Justice, Blair, *Who Gets Sick* (Houston: Peak Press, 1987), 79–80.
8. Personal Communication, November 14, 1994.

Chapter 24

1. "Thyroid Hormone Missing from Menopause Discussion for Millions of Women," news release from the American of Association of Clinical Endocrinologists, January 13, 1999.
2. Ibid.

3. "Give Yourself the Thyroid 'Neck Check!' It Could Save Your Life," news release from the American Association of Clinical Endocrinologists, January 13, 1999.

Chapter 25

1. Shiroky, J. B., et al., "Thyroid Dysfunction in Rheumatoid Arthritis," *Annals of Rheumatic Diseases* 52 (1993): 454–56.
2. Lowe, John C., Personal Communication, July 1999.
3. Lowe, John C., "Thyroid Status of 38 Fibromyalgia Patients: Implications for the Etiology of Fibromyalgia," *Clinical Bulletin of Myofascial Therapy* 2, no. 1 (1997): 47–64.
4. Lowe, John C. Lowe et al., "Effectiveness and Safety of T3 (Triiodothyronine) Therapy for Euthyroid Fibromyalgia: A Double-Blind Placebo-Controlled Response-Driven Crossover Study," *Clinical Bulletin of Myofascial Therapy* 2, no. 2/3 (1997): 31–57.
5. Lowe, John C., Personal Communication, July 1999.
6. Shomon, Mary, "Fibromyalgia Aches and Pains as a 'Symptom' of Hypothyroidism: A Look at the Theories of Dr. John Lowe," About.com Guide to Thyroid Disease, April 27, 1999.
7. Ibid.
8. Lowe, John C., Personal Communication, July 1999.

Chapter 26

1. Personal Communication.
2. Ali, Majid, "Temperature Dysregulation in Stress," http//:majidali.com/tempera.htm, February 9, 2005.

Chapter 28

1. Mueller, Beat, et al., "Impaired Action of Thyroid Hormone Associated with Smoking in Women with Hypothyroidism," *New England Journal of Medicine* 333, no. 15 (October 12, 1995): 964–69.
2. Utiger, Robert D., "Cigarette Smoking and the Thyroid," *New England Journal of Medicine* 333, no. 15 (October 12, 1995): 1001–2.
3. Fukata, S., et al., "Relationship Between Cigarette Smoking and Hypothyroidism in Patients with Hashimoto's Thyroiditis," *Journal of Endocrinological Investigation* 19, no. 9 (October, 1996): 697–712.
4. Cooper, David S., "Smoking and the Thyroid," *The Bridge* (newsletter of the Thyroid Foundation of America) 8, no. 1 (Spring 1993).

5. Shomon, Mary, "Does Quitting Smoking Trigger Thyroid Disease?" About.com Guide to Thyroid Disease, October 13, 1997.
6. Ibid.
7. Nikodemov, M., et al., "Chronic Ethanol Drinking and Food Deprivation Affect Rat Hypothalmic-Pituitary-Thyroid Axis and TRH in Septum," *Endocrine* 9 (October 1998): 213–18.
8. Coiro, V., and P. P. Vescovi, "Effect of Pyridostigmine on the Thyroid-Stimulating Hormone in Abstinent Alcoholics," *Clinical Experimental Research* 21 (October 1997): 1308–11.
9. Williams, Roger J., *Nutrition Against Disease* (New York: Bantam Books, 1981), 177–78.

Chapter 29

1. Miller, Walter, "Health Risks from Fluoridation," newsletter, August 1997.
2. Mullenix, Phyllis J., et al., "Neurotoxicity and Teratology," *Trends in Neuroscience* 17, no. 2 (1995).
3. Machoy-Mokrzynska, A., "Fluoride-Magnesium Interaction," *Journal of the International Society for Fluoride Research* 28, no. 24 (November 1995): 175–77.
4. Challoner, Alan, "Fluoride and Lead," *British Medical Journal* (September 15, 2002).
5. "Perchlorate: The Quiet Contaminant," news release from Zero Waste America, December 5, 1998.
6. Winegar, Karin, "Danger in the Air," *Mother Jones* magazine, July/August 1998.
7. *The Encyclopedia of Common Diseases* (Emmaus, PA: Rodale Press, 1976), 312–13.
8. Monastersky, R., "Asian Pollution Drifts Over North America," *Science News* (December 12, 1998), 370.
9. Wirth, Timothy, National Academy of Sciences' Round Table on Environmental Health, June 29, 2000.
10. Faelten, Sharon, and editors of *Prevention* magazine, *The Complete Book of Minerals for Health* (Emmaus, PA: Rodale Press, 1981), 175.
11. O'Brien, Jim, "Mercury Amalgam Toxicity," Global Healing Center, Inc., Houston, Texas, April 6, 2003.
12. Kennedy, David, "The Opinion of David Kennedy, DDS," undated, released by tuberose.com/Mercury.html.

13. Faelten, Sharon, and editors of *Prevention* magazine, *The Complete Book of Minerals for Health* (Emmaus, PA: Rodale Press, 1981), 176.
14. Murray, Frank, *The Big Family Guide to All Minerals* (New Canaan, CT: Keats Publishing, Inc.1995), 387.
15. Huag, A., "Composition and Properties of Alginates," Report #30, Norwegian Seaweed Research Institute (Trondheim), 1964.
16. Wirth, Timothy E., "Environment and Health: A Connection to the Current Debate," Speech to the National Academy of Sciences Round Table on Environmental Health Science, June 20, 2000.
17. Quaid, Libby, "Pesticide Fears Turn Families Organic," Associated Press, November 3, 2005.
18. "Pesticides Vanish from the Body After Change in Diet," *Science News* (September 24, 2005), 197.
19 "Chemical Pollution and Health Problems," The Union of Concerned Scientists, Web of Creation, http:/www.ucsusa.org/transportation index.

Chapter 30

1. Pitskhelauri, G. Z., "The Long-Living of Soviet Georgia," *The Gerontologist* 22, no. 2 (February 1982): 117–18.
2. *Nutrition and the M.D.* 7, no. 10 (October 1981): 5.
3. "Keep Your Brain Young at Any Age," *Los Angeles Times*, part 3, April 26, 1983.
4. "Of Life Extension, Mice, and Men," *Los Angeles Times,* June 21, 1982.
5. Swaim, L. T., "Chronic Arthritis," *Journal of the American Medical Association* 93 (1929): 259.
6. Barnes, Broda O., and Lawrence Galton, *Hypothyroidism: The Unsuspected Illness* (New York: Thomas Y. Crowell Company, 1976), 204, 205.

Chapter 31

1. McCowen, K. C., et al., "Elevated Serum Thyrotropin in Thyroxine-Treated Patients with Hypothyroidism Given Sertraline," *New England Journal of Medicine* 14 (October 2, 1997): 1010–11.
2. Ibid.
3. Schneyer, Christine R., "Calcium Carbonate and Reduction of Levothyroxine Efficacy," *Journal of the American Medical Association* (March 11, 1998).

4. Baker, Barbara, "Hypothyroidism, Allergic Rhinitis Tied to Apnea," *Family Practice News* (August 1, 1999).
5. Langer, Stephen E., "The Reason Behind Weight Gain, Fatigue, Muscle Pain, Depression, Food Allergies, Infections," *Alternative Medicine* 16, (1998).

Chapter 32

1. Barnes, B. O., "Basal Temperature versus Basal Metabolism," *Journal of the American Medical Association* 119 (August 1942): 1072.
2. Scott, J. C., Jr., and Elizabeth Mussey, "Menstrual Patterns and Myxedema," *American Journal of Obstetrics and Gynecology* 90 (1965): 161.
3. Gold, M. S., H. R. Pearsall, and A. C. Pottash, "Hypothyroidism and Depression: The Causal Connection," *Diagnosis* (December 1983): 77–80.
4. Levey, Gerald S., "Hypothyroidism: A Treacherous Masquerader," *Acute Care Medicine* (May 1984), 34–36.

Bibliography

Adams, Ruth. *The Complete Home Guide to All the Vitamins*. New York: Larchmont Books, 1976.

Balch, James F., and Phyllis A. Balch. *Prescription for Nutritional Healing*. Garden City Park, N.Y.: Avery Publishing Group, Inc., 1990.

Bricklin, Mark. *The Practical Encyclopedia of Natural Healing*. Emmaus, PA: Rodale Press, Inc., 1976.

Clark, Guy W. *A Vitamin Digest*. Springfield, IL: Charles C Thomas, 1953.

Crook, William G. *The Yeast Connection*. Jackson, TN: Professional Books

Davies, Stephen, and Alan Stewart. *Nutritional Medicine*. London: Pan Books, 1987.

Davis, Adelle. *Let's Get Well*. New York: Harcourt Brace & World, Inc., 1965.

Elwood, Cathryn. *Feel Like a Million*. New York: The Devin-Adair Company, 1952.

Fredericks, Carlton. *Psycho-Nutrition*. New York: Grosset & Dunlap, 1976.

Fredericks, Carlton, and Herman Goodman. *Low Blood Sugar and You*. New York: Constellations International, 1969.

Gerras, Charles. *The Complete Book of Vitamins*. Emmaus, PA: Rodale Press, Inc., 1977.

Jeffries, William McKendree. *Safe Uses of Cortisone*. Springfield, IL: Charles C Thomas, 1981.

Justice, Blair. *Who Gets Sick*. Houston: Peak Press, 1987.

Kugler, Hans, et al. *Life Extenders and Memory Boosters*. Reno, NV: Health Quest Publications, 1993.

Langer, Stephen, and James F. Scheer. *Raise Your I.Q.* New York: Kensington Books, 1999.

Langer, Stephen, and James Scheer. *Solved: The Riddle of Weight Loss*. Rochester, VT: Healing Arts Press, 1989.

Mandell, Marshall, and Lynne Waller Scanlon. *Dr. Mandell's 5 Day Allergy Relief System*. New York: Pocket Books, 1980.

Masor, Nathan. *The New Psychiatry*. New York: Philosophical Library, 1959.

Passwater, Richard. *Supernutrition for Healthy Hearts*. New York: The Dial Press, 1977.

Philpott, William H., and Dwight K. Kalita. *Victory over Diabetes*. New Canaan, CT: Keats Publishing, Inc., 1983.

Pinckney, Cathey, and Edward R. Pinckney. *Do-It-Yourself Medical Testing*. New York: Facts on File, 1983.

Pinckney, Edward R., and Cathey Pinckney. *The Fallacy of Freud and Psychoanalysis*. Englewood Cliffs, NJ: Prentice-Hall, Inc., 1965.

———. *The Cholesterol Controversy*. Los Angeles: Sherbourne Press, 1973.

Price, Weston A. *Nutrition and Physical Degeneration*, 6th ed. Los Angeles: Keats Publishing, 1997.

Staff of *Prevention*. *The Encyclopedia of Common Diseases*. Emmaus, PA: Rodale Press, Inc., 1976.

Quillin, Patrick. *Healing Nutrients*. Chicago, IL: Contemporary Books, 1987.

Randolph, Theron G., and Ralph W. Moss. *An Alternative Approach to Allergies*. New York: Bantam Books, 1982.

Riedman, Sarah R. *Our Hormones and How They Work*. New York: Collier Books, 1962.

Arem, Ridha. *The Thyroid Solution*. New York: Ballantine Books, 1999.

Rubin, Herman H. *Glands, Sex, and Personality*. New York: Wilfred Funk, Inc., 1952.

Vogel, H. C. A. *The Nature Doctor*. New Canaan, CT: Keats Publishing, Inc., 1991.

Werbach, Melvyn R. *Nutritional Influences on Illness*. New Canaan, CT: Keats Publishing. Inc., 1988.

Williams, Roger J. *Free and Unequal*. Austin, TX: University of Texas Press, 1953.

———. *Biochemical Individuality*. New York: John Wiley & Sons, Inc., 1956.

———. *Nutrition Against Disease*. New York: Bantam Books, 1981.

Williams, Roger J., and Dwight K. Kalita. *A Physician's Handbook on Orthomolecular Medicine*. New York: Pergamon Press, 1977.

Index

AACE. *See* American Association of
    Clinical Endocrinologists
Acne, 109, 111–12
Addanki, Somasundaram, 135–36
Addictions, 138
Adrenal glands, 45, 46, 68, 128–30
Age-related changes, 69, 179–87, 200.
    See also Longevity
Ahrens, Edward, 145
Air pollution, 41, 218–19
Albrecht, William A., 35
Alcohol, 212–13
Alfin-Slater, Roslyn, 149
Ali, Majid, 198
Allergies, 207–8, 240–41
Alpha cells, 133
Aluminum, 182–83
Alzheimer's disease, 180, 182, 184
Amalgam fillings, 224
Amenorrhea, 58
American Association of Clinical
    Endocrinologists (AACE), 188–89
American College of Physicians, 14
Amino acids, 78, 138
Amiodarone HC1, 30
Anderson, James, 135
Anemia, 48, 68, 256
Animal thyroid supplements, 144
Anitschkov, Nikolai, 146
Antibiotics, 22
Antibodies, 52, 88
Antidepressants, 239
Antidiabetic agents, 30, 42, 256
Antioxidants, 97, 152, 185, 200, 201,
    235. *See also specific antioxidants*
Anxiety attacks, 94
Appendix, 44–45
Armour natural desiccated thyroid
    supplement, 3, 23
Arterial plaque, 161
Arteries, 160–64, 167, 182
Arteriosclerosis, 167–68
Arthritis, 237
Aspirin, 30
Atherosclerosis
    and blood cholesterol, 161–63
    defined, 70
    gender differences in, 176

and heart attacks, 142–44, 146, 147,
    154
and hypothyroidism, 15
Autoimmune thyroiditis, 28. *See also*
    Hashimoto's thyroiditis

Banting, Sir Frederick G., 167
Barbiturates, 29
Barnes, Broda O., xvii–xx, 4–15, 244
    on arthritis, 237
    and B vitamin use, 24
    on birth control pills, 62–63
    and blood cell production, 47–48
    on blood fat and cholesterol, 147
    on cellular health, 249
    on cholesterol in pregnancy, 158
    on competition of diseases, 22
    cretinism reversal, 105–6
    and diabetic complications, 166–70
    and hypoglycemia vs.
        hypothyroidism, 128–30
    infertility cases, 74
    and iodine supplementation, 23
    on low-cholesterol diets, 154–55
    menstrual problem treatment, 57–59
    natural thyroid supplementation, 44
    and subnormal temperatures, 47
    temperature test, 244–45
    on underweight hypothyroids, 205
Barnes Basal Temperature Test, 2–3,
    12–13, 124, 244–45
Behavior in hypothyroids, 252
Belief systems, 4
Bennett, I. L., Jr., 51
Berman, Louis, 11
Best, Charles H., 167
Beta blockers, 65
Beta carotene, 37–38
Beta cells, 133
Billroth, Theodor, 143
The Biochemistry of Disease (Meyer
    and Oscar Bodansky), 156–57
Bioflavonoids, 82, 83
Birth control, 65–66, 258
Birth control pills, 42, 56, 61–63, 126
Bland, Jeffrey, 67–70, 197, 258
Bleehan, S. S., 114–15
Block, Gladys, 36

Blood cells, 47–48, 121
Blood circulation, 111–12
Blood sugar, 259
    diabetes, 36, 132–41
    hypoglycemia, 70, 127–31
Bodansky, Meyer, 156–57
Bodansky, Oscar, 156–57
Body temperature. See Temperature
Bone mass, 98–99
Boron, 98
Brain, 120–21, 158
Bromoform, 28
Brugge, Doug, 227–28
Bruhn, John, 150
Bugleweed, 96
Butterfield, John H., 134–35

Cabbage, 31
Cadmium, 225–26
Calcium, 98–99, 184, 215, 221–22
Calcium supplements, 42, 239–40
Cancer, 173–78
    bone, 214, 215
    breast, 41, 101, 173–75, 189
    colon, 41
    and hormone replacement therapy,
        189
    lung, 118
    prostate, 41
    protection against, 36, 41, 45, 101
    uterine, 59
Capillaries, 83
Carbohydrate metabolism, 253
Carlson, Anton J., xix, 6
Carotene, 33–36, 38, 129
Carpal tunnel syndrome, 255
Casdorph, Richard, 183–84
Celiac disease, 80–81
Cellulitis, 111–13
Centers for Disease Control, 13
Chelation, 182–84, 221
Chemicals. See also Pollutants
    environmental, 218
    suppressing thyroid function, 30
    synthetic, 226
    in water, 28–29
Children
    diabetes in, 133
    goiter in, 27
    Hashimoto's thyroiditis in, 88
    hypothyroidism in, 85–86, 253
    iodine for, 105
    IQ of, 107–8
Cholesterol, 129
    in the body, 157–58
    effect on arteries, 160–64
    and HDL vs. LDL control, 159–60
    and heart attacks, 145–50
    and low thyroid function, 156–57

and low-cholesterol diets, 154–56
    uses of, 158–59
Choline, 149, 186
Chromium, 133–34
Circulatory problems, 165–72
Coenzymes, 68
Colds, 53–54
Coltsfoot, 211
Commission E, 96
Cooksey, Robert, 31–32
Cooper, David S., 210
Copper, 49, 66–70, 98, 222, 223
Cordarone, 30
Corticosteroids, 30, 237, 256
Cortisol, 129–30
Cough medicines, 30
C-reactive protein, 152
Cretinism, 27–28, 105–6
Crook, William G., 266
Curtis, A. H., 57
Cyanide, 29, 258
Cystic fibrosis, 178
Cystine, 258

Daar, Sheila, 218
Dairy products, 98
Dawson, Earl B., 76
Degenerative diseases, 106
Dementia. See Age-related changes
Depression, 117, 122–27
Dern, Raymond J., 48
DeVries, Herbert, 236
Diabetes, 36, 132–41, 255
    circulatory problems with, 165–72
    development of, 133–34, 136–37
    diet for, 135–36
    and impotence, 136
    and obesity, 134–35
    and pancreas function, 137–40
    prevention or control of, 140–41
    symptoms of, 132
Diamond, Marian C., 232–33
Digestive change, 251
Digoxin, 255
Dihydroxybenzoic acids, 28
Diiodothyronine (T2), 44, 176
Diseases of the Endocrine Glands
    (Hermann Zondek), 148
Donchin, Emanuel, 49–50
Dopamine, 30, 70
Drugs, 30, 255, 256
Duff, G. W., 52
Durum, S. K., 52

Eaton, C. D., 140
Eczema, 110, 112
EDTA, 184, 221
Eggleston, David W., 224
Eggs (food), 148–49

Eggs (ovulation), 78
Ehrlich, Joseph, 12
Elastin, 69
Emotions. *See* Mental and emotional
   symptoms
Energy, 11
Environmental Protection Agency (EPA),
   214, 216, 218, 219
Environmental Working Group, 227
Enzymes, 68–69, 138–40, 198
EPA. *See* Environmental Protection
   Agency
Epinephrine, 134
Erysipelas, 111, 113
Eskimos, 106–7
Eskin, Bernard, 173
Essentials of Gynecology (E. Stewart
   Taylor), 57–58
Estrogen, 30, 42, 75–76, 78, 136, 176,
   258
Evans, D. C., 126
Evening primrose oil, 206
Exercise, 120, 160, 207, 236–37
Eyesight, 165–66, 170–72, 252

*The Fallacy of Freud and
   Psychoanalysis* (Edward R. and
   Cathey Pinckney), 118
Feld, Stanley, 189
Feldman, David, 41
Female sexual dysfunction syndrome,
   59–60
Fertility, 72–81
   in men, 74–78
   in women, 61, 78–81
Fever, 51–52
Fibrin, 161
Fibromyalgia, 191–95
Fingernails, 110, 111, 250
Fish, 37, 41, 98, 105, 223
Fish liver oils, 37
Fish skin, 110
Flavonoids, 82, 83
Fluid accumulation, 250
Fluoride, 29, 91, 214–16
Folic acid, 84
Food additives, 30
Food allergies, 207–8
Food restriction, 236
Foods. *See also* Nutrition
   digestive enzymes in, 139
   eggs, 148–49
   organic, 226–28
   raw, 139
   and thyroid function, 31–32, 97
   and thyroid hormone synthesis, 91
Foster, Harold D., 100–102
Frank, Benjamin, 235
Free and Unequal (Roger J. Williams), 21

Free radicals, 76, 77, 96–97, 152, 153,
   196–202, 260
Freud, Sigmund, 117
Friedland, I. B., 147

Gaitan, Eduardo, 19–20, 27–28
Galen, 7
Gangrene, 168–69
Gildea, E. F., 156
Glucagon, 133
Glucocorticoids, 186
Glucose, 129, 132, 133, 259
Glutathione, 258
Glutathione peroxidase, 100
Glycogen, 133
Goiter, 18–21
   learning deficiencies with, 103–4
   and lithium therapy, 126
   in rural areas, 29
   sources of, 27–28, 31
   thyroidectomies and heart attacks,
      143–44
Goiter belts, 19, 27, 104, 173
Goitrin, 31
Gold, Mark, 122–23, 247
Goldstein, Allan L., 233–34
Graves disease, 94–95
Greenblatt, Robert, 82, 83
Gwinup, Grant, 236

Haddow, James E., 107
Haeger, Knut, 164
Hair loss, 110, 111, 250
HAIT. *See* Hashimoto's thyroiditis
Harman, Denham, 200
Hashimoto's thyroiditis, 88–92, 94, 104,
   122–23, 210, 241–43, 262
Hass, Elson, 104
HDL. *See* High-density lipoproteins
Headaches, 54
Healing Nutrients (Patrick Quillin), 101
Heart attacks, 142–53, 250
   and cholesterol intake, 145–50,
      154–55
   and C-reactive protein, 152
   and homocysteine, 150–52
   and isoprostane, 152–53
   and thyroid supplementation, 145
   and vitamin C intake, 162–63
Heart irregularity, 67
Heat regulation. *See* Temperature
Heinerman, John, 97
Heredity
   and diabetes, 134, 135
   and high blood cholesterol, 159
   and longevity, 230
   and thyroid function, 19, 21
Herrell, Ruth Flinn, 120
Hertoghe, Eugene, 57

High blood pressure, 70–71
High-density lipoproteins (HDL),
    159–60
High-fiber diets, 135
Hippocratic oath, 7
Hoffer, Abram, 185
Holmes, J. MacDonald, 120
Homocysteine, 150–52
Hormone replacement therapy, 42,
    189–90
Hoskins, Roy G., 116
Huffman, John W., 57
Humphreys, W. Griffith, 183
Hurxthan, L. M., 156
Hyaluronic acid, 250
Hydrocortisone, 46
Hydrocyanic acid, 29
Hyperinsulinism, 127. See also
    Hypoglycemia
Hypertension, 70–71
Hyperthyroidism, 11, 93–99
    and cancer susceptibility, 174
    during pregnancy, 86–87
    and shortage of vitamins C and E, 40
    and vitamin E supplementation, 77
Hypoglycemia, 70, 127–31
Hypothalamus gland, 23, 212
Hypothyroidism
    causes of, 18–22, 27–31
    diagnosing, 5, 13–17, 244–48
    effects of, 7, 9 (See also specific
        diseases)
    EKG and blood chemistry changes
        from, 250
    false beliefs related to, 193
    in infants, 85–86
    iodine supplements for, 23
    in Japan, 19
    prevalence of, 5–6, 16
    primary, 24
    secondary, 24
    and sexuality, 70
    symptoms of, 1–2, 8–12, 15–16, 244,
        248, 250–56
    temperature test for, 2–3, 12–13
    tests for, 26
    treatment of, 23, 24, 246, 249
    undetected, 5, 15, 26, 124, 262
Hypothyroids
    cancer susceptibility of, 174
    marriages between, 21–22
    and resistance to infectious diseases,
        22

Ichthyosis, 110–11
Immune system, 233–35
Impetigo, 111, 113
Infections, 51–52
Ingbar, Sidney H., 129–30

Insulin, 127–28, 132–38
Interleukin-1, 52
Intermittent claudication, 164
Iodine, 18–19, 103–8
    and breast cancer, 173–74
    drugs interfering with, 42
    in hypothyroidism treatment, 23
    radioactive, 95
    and thyroid function, 32, 45
    and vitamin B6, 39
Iodized salt, 18, 104
IQ, 105, 107–8, 120
Iron, 37, 48–49, 91, 256
Islets of Langerhans, 133
Ismail, A. H., 149
Isoprostane, 152–53, 201, 260
Israel, Murray, 24–25, 170–71

Jackson, A. S., 15
Jaffe, Daniel A., 219–20
Japan, 19, 135, 173–74
Javert, Carl, 82
Jeffries, William McKendree, 46
Jenner, Edward, 22
Jennings, Isobel, 37–38, 212
Joint pains, 255
Joslin, Elliott P., 167
Jung, Carl, 117

Kalita, Dwight K., 136–37
Kannel, William B., 148
Kennedy, David, 224
Kerkhof, G. A., 50
Khoe, Willem, 224
Kidneys, 168, 184
Kluger, M. J., 51
Kocher, Theodor, 143
Kountz, William B., 161–62
Kwashiorkor, 34–35
Kyo-Dophilus 9, 91

L-arginine, 76, 78
L-carnitine, 99
LDL. See Low-density lipoproteins
Lead, 220–23
Learning, thyroid and, 103–5
Lecithin, 186
Leslie, Constance Spittle, 163
Levey, Gerald S., 15, 248
Levothyroxine, 43
L-glutamine, 213
Lithium, 30, 126
Liver, 128–29, 137, 157, 184, 257
L-lysine, 78
Lobelia, 211
London Clinical Society, 142
Longevity, 229–38
    exercise for, 236–37
    food restriction for, 236

guidelines for, 230–31
and hypothyroidism, 237–38
and immune system energy, 233–35
and protection of body cells, 235–36
and stimulation, 232–33
Lorge, Irving, 231
Low-cholesterol diets, 148–50, 154
Low-density lipoproteins (LDL), 151,
159–60
Lowe, John C., 192–95
Low-sodium diets, 104
Lu, Cheshong, 227
Lupus erythematosus, 111, 113–14

MacDonald, Timothy L., 183
Magnesium, 42, 98, 183, 184, 186, 215
Malpractice suits, 14
Malysheva, L. V., 146
Manganese, 98, 99, 184
Mann, C. B., 156
Mann, George V., 145–46
Maria Theresa, Empress (Austria), 143
Marshall, Noel K., 49–50
Martin, R. Bruce, 183
Masor, Nathan, 25–26, 117, 119–21
Mayer, Karl, 117
McCarrison, Sir Robert, 28–29
McCurdy, Paul R., 48
Medical tests, 13–14
    blood, 257–58
    bone mineral density, 99
    fertility, 73, 74
    for fibromyalgic symptoms, 192–93
    during pregnancy, 85
    for thyroid function, 26
Medications, 30
Men
    diabetic impotence in, 136
    fertility in, 74–78
    Hashimoto's thyroiditis in, 89
    hypothyroidism in, 253
    sexuality in, 64–71
Menopause, 188–90
Menstrual problems, 56–59
Mental and emotional symptoms,
    116–21, 180–81
Mercola, Joseph, 223
Mercury, 223–25
Mertz, Walter, 133
Metalloenzymes, 68–69
Methoxyanthracene, 28
Microtubules, 183
Milk, 98
Miller, Walter, 214
Millet, 31–32
Mind-body connection, 4
Minerals, 66–70, 75–78, 91. *See also
    specific minerals*
Miscarriages, 81–83

Monoiodothyronine (T1), 44
Morehouse, Lawrence, 236
Movement, speed of, 49
Mueller, Beat, 209
Murray, G. R., 144, 145
Musculoskeletal problems, 255–56
Mussey, Elizabeth, 13, 247
Myers, John A., 175–78
Myxedema, 9, 57, 116, 119, 128–29,
    147–48

Natural thyroid, 43–46
Needleman, Herbert L., 220–21
Nerve cells, 232–33
Neuropathies, hypothyroidism and,
    169–72, 251–52
Neurotics, 117, 118
The New Psychiatry (Nathan Masor),
    26
Nicastri, A., 51
Nichols, Allen B., 155, 156
Night blindness, 252
Norepinephrine, 68
Novak, Emil, 61
Nucleic acids, 235
Nutrition, 33–42. *See also* Minerals;
    Vitamins
    beta carotene, 37–38
    and celiac disease, 80–81
    cholesterol intake, 145–50
    to combat air pollution, 219
    and diabetes, 135–36, 140–41
    and disease, 106
    flavonoids, 82, 83
    for hyperthyroid patients, 96–98
    and hypoglycemia, 130–31
    and immune system, 92
    for lead elimination therapy, 222–23
    for longevity, 235–36
    and male infertility, 75–78
    and men's sexual performance, 67–68
    minerals, 66–70
    and old age symptoms, 69
    omega-3, 37
    during pregnancy, 83, 84, 106
    protein, 34–35
    and pseudosenility, 184–86
    suboptimal, 42
    and thyroid function, 31–32
    vegetarianism, 33–37
    vitamins, 33–36
    and weight loss, 203–6
Nutrition and Physical Degeneration
    (Weston Price), 106
Nux vomica, 211

Obesity, 134–35, 155–56, 236
Oliver, Michael, 145–46
Omega-3 fatty acids, 37

Omega-6 fatty acids, 37
Ord, William, 8–9, 142
Organic foods, 226–28
Ornish, Dean, 182
Osler, Sir William, 51
Osmond, Sir Humphrey, 185
Osteoporosis, 255
Ovaries, 175–77
Ovulation, 78
Owens, William A., Jr., 231–32

Palludan, Birthe, 38
Pancreas, 133, 136–40
Papaioannou, Rhoda, 222
Passwater, Richard, 37, 100
Patsch, Josef, 160
Pauling, Linus, 235
PCBs (polychlorinated biphenyls), 226
Pearsall, H. Rowland, 247
Perchlorate, 216
Pesticides, 216–18, 227
Peters, J. P., 156
Philpott, William H., 136–40, 254
Phthalates, 20, 28
Pick E. P., 144
Pinckney, Cathey, 118
Pinckney, Edward R., 13–15, 118,
   146, 150
Pineless, F., 144
Pitskhelauri, G. Z., 230
Pituitary gland, 11, 30, 38, 212
Pituitary hormone, 70
Pollutants, 214–28, 258
   and access to wholesome foods,
      226–28
   air, 41, 218–19
   cadmium, 225–26
   and chelation treatment, 221
   environmental chemicals, 218
   fluoride, 214–16
   insecticides, 217
   lead, 220–23
   and male fertility, 75–76
   mercury, 223–25
   perchlorate, 216
   pesticides, 216–18
   spread of, 219–20
Polychlorinated biphenyls (PCBs), 226
Postpartum depression, 117, 126
Postpartum thyroiditis, 86
Posture, 120
Potassium, 104
Pottash, A. Carter, 247
Power, Lawrence, 36
Prediabetics, 129
Prednisone, 30, 42, 256
Pregnancy, 78, 81–87. See also Fertility
   cholesterol during, 158
   diagnosis of hypothyroidism in, 253

iodine intake during, 105
mercury exposure during, 223–24
nutrition during, 106
preparing for, 106–8
selenium during, 101–2
Price, Weston, 106
Primary hypothyroidism, 24
Probiotics, 91
Progesterone, 78
Progoitrin, 31
Prolactin, 71
Propylthiouracil, 95
Prostate gland, 66
Protein, 34–35, 249
Proteolytic enzymes, 133, 138–40, 255
Pseudosenility, 183–87
Psoriasis, 111, 114–15

Quillin, Patrick, 101

Rabin, P. L., 126
Radioactive iodine, 95
Radishes, 97
Raise Your IQ! (Jim Scheer), 106
Raley's stores, 226–27
Rath, Matthias, 162
Reaction time, 49
Red blood cells, 47–48
Regelson, William, 235
Resorcinol, 20, 28, 31
Respiratory ailments, 53–54
Retinine, 249
Retinopathy, 171–72
Riccitelli, M. L., 163
Ridha, Arem, 45
Riley, Becky, 217
Rivera, Robert, 120
Rodbard, Helena, 188–89
Rosenthal, Mark, 186–87
Ross, I. R., 170–71
Rubin, Herman H., 11

Safe Uses of Cortisone (William
   McKendree Jeffries), 46
Saffioti, Umberto, 218–19
Salicylates, 30
Salt, 18, 104
Sanchez, Clare Jeanne, 186–87
Schachter, Michael, 45
Scheer, Jim, 106, 224
Schneyer, Christine, 240
Schon, Martha, 117
Scott, Joseph C., Jr., 13, 247
Scrotal pouch, 75
Secondary hypothyroidism, 24
Selenium, 45, 76, 77, 84, 100–102, 225
Selenium yeast, 100
Senility, 180
Serum amylase, 254

Sexuality
  erogenous zones, 54, 55
  as expression of energy, 11
  in men, 64–71
  in women, 56–63
Sharpe, Richard, 78–79
Shiroky, J. B., 192
Shomon, Mary, 46, 211–12
Sigal, Leonard H., 191–92
Silica, 98
Singer, Peter, 71
Skeletal system, 255
Skin, 54–55, 68, 109–15, 250
Sleep apnea, 241
Smoking, 30, 78–79, 83–84,
    209–12
SOD (superoxide dismutase), 69
Somastatin, 136
Soy products, 31
Spencer, J. G. C., 173
Sperm cells, 74–77
Sperm counts, 75–76
Stambul, Joseph, 176
Staphisagria, 211
Stoll, H. F., 116
Story, John, 145
Stout, R. W., 137
Stress, 52–53
  and cholesterol, 159
  and diabetes, 134
  and female infertility, 79–80
  and free radicals, 152, 196–202
  and low sex drive, 71
  and pseudosenility, 186
  symptoms caused by, 200–201
Subnormal temperature, 12, 47–48,
    140
Subtle albinism, 68
Sulfa drugs, 30, 42, 256
Sunshine, 41–42
Superoxide dismutase (SOD), 69
Surgery, thyroid, 95–96
Swaim, Loring T., 237
Swan, Shanna, 76
Synthetic thyroid, 43–46

T cells, 52, 234
T1. *See* Monoiodothyronine
T2. *See* Diiodothyronine
T3. *See* Triiodothyronine
T4. *See* Thyroxine
Tabacum, 211
Tapazole, 86–87, 95
Taylor, E. Stewart, 57–58
Temperature, 257–58
  fever, 51–52
  subnormal, 12, 47–48, 140
  testicular, 75
Testosterone, 71, 136

Textbook of Gynecology (A. H. Curtis
    and John W. Huffman), 57
Thought processes, 49. *See also* Age-
    related changes
Thrasher, Jack, 217
Thymosins, 234–35
Thymus gland, 234–35
Thyocyanide, 30
The Thyroid (Sidney C. Werner and
    Sidney H. Ingbar), 129–30
Thyroid function
  chemicals harmful to, 28–29
  diagnosing, 245–47
  foods interfering with, 97
  hereditary influence on, 21
  medical tests for, 26
  routine screening for, 16
Thyroid gland, 10–12
  alcohol's effect on, 212–13
  and blood sugar levels, 130
  control of, 38
  influence of, 17
  self-examination of, 190
  size of, 95
  smoking and changes to, 209
Thyroid hormone, 10–11, 256–57
  and control of thyroid, 38
  drugs affecting, 30
  foods affecting, 31–32, 91
  and protein synthesis, 249
  water-based solution of, 261
The Thyroid Solution (Arem Ridha), 45
Thyroid storms, 93
Thyroid supplements
  after thyroidectomy, 144–45
  and atherosclerosis, 15
  with calcium supplements,
      239–40
  dosage of, 24
  natural, 3, 23, 24, 43–46
  rejuvenative effect of, 25
  result of too much, 11
  synthetic, 43–46, 240–41
  with T4 and T3, 43–46
  as treatment, 16
Thyroiditis
  ages of those affected by, 92
  autoimmune, 28 (*See also*
      Hashimoto's thyroiditis)
  postpartum, 86
  signs of, 91
Thyroid-releasing hormone (TRH), 23,
    69, 212
Thyroid-stimulating hormone (TSH)
  and alcohol consumption, 212
  and diagnosis of thyroid function,
      258–59
  levels of, 258, 263
  release of, 23, 69

Thyroid-stimulating hormone (TSH), *continued*
  suppression of, 30
  and vitamin A, 38
Thyroxine (T4), 30–32
  conversion of, 198, 257
  and selenium, 100–102
  and stress, 71
  synthetic vs. natural supplements, 43–46
  and zinc-copper ratio, 69, 70
Tiwari, Banarasi D., 103
Tralomethrin, 217
TRH. *See* Thyroid-releasing hormone
Triglycerides, 155–56
Triiodothyronine (T3), 30–32
  conversion of T4 to, 198, 257
  and fibromyalgia, 193
  and hypertension, 151
  and selenium, 100, 101
  and stress, 71
  synthetic vs. natural supplements, 43–46
  and zinc-copper ratio, 70
TSH. *See* Thyroid-stimulating hormone
Tubulin, 183
Turnips, 31
Tyrosine, 45

Union of Concerned Scientists, 228
Utiger, Robert D., 209

Vaginal infections, 177
Vasectomy, 65
Vegetarianism, 33–37, 206–7
Verlangieri, Anthony J., 162
Vestigial organs, 44–45
Victory over Diabetes (William H. Philpott and Dwight K. Kalita), 136–40, 254
Virchow, Rudolph, 147, 161
Vitamins, 33–42
  A, 33–36, 38, 91, 129, 218, 219
  B complex, 25, 33–40, 59, 66, 119–20, 126, 151, 163, 185, 212, 213, 258
  C, 37, 40, 48–49, 76, 77, 82–83, 98, 162–63, 184, 222, 223, 235
  D, 37, 40–42, 91, 99, 159
  E, 40, 76, 77, 91, 163–64, 197, 219
  for free radical control, 200
  K, 91, 98
  and male infertility, 75–77
Vitamins in Endocrine Metabolism (Isobel Jennings), 37–38

Wagner, Hans, 210
Walczak, Michael, 170–72

Walford, Roy L., 236
Walnuts, 31
Walraven, Philip A., 222
Water
  chemicals in, 20–21, 28–29
  fluoridated, 29, 214–15
  pollution of, 27
Weight. *See also* Obesity
  and diabetes, 134–35
  and fertility, 79
Weight loss, 203–8
Wellness Index, 153, 201, 260–61
Welsh, JoEllen, 41
Werner, Sidney C., 71, 129–30
White blood cells, 47–48
Whybrow, P. C., 118–19
Williams, Roger J., 15, 21, 95, 163, 213
Williamson, Charles, 223–24
Winegar, Karin, 217, 218
Wirth, Timothy E., 220, 226
Wittman, Rita, 241
Wolf, Stewart, 150
Women
  depression in, 126
  fertility in, 78–81
  fibromyalgia in, 191
  Hashimoto's thyroiditis in, 88
  menopause, 188–90
  myxedema in, 119
  nursing, 176
  pregnancy, 81–87
  selenium intake by, 101–2
  sexuality in, 56–63
  undetected hypothyroidism in, 253
  vaginal infections, 177
Wong, William, 75–76
Wren, James C., 15
Wurtman, Richard, 184

Xerophthalmia, 38

The Yeast Connection (William G. Crook), 266

Zero Waste America, 216
Zinc
  absorption of, 84
  and aluminum absorption, 184
  and cadmium level, 225
  and lead exposure, 222
  and male sexuality, 66–70, 76–78
  and pseudosenility, 186
  sources of, 222–23, 225
  in vegetarian diets, 37
Zondek, Hermann, 147–48

About the Authors

STEPHEN E. LANGER, MD, received his medical training at the State University of New York, Buffalo, College of Medicine. He is president of the American Nutritional Medical Association, and has a medical practice specializing in thyroid replacement therapy, clinical nutrition, and antiaging medicine in Berkeley, California.

Dr. Langer has produced and hosted his own nationally syndicated TV and radio programs and has authored six books and hundreds of articles for major health and medical publications.

Dr. Langer is available for personal telephone consultations and may be reached at (510) 548-7384 or written to at 3031 Telegraph Avenue, Suite 230, Berkeley, CA 94705. His Web site is: www.thyroidmd.com.

JAMES F. SCHEER has authored or coauthored twenty-four published books, many in nutrition and health. He is the coauthor of *Foods That Heal,* whose sales topped a million copies.

More than 2,500 of his articles—one thousand in nutrition and health—have appeared in leading magazines throughout the world. He is past editor of three health publications: *Let's LIVE, Food-Wise,* and *Health Freedom News.*

One of his books served as the basis for a David Wolper–produced sixty-minute documentary, "The Race for Space," which was nominated for an Academy Award.